THAT SENSE OF WONDER

How to Capture the Miracles of Everyday Life

FRANCESCO DIMITRI

HEAD
ZEUS

An Anima Book

THAT SENSE
OF WONDER

Francesco Dimitri is the
author of *To Read Aloud* (2017),
the novel *The Book of Hidden
Things* (2018), and eight books
in Italian. He is on the faculty of
the School of Life.

For Paola.
It is kind of a trilogy, isn't it?

This is an Anima book, first published in the UK in 2018
by Head of Zeus Ltd

9 7 5 3 1 2 4 6 8

A catalogue record for this book is available
from the British Library.

ISBN (HB): 9781786699893
ISBN (E): 9781786699886

Illusrations by Kate Bayley

Typeset by Lindsay Nash

Printed and bound in Great Britain by
CPI Group (UK) Ltd, Croydon CR0 4YY

Head of Zeus Ltd
First Floor East
5–8 Hardwick Street
London ECIR 4RG

WWW.HEADOFZEUS.COM

Contents

The Threshold

I remember when my older brothers told me that Father Christmas was real. I can't be sure whether it is an actual memory or a patchwork of truth and fiction I conjured up later, but the mental picture is there, crystal clear. I was sitting on a bed under a huge Duran Duran poster, my legs dangling a good distance from the floor. Though it must have been late autumn, the day was warm. My two brothers were standing right in front of me and I was craning my neck to be sure I took in their every word. I looked up at them. You would have done the same: they wore the coolest sunglasses, listened to the best music and hung out with the smartest kids in town; and yet they still took time off from their busy schedules to kick a football with me.

'He has a big belly,' said Gigi.

'Like dad's?' I asked. My father was still in perfect health and I thought that would never change.

'Bigger!' replied Gigi, air-drawing a seriously prodigious belly with an expansive circular movement of his arms.

Arcangelo added, 'He needs all that fat to keep warm.

1

He lives at the North Pole, you know. With penguins.'

I *so* wanted to believe. But due diligence was required here, and I probed further: 'And he's the one who brings us presents at Christmas? Are you sure about that?'

'Yes, that's right.'

'To all children? Across the whole world?'

'Yup.'

'He goes around the world in *one night*?'

'He travels on a sledge,' said Gigi, as if that settled the matter.

I looked at the sunny day outside, and doubts began to creep into my mind. Sledges ran on snow, I knew that much. But I also knew we didn't see a lot of snow in southern Italy. No, wait, we didn't see *any* snow. My Christmas presents were at risk.

Arcangelo seemed to detect my concern. 'It's a *flying* sledge,' he explained. 'It doesn't need any snow.'

'But how's that possible?'

'Because it flies.'

'Yes, but how?'

'It flies by magic,' said Gigi.

And *that* settled the matter; magic made sense to me back then, as it still does, albeit in a different fashion.

That was the first Christmas I can remember. On Christmas Eve, I left out biscuits and a glass of milk for Father Christmas, then lay awake for hours, tossing and turning under the covers. I awoke the next morning at six o'clock, leaped out of bed, roused the other members of my family – and dashed to the Christmas tree, where, sure enough, presents had appeared, the glass had been emptied and the biscuits had been eaten, only crumbs remaining.

I don't remember what I got. But I remember very clearly the crumbs and the empty glass.

Presents were only presents, only *things*, and the novelty of things wears off quickly. But the empty glass and the crumbs – they were something *more*. They proved that Father Christmas had actually flown across the sky and slid down my chimney. The crumbs and the glass – they were *magic*.

It might be tempting to explain children's excitement at the presents Father Christmas brings as the greed of spoiled brats. That is true, in part. There is another truth, and this is the one that matters. Children are excited because Father Christmas comes from a world of magic. The stuff they get for their birthday is not remotely as exciting: they know where it comes from, and it is not from a magic man on a flying sledge. The story of Father Christmas is a lot more than a white lie: it is a different sort of truth, a sprinkle of fairy dust that turns plastic dolls into talismans and teddy bears into totems. In short, into objects of wonder.

Time went by. The Eighties marched on with their madness of inglorious politics, horror films and synth music, and at some point the harsh truth sank in: it was Mum and Dad who bought – and brought – me the presents; there was no magic involved, only a cold exchange of cash for goods. I don't remember when or how I learned that this was the case, perhaps because the discovery caused me such disappointment. The merciless light of reason had broken the spell, and Christmas would never be the same again.

Don't get me wrong, I continued to like Christmas, and I still do. I enjoy the warmth, the coming together of family and friends, even with the seasonal feuds and fights and cutting remarks fuelled by drink. Although I grumble and whine, as busy adults are required to do, I still have a good time. And I still get presents.

But they are never *quite* as good as the ones I received as a child. How could they be? They don't come down the chimney any more. I am happy to be a functioning adult and I would never want to be a child again, but when I am feeling a bit down, when the going is getting tough on a cold night in February, I miss the crumbs and the empty glass.

Sometimes, I'll admit, I miss Father Christmas.

✳

All of us experience a sense of wonder at some point in our lives. Perhaps you felt it when you gave your first kiss; when you grasped the perfectly balanced beauty of an equation; when you glimpsed the divine in the rose windows of Chartres Cathedral; when you poured your soul into a painting; when you surprised yourself by taking part in an orgy;

or was it when you went sky-diving and then drummed until dawn? Whatever the circumstance that triggered the feeling, you were left speechless by this extraordinary world of ours. We speak different languages, cling to different ideas about politics and spirituality, even different notions of love, but a longing for wonder connects us all through space and time: the cabbie who slows down at night to look at the skyline over the Thames; the sage working towards his next reincarnation; the atheist sociologist. *Amaze me*, we ask of magicians, artists and writers. *Make me wonder, make me wise*, we ask of scientists, philosophers and gods. 'To survive is not enough,' said Roga Danar in a memorable episode of *Star Trek: The Next Generation*. 'To simply exist is not enough.' Our survival instinct might keep us going, but we need a sense of wonder to be fully alive. Your sense of wonder is the most powerful fuel you have.

So what do you do when you have used it all up?

✳

On 23 May 2016 I hit thirty-five, and that night, as I blew out my candles, I realized that they covered the entire cake. I was now closer to middle age than childhood.

By any reckoning I didn't have a bad life, but neither was I happy. The thing is, I was stuck. I seemed unable to move things forward: over the past few years, all my most exciting projects had been shot down like a sleepy row of sitting ducks.

I was ready for new challenges but no one seemed particularly eager to challenge me.

I attributed my dissatisfaction in part, at least, to the political climate: the United Kingdom was at that time locked in a dismal debate about the pros and cons of remaining in or leaving the European Union. The referendum campaign was big on empty sloganizing and short on truth-based argument. A little fighting cock of a man who seemed to me to lack imagination, generosity and any trace of intelligence was clocking up far too much airtime. But at least, I told myself, it would all soon be over. Britain, in that sensible, pragmatic way for which she is famous, would make the right decision. And life would go on as before.

Summer 2016, I decided, was going to be great.

*

For an Italian in London, waking up on 24 June 2016 was *not* great. Whatever the ultimate wisdom of leaving or remaining, I can confidently say that the morning after the referendum sucked. I had become a stranger overnight.

The day was a blur of texts, phone calls and emails from my British friends expressing their solidarity, their horror, their love; one who had voted Leave called to make it clear it wasn't about me, it wasn't about racism or any form of nastiness, and she honestly believed that. My very English neighbour knocked at my door with a slice of lemon cake and a long rant against the result. Paola, my wife (also an Italian, and a psychotherapist working for the NHS), received pretty much the same treatment. I felt very loved.

And also very lonely.

I had been living in London for eight years and until that day I never realized I was an *Italian*. Not that I thought of myself as English, or as a European for that matter, or as a 'citizen of nowhere', to use a slur that a spiteful woman would slap on the likes of me a few months later. I was just a guy. I never cared about politics, I never cared about national identities, and I had been naive enough to think that when people looked at me, they didn't see an *Italian man*, they saw just a person.

All at once I became obsessed with politics. I wasn't worried about the personal consequences of the vote, I was worried about the State of Things, Things in General, Thing-y Things. I went from reading articles on the exploration of Mars and the nature of consciousness to reading articles about trade deals that might never come to pass. I tweeted and retweeted furiously, and talked and talked. I made my voice heard. Surely, through the very quantity of my words, I was making a difference, wasn't I...? Time passed, and anti-EU sentiment became commonplace, and I felt a little lonelier. I tweeted more furiously than ever, but the more I tweeted, the darker the horizon looked. But there was still hope, I told myself. The US presidential elections were just around the corner, and they would restore sanity to the world.

I couldn't wait.

I am a terrible political pundit.

*

A new winter came, and my mood plummeted with the temperature. I was anxious about my finances, my health, the possibility of the Third World War breaking out, and the declining quality of superhero films.

'Do you think I'm depressed?' I asked my wife one morning over breakfast. 'If I were your patient, what would you say to me?'

She lifted her eyes from her yogurt to look at me. 'Honestly?'

'Yes, but kindly too.'

'You're fine. For now.'

'You're saying I might *become* depressed then.'

'I'm saying you're worrying too much.'

'How could I not?' I started to heat up. 'Have you seen *the state of the world*?'

'Yes.'

'It's horrendous! Modern politics is…'

She raised a hand to stop me, and said, 'Plato.'

'What about Plato?'

'The *Theaetetus*, specifically.'

'I've *read* Plato's *Theaetetus*.'

'Read it again.'

'But…'

'Please?'

At the time, I thought Paola had said it only to stop me whining. But I was being unfair.

✳

The dialogue known as *Theaetetus* is Plato at his best, for three reasons. First, its main character is Socrates, and Socrates is always fun. Second, it asks the sort of heavy questions that only a writer like Plato could make engrossing (namely: What is knowledge? What do you mean when you say you 'know' something?). Third, it ends with a cliffhanger: Socrates, after helping a young man called Theaetetus to become wiser, just drops into the conversation that he has to go to court, as if it were a minor inconvenience. It was actually a major one: Socrates ended up being condemned to death for doing exactly what he has just done with Theaetetus, that is, teaching a young person to think for themselves. Or, as his prosecutors put it, *corrupting their minds*, which from his accusers' point of view was entirely reasonable, considering that after talking with Socrates young people became much less willing to shut up and do as they were told.

There is a moment when Socrates shows the clever Theaetetus that he shouldn't take anything for granted. Socrates says, let's start with something obvious. We can agree that nothing can become bigger or smaller without *changing*. If you get bigger, you have changed; likewise if you get smaller. And if you don't get bigger and don't get smaller, well, you don't change. A no-brainer, surely?

Not so fast. Next year, Theaetetus, being a growing boy, will be bigger, while Socrates, being already a grown-up, will not. Socrates hasn't changed, and yet, when seen from the – now taller – Theaetetus's point of view, Socrates will be smaller. Socrates will have changed, without changing. See? It is all a matter of perspective.

When Theaetetus admits that he is 'amazed', Socrates declares that he must be a philosopher, because 'wonder is the feeling of a philosopher, and philosophy begins in wonder'.

Philosophy begins in wonder.

As Paola knew only too well, these words were very important to me. I have always sought wonder. I see myself as a wonder-oriented person. And here were none other than *Plato and Socrates* stating unambiguously that wonder is – quite literally – *fundamental*. In cherishing wonder, I was mixing with a very cool crowd indeed.

For an ancient Greek, the word 'philosophy' ('love of wisdom') had a quite different meaning from the one it has for us today. While for us 'philosophy' is a specific discipline, different, say, from physics or theology, for the Greeks a 'philosopher' was more of a general knowledge geek, and 'philosophy' could express itself in theories about the cosmos, in poems and in riddles, and often in a mix of all three. So, when Socrates says that philosophy begins in wonder, he is actually saying that *everything that makes us human – science, art, religion, you name it – begins in wonder.* From practical questions about tool-making and house-building to spiritual ones about the nature and power of the gods, it all stems from there. Socrates' questions to Theaetetus weren't intended to be answered, but to awaken the boy's sense of wonder.

Or, in other words, to make him journey back to the source.

✳

I had run out of wonder. I knew, intellectually, that wonder was good for me, but how long had it been since the last time I felt amazed, in my guts, in my flesh? I had stopped asking the sort of questions that made me wonder (*how will Father Christmas's sledge reach southern Italy without snow?*), because I had too many questions to answer about the mundane matters of life (*will my car hang on for another six months?*).

It had happened gradually, without my noticing it. You start fretting about tax returns and after a while you don't have a lot of time left to worry about monsters in the dark: HMRC bureaucrats are scary enough. When I was a child, I used to spend hours sitting on the beach, gazing out to sea. I imagined myself living the life of a pirate, sailing in a ship with Long John Silver and his parrot, making landfall on islands remote and strange. But now I know that I was simply looking at a stretch of the Mediterranean, and that what I saw in the distance was not the jagged masts of the *Hispaniola*, but the coast of Calabria. With every new thing I learned, another speck of fairy dust was wiped from the surface of my existence, until I was ready, finally, to function in a wholly adult world, and my life was a more or less spotless house. Orderly, cleaned twice a week, no dust at all. Tidy, safe and mind-numbingly boring. Ye gods!

I wanted my wonder back.

✳

You have a vague feeling of what I mean by *wonder*, but you might want a better definition. Let me answer with another question...

...*Where are you?*

Let's say you are sitting somewhere. Or standing in an over-crowded train.

All right, but in a wider sense – where are you, now? In a town, or city, or, if you are lucky, somewhere deep in the countryside, reading these words in the shade of a tree. In your imagination, take a step away – and rise. You are looking at the scene from above. Let your eyes get used to this new perspective. You can see a chunk of the planet, defined by geographical boundaries – mountains and rivers and sea. But there are no boundaries if you keep stepping away, because now you are looking at the entire planet from above, and it is a miraculous sphere coloured in blue, white and green – small, fragile and beautiful. And arguing over European Union regulations regarding the curvature of bananas seems completely pointless.

But hang on – did I just say *above*?

My mistake. There is no *above* where you are now, because out here, in empty space, there is no *up* and *down*. You are just *here*, floating, lost, pleasantly shipwrecked.

You haven't stepped away far enough.

Keep stepping away. And look at the solar system: eight tiny marbles circling a bigger one, and all of them moving… you were almost tempted to say 'forward', but there is no 'forward', only space, and a game of marbles.

Step even further away. Look at the other solar systems surrounding the first one, all dancing and partying to a music you can't hear (or can you?). Now step away some more, and look at the Milky Way, just one galaxy among many. The further you step away, the more you can see. Galaxies and nebulae and star clusters and planetary systems without number. And then what?

Stay there a few moments.

Stay there.

✳

And now dive back in. Jump back to the here and now, to your body, come back to a place where 'here' and 'now' have a meaning, this human-made town, this small spot of wilderness.

Think about this: all that you have just seen is, in terms of our basic scientific understanding, perfectly real. In a very practical sense, you are twirling in a cosmic dance. Planet Earth is a spaceship, but it is big enough for you to forget what it does. Right now, Spaceship Earth is carrying you through space and time in a vast, vast universe that you know very little about. You think you stand on solid ground? Think again. To say that you are at this moment *floating off into space* is every bit as true as saying that you have your buttocks on a chair.

That is wonder. Wonder is the emotion you feel when your jaw drops: when you hear music so heart-stopping that it makes the hair stand up on the back of your neck; when an unexpected brainwave makes your head spin; when someone you have always fancied stands stark naked in front of you. Wonder is more than surprise, though of course it contains *an element of surprise*. Wonder can make you happy, but it can also be terrifying. Wonder shatters what you think about the world. Wonder inspires both the best decisions and the worst mistakes you make in life.

That was what I'd lost.

※

In *The World as I See It*, Albert Einstein went even further than Plato in defending wonder. He said that 'the mysterious' is not only 'the most beautiful experience we can have', but also 'the fundamental emotion that stands at the cradle of true art and true science'. He then adds, rather ominously: 'Whoever does not know it and can no longer wonder, no longer marvel, is as good as dead, and his eyes are dimmed.' So not only does wonder act as an inspiration for your best endeavours, but also the loss of it *kills* you, in a way. You survive, but you don't really *live*. It's that *Star Trek* quotation again.

And yet our society, our schools, our workplaces, go to great lengths to teach us that the opposite is true. They tell us it is important to 'grow up' – that's what you have to do if you want to 'get on in life'. Growing up means focusing on practical matters; on getting things done; on being a hard-working professional doing a busy job. It means being sensible; it means losing our sense of wonder.

Whoever taught you that, I bet he wasn't as clever as Albert Einstein.

Einstein's words tell us that the loss of wonder is not an unavoidable feature of growing up, but a bug – a temporary malfunction. It happens, sure; that doesn't mean it's good. Of course we need to develop the skills and behaviours that allow us to take our place as responsible, well-adjusted citizens of the adult world. But we don't have to throw out our sense of wonder with our childhood toys. Even an accountant can temper the rigours of the balance sheet with nights spent debating the meaning of life.

There is a widespread notion that the older we get, the less creative we become. This is probably true for most of us; but it is not our inevitable fate. Loss of creativity doesn't happen because of some unstoppable mechanism of ageing, it happens because our sense of wonder fades. We are not as enthusiastic as we once were. We become wearier, less daring, and thus less able to imagine and to create new stuff. And this makes us more prone to anxiety, because *our eyes are dimmed*, and we can't see the myriad paths to a better life that are well within our reach, if only we had eyes to see them.

Viktor Frankl, an Austrian psychiatrist, quoted the words of the philosopher Friedrich Nietzsche that 'those who have a *why* to live can bear with almost any *how*'. Frankl had survived several months' incarceration in Nazi concentration camps during the Second World War, so he knew what he was talking about. But before finding your *why*, you first need to *wonder* about it. Lose your sense of wonder, and you'll end up wasting time fretting over your career prospects, your social status and the size of your bank account, or even sending angry tweets about little fighting cocks of men; reclaim it, and you will enrich immeasurably your experience of the world; you will find the strength and courage to change yourself, and – who knows? – even to change the world. Einstein did. That may be because he was cleverer than most people, including you. Or perhaps he just wondered more.

So, the question is: *how?*

✳

Certainly not by reverting to your inner child. To claim we can only find a sense of wonder by finding the child within is to follow the logic of believing that we are bound to lose wonder as we grow up. If that were really the case, then of course we would have to go back to our childhood as the only enchanted place we had ever known. But there must be a better option than returning to a state in which we were barely potty-trained.

Social convention holds children to be sweet, reasonably clean and adorably mischievous, but if you have ever seen a real child, or you have the faintest memory of what being one was really like, you know the truth. Children are brutes. They are self-centred, demanding and unscrupulous, or, as J. M. Barrie put it at the end of *Peter Pan*, 'heartless'. But let's cut them some slack: they have to be like that in order to survive, vulnerable and dependent as they are. They are fumbling around in a bewildering new world where everything and everyone is bigger and stronger than they are. Their sense of wonder grows in dark, shadowy places.

As a child, I felt in awe of my big brothers. They were role models to me; more than that, inspirations. I didn't make *my* choices, I made the choices I thought *they* would make. They loved me truly, but our power dynamic was imbalanced. I was utterly helpless in the face of their whims. If they decided to hang out with their girlfriends on a Sunday afternoon rather than stay at home and watch cartoons with me, my world would crumble, and I would be desperate, lonely and forlorn. Children must go with the tide, like the servants of feudal masters. Part of the reason they *feel* magic so intensely is that they hope magic will give them a level of power they do not, in fact, possess.

Anthropologists say that magic is (among other things) a strategy used by the dispossessed to make their existence bearable. Take, for example, the peasants of southern Italy, the hardened line of labourers of the region I come from. They were poor, they were at the bottom of a feudal hierarchy and they toiled in a harsh land. They had no money, no power, no hope of improving their situation. Magic was all they had. The same goes for children.

A child's enchantment comes with the steep price of helplessness. As grown-ups we are not helpless, not in the way children are, and we should be happy about that. Receiving magical gifts was great, but now you can have more or less what you want (within certain limits, of course), more or less when you want it. You don't like broccoli? Fine, you don't have to eat it. Children might *feel* magic, but adults can *work* it. They get to *be* Father Christmas.

You see the paradox here. You get to be Father Christmas only when you realize that Father Christmas is not real, and by then, you don't have a reason to bother being Father Christmas any more. You would rather be rich, for example. Magic is an escape at best, a delusion at worst: you know that real power lies elsewhere. You dress up like Father Christmas, but only a seriously maladjusted adult would believe they *are*, indeed, Father Christmas. The cliché of childlike wonder is worse than useless, it is detrimental, since it denies the facts of life. You are a grown-up; you have bills to pay and you will have to go on paying for ever; you know that your imaginary friend is imaginary, because one of your real friends got cancer last year and you can damn well tell the difference.

We can't bring back enchantment just by telling ourselves that we really, really should do so. All we can achieve that way is to create a manic simulacrum of a state we have lost, and to which we can never return. The magic of childhood is a lost domain, to which the paths are barred.

We have come to a dead end. Enchanted or powerless. A dreamer or a doer. A wild fantasist or a cog in the machine. Which one are you?

You are someone who will find a way out.

✳

I closed the *Theaetetus* filled with a tremendous sense of purpose. I was determined to start out on a journey to the heart of wonder. To storm the castle and take back what is ours!

I started by travelling all the way to the kitchen, where I filled a Moka pot with coffee and put it on the stove. How can you inhabit a world of enchantment when you know that Father Christmas was your dad, that the Mediterranean is a glorified pond, and that crime sometimes does pay?

By talking to those who do it every day.

The expression 'sense of wonder' comes from literary criticism: it was first used by science-fiction enthusiasts. One of the main triggers of my lifelong love affair with wonder was reading *The Lord of the Rings* when I was ten. The beauty of its enchanted woods and the mystery of its ancient ruins remained with me.

The first thing *Homo sapiens* did, as soon as it was smart enough to do something other than sleep, hunt and copulate, was tell stories. Stories are the way our cultures came to define themselves. They are the cornerstone of philosophy, religion, art and science. If wonder is raw energy, stories are the first shape that energy took – and storytellers were always in the business of shaping wonder.

But stories were not only made of words. Take the Lascaux cave, the prehistoric site in southern France whose walls are decorated with around 6,000 depictions of animals (bulls, horses, stags, big cats and the odd human), drawn some 20,000 years ago. The images are clearly telling us something, and anthropologists and art historians have been theorizing about what that might be ever since the cave was discovered in 1940. Lascaux had no practical function to speak of, and, when you consider how small and vulnerable were the tribes of the Late Stone Age, you could be forgiven for thinking that they had more pressing tasks than walking underground, in the dark, for hours on end, etching figures on a cave wall. And yet that is exactly what they did. But why? Those who took the trouble to create these beautiful paintings must have been driven by motivations more mysterious than the functional depiction of animals slaughtered in the hunt. There is magic at work here. These cave artists were past masters of wonder.

Such people are still among us. Even in our disenchanted age there are people who *do things with wonder*, as a profession, a calling, or both. Artists, scientists and magicians, to name but three. They could give me important lessons.

Not lessons, I thought. *Training.*

All of our senses can be trained: we can become better at spotting things, we can develop a musical ear, we can learn to improve our sense of touch, taste and smell.

And we can train our emotions also. We can train ourselves to be calmer, to cope better with heartbreak, to carry on when the going gets tough.

I didn't see why our sense of wonder should be any different. I could search for wisdom in various different fields, and come up with a training programme, a workout to strengthen our wonder muscles.

I drank my coffee as a potion and returned to my books.

Somewhere on my shelves I had a book about the history of theatrical magic.

✳

And so I took the first step on a journey that would bring me to marvellous shores. My aim was to distil the lessons learned along the way into a form of practical wisdom, a new kind of magic with the power to re-enchant our lives: I wasn't after a temporary fix to help me shake off the blues, I wanted to learn something that would stay with me, something that would strengthen me and help me cope with future crises.

At each step of my journey I tried to clarify, to myself in the first place, what was the lesson. It was like finding keys on a quest. Once I had them all, I would be able to open the doors to a new sense of wonder. I gave a name to each of these keys, and for each key I prepared a workout, a series of practical exercises. The order in which the keys appear is not random: there is a rhyme and a reason to their sequence. I recommend, therefore, that you read the chapters in this book, and do the associated workouts, in the order in which they are presented. There are doors that cannot be unlocked until others have first been opened.

I started with the firm view that wonder is not a zero-sum game, that we can be both accomplished and wide-eyed. I have found ways to embrace both the inevitable weariness of life and its glorious potential for wonder – ways that worked for me and might work for you. I claim no ultimate wisdom, but I have learned a few secrets, and I think you might want to learn them too.

Come on, let me show you.

The First Key

The Mystery

You feel, for an extraordinary moment,
that there is *more* to them than you
can ever dream of explaining

I ra and William Davenport never said they were mediums; nonetheless, they raised ghosts on the stages of the USA and Europe. They awed or enraged their audiences, but either way, they never failed to cause a stir. Their act was, in the mid-nineteenth century, cutting-edge magic.

On stage, the Davenport brothers would not utter a word, and they would always keep a calm demeanour: the otherworldly powers they raised left them unfazed. The shows themselves were quite slow by today's standards. The brothers would be introduced by a third person as master spiritualists, capable of forcing spirits to do their bidding. Then they would sit in a dark wooden cabinet, and be tied up. Their helper would close the door of the cabinet and then all hell would break loose. A guitar, a tambourine, a trumpet and a violin (sometimes called 'the devil's instrument') would play; thumping would be heard, and ghostly arms would be seen. Surely, nothing of the sort could happen without supernatural intervention? Surely the Davenports were calling forth spirits from the Otherworld? Or not, depending on whom you asked.

Spiritualism was born in 1848 in Hydesville, New York, where spirits started to communicate with two young girls, Margaret, fourteen, and Kate, eleven, by thumping on the walls. An older sister, Leah, spotted the business opportunity and helped Margaret and Kate to become celebrities in nearby Rochester, giving performances for paying audiences. Others saw there was money to be made from claiming to communicate with the spirits of the dead. An entire industry developed, offering what was, simultaneously, both a spiritual experience and a form of popular entertainment. Spiritualism became a worldwide phenomenon, and hundreds of people suddenly found supernatural abilities and cashed in on them.

People were hungry for ghosts, so the Davenports gave ghosts to people. Their tricks were far from perfect and were often exposed – which only added to the brothers' mystique. Were they prophets or scoundrels? Their act excited the audience's imagination: sceptics and believers alike wanted to see the Davenports' magic with their own eyes, and the believers would find confirmation that the spirit world was real, and the sceptics would find confirmation that it was not. At the height of their fame, the Davenports performed for Queen Victoria.

Many years later, an up-and-coming magician by the name of Harry Houdini visited the surviving brother, Ira, now an old man in retirement. Ira had words of praise for the young artist, taught him his favourite rope trick, and after a conversation that both men greatly enjoyed, he said goodbye to Harry with the words: 'Houdini, we started it, you finish it.'

Historians have long debated what Ira meant by this. Some argue that he meant that Ira and William had helped transform the spiritualist craze into a global phenomenon, and now it was up to Houdini to make it go away: what had started as showmanship was ruining lives, as people blew their hard-earned savings on attempts to talk to dead relatives. Harry would become a fierce opponent of mediums, but he would always defend the Davenports, who had never claimed explicitly to have spiritual powers.

Still, only a star-struck young artist could ignore the ambiguity at the core of their act. Were the two magicians pretending to be mediums for the sake of the show, or were they just two more swindlers pretending to be mediums by using tricks? Drawing the line is not easy.

Magic has changed since the nineteenth century.

This ambiguity still lies at its core.

Imagine you have been feeling downcast for quite some time – for several years, in fact. You haven't been through any major traumas, but a thousand small things have piled up: you never seem to get the praise you deserve at work; you and your partner have sex that's sort of okay, but hardly mind-blowing; and it's even been quite a while since you came by a novel that kept you reading late into the night. In fact, you can't remember the last time that something truly excited you – the last time, if you dare put it this way, that you were really *happy*. You don't feel exactly sad (you have food on your table, and a roof over your head), just... downcast.

What happens next is that you get used to it. You take your current mood for granted, and slowly but surely that mood becomes a rock-solid fact of life. To the point that when – at last! – you have the chance to feel better, you can't even see it. Your boss praises you lavishly for closing that deal with Shanghai, but you do not take her seriously. Nothing can brighten your mood because by now you have come to believe that the problem is not just your downcast mood – it is your whole life, it is *you*.

This is a dangerous spiral, one that might extend your grim times for ever. At every turn it gets more and more difficult for you to get better, because *you don't remember what better feels like*. You know there is a sunnier place, somewhere, but you haven't a clue where to look.

It is hard to cook a recipe that you tried only once, ten years ago. And the same goes for emotions. The less we recall how they feel, the more difficult it is to feel them again: it took three ghostly visitations – plus some time travel – to remind Ebenezer Scrooge what compassion looked like. The part of him that used to nurture such emotions was out of shape, worn out by greed and anxiety. Emotions, like plants, wither if you do not tend them.

You cannot search for your sense of wonder if you don't remember what it looks and feels like. You might still stumble upon it by chance, but the more time passes, the less likely that becomes. You reach a point where your memories of wonder are too remote, too vague, to be of any use.

Sense of wonder is like an ancient motorbike that we have left out in the cold for too long. Its battery is drained, so before we can think about taking it for a spin, it needs to be jump-started. But the motorbike is sturdy, and a spark is all it takes.

I searched for my spark among the magicians.

✳

Growing up is a lot like training to be a magician: you have to learn your tricks. Take shadows, for example. I used to be sure that the shifting shadows on my walls were unearthly creatures: they had crooked limbs (too many of them) and sharp talons, and they only moved when I wasn't watching them. Night after night I observed them. Night after night I tried to make sense of them. Until, at last, I came to realize that those ever-changing monsters were an illusion caused by light from the street and the clothes I would always put in a piled-up heap on the floor. It was a reassuring find, but also more than a little disappointing. Because if there were no monsters lurking in the darkness, that meant there were no heroes to fight them. The price of a world with no demons is a world with no angels.

And this is the reality of the world we live in. In time, we learn that the only monsters are human ones, and that the people who seemed to be heroes are just people we didn't know well enough. We learn the tricks of life, we practise them tirelessly, and come to believe that we have little left *to wonder at*. By the time we know enough to be able to function as a grown-up, words like *jaded* and *world-weary* apply to us. Disenchantment coils its tentacles around our throat, and we only notice them when we are halfway to being strangled.

Of course, we know we will never get to a point where we understand all the tricks that make the world function. But we understand so many of them that we can confidently say that there is always a trick at play, even when we can't pin down its exact nature. You might not be able to describe how data reaches your tablet, but you know that the powers that make it happen are not at all *mysterious*. You might not be able to explain the mechanics of a solar eclipse, but you know that it does not involve dragons eating up the sun. And you might already be fondling your phone, eager to check Wikipedia the moment this paragraph ends. We live in a world where good, solid, reliable information is never more than a few taps away.

Or a few discoveries away. There are still plenty of unexplained phenomena in our old universe, things that even Nobel prize-winning scientists don't understand yet. But what we don't know, as a species, we shall learn. Again, the one fundamentally important thing we *do* know, you and I and everybody else, is that *there is always a trick at play*. Moonlight might inspire poets, but when all is said and done it is nothing more than the reflected light of the sun. The moon? A barren grey rock in the sky, as bewitching, in and of itself, as a paperweight.

This kind of thinking led the sociologist Max Weber to say that society has been through a process of disenchantment, brought about by modern science and rationality. We became too clever to believe in fairy tales. Society as a whole stopped believing in mystery in the same way we, as individuals, stopped believing in Father Christmas. With the same rewards, and also paying the same price.

As a society, we know that we can calculate our way out of our troubles; if not today, then tomorrow. It seems that we have no use for gods, spirits and miracles any more. Once upon a time, adults and children alike cultivated an enchanted view of apparently unexplainable phenomena, but the *unexplainable* has ceased to exist. All that we are left with is the *unexplained*, and we know perfectly well how we are going to explain it: through science. We might get something wrong along the way, but science is beautifully willing to correct itself. The method as a whole never fails.

And yet.

Imagine you are walking through a street market. At one of the stalls, a young woman with pinched cheeks and a runny nose is showing a magic trick to a bunch of teenagers herded by a weary-looking teacher. You know perfectly well what is happening: an underpaid performer is bamboozling tourists into buying cheap gadgets. But all the same, you stop in your tracks. You forget the freezing wind, your ridiculously busy day, your in-laws coming for lunch next Sunday. You forget all of that when the woman guesses the name of one of her punters, a French student she couldn't possibly have met before. You gape at her, and your lips move in spite of yourself, and before you know it you find yourself smiling, and then clapping her, just a bit.

The young woman is a magician. Her day job is to inspire a sense of wonder. All of the other people we are going to meet on the road – occultists and scientists, fairy experts and story-tellers – do wondrous things, but inspiring wonder is explicitly a magician's job.

Sure, seeing someone change an Ace of Spades into a Ten of Hearts is not necessarily a wonderful experience, and you don't stare in awe every time a trickster joins two rings of apparently solid steel, but, on a good day, when the magician knows what she is doing, and you are in the right frame of mind, something happens, the wires touch, and a spark hits you. Whether the trick is carried out by a celebrated illusionist or a nameless street magician, or by a drunk friend who knows only one trick but delivers it with seamless grace, it comes like a bolt from the blue, and when it does, it makes you feel unmoored, slightly dizzy. You forget for the briefest moment that it *is* an illusion after all.

Immediately, common sense takes the reins again: there is always a trick! What the magician did is *unexplained*, yes, but far from *unexplainable*. And indeed, your mind is already busily trying to work out the trick. Yet for a brief moment before that, you had the experience of a bona fide miracle. Magic pulled you into another world, an enchanted one, where prodigies happen at market stalls.

So, how can we bottle that?

✳

'Sometimes,' says a man with a white beard and a polished accent, 'things that seem simple aren't so simple after all.' He sits in a dark, but not too dark, room. There is a thin candle on the table in front of him, and he holds in his hands a length of string. He starts talking about how life can be great, but also difficult, and every time he mentions trouble, he passes the piece of string through the flame, until all he is left with is a small handful of charred threads. 'The bonds between us,' the man sighs, shaking the burned threads in his clasped hands, 'seem broken for ever.' Then he makes a tiny ball of the blackened remains of the string. 'We hope that's not so,' he says. 'We want something more. The universal dream is a dream of magic... and transformation.' Widening his lips in a Cheshire cat grin, he uses two hands to unravel the ball, revealing a single thread, perfectly whole again.

This extraordinary performance, less than two minutes

long on my laptop's screen, leaves me elated. It shuts down my rational inner chattering for the time it lasts. I don't care how the man in the video managed to restore the wholeness of the string. I only wish he could do the same to our divided, bitter society – and, if I am honest, to my divided, bitter self.

But I am supposed to be carrying out research. Magicians have their jargon: technically a 'trick' is made of two parts, an 'effect' and a 'method'. What we see (a rabbit coming out of a top hat) is the 'effect'; the way they accomplish it (which I won't reveal here, sorry) is the 'method'. I search online for an explanation of the method, which takes me all of fifty seconds to find, and yes, it is as trivial as you would expect. Fortified with my adult understanding of how things are done, I go back to the bearded man's performance.

I make a point of looking for the method at work, and I manage, but just for a few seconds. Then I forget. The magician's voice lulls me into a daze again, and my rational faculties, again, shut down. His magic is not literally *real*, nor does he pretend otherwise, but I believe in it all the same. It is not that I *want* to. It is more that his magic just *is*, it exists, regardless of what I believe, or want to believe. The effect is much more powerful than the method, and the result is impressive enough to make me stop thinking about its petty mechanics.

The performance is on YouTube, and the man is called Eugene Burger. He is not with us any more, but his name lives on as one of the most powerful magicians who ever walked this planet.

You have probably never heard of him.

✳

In the underground community of magicians, Eugene Burger has the semi-divine fame of a Greek hero. In this community, masters, apprentices, hobbyists and collectors come together to exchange tips, ideas and routines; they write books, they make videos, they get drunk, they make love, war, or both. The community has its private clubs, like the Magic Castle in California and the Magic Circle in London, and its online forums. It has an unofficial but strict hierarchy, with the professionals on top, and the most revered of them on top of the top. There is no straightforward path to these rarefied realms of arch-wizardry: the community must put you there. Working hard does help, though. You want to be someone in the field of card magic? Then you had better go and study with the legendary Spanish cardician Juan Tamariz. Achieving fame in the wider world, by having your own successful TV show, can help boost your reputation, but only to an extent. Illusion designer Jim Steinmeyer, who is not a performer, is virtually unknown among us laypeople, but has rock-star status among magicians. The respect of your peers is the only currency that matters. To rise up the ranks you need street cred, and you only gain it by word of mouth.

The community has its own classics, printed in small quantities and very hard to find. Magicians are true believers in wonder. They talk of it at every occasion. They cultivate wonder, they cherish it, they passionately argue that awakening a sense of wonder is *the* point of their craft – and if not the only one, then by far the most important. When a magician is doing his thing, the audience should be amazed, astonished, flummoxed. A famous and articulate Dutch magician adopted the stage name of Tommy Wonder, just in case his audience hadn't cottoned on. Jim Steinmeyer says that magic properly done gives 'a redemptive feeling, a reminder of many potential wonders'. Wonder is a benign obsession for most magicians, the reason they dedicate their life to a niche, misunderstood and often ridiculed art. They train every day, with mirrors and family members, neglecting to study sensible subjects like law and economics, forgetting to go out with their friends, not bothering with the beach – and all they have to show for their efforts is nimble fingers that can shuffle cards in two dozen ways. They do that because shuffling cards is not the endgame.

A sense of wonder is.

✳

Even with their extensive international community, magicians are not what they once were. Historically, the *magoi*, or *magi*, were ancient Persian priests, followers of the prophet Zoroaster, and custodians of a sacred knowledge of fire. They spoke with gods and humans alike, and were endowed with fabulous powers (and it is, of course, from *magoi*, the Greek word for this strange priestly caste, that our word 'magic' ultimately derives). The *magoi* could make or break empires.

Today they make a living in Las Vegas.

Day in, day out, they step out in front of a hyper-aware public who know that it is all done with smoke and mirrors. These are audiences of the hard-bitten – gamblers, drinkers, high-livers, people who think they have seen it all. It takes hard work, not to mention an immense amount of chutzpah, to perform for these people with a smile and a bow, and then proceed to fool them into wonder.

I was sure that there was a lesson here for me and I took the obvious next step and decided to learn some tricks. As is often the case, the obvious next step proved to be a mistake.

I started by scouring videos online to find performances that struck a chord with me, and selected three. Eugene Burger's trick with a piece of string; a coin 'vanish' you can practise in a sleeveless shirt; and a card routine, one of countless variations on a trick that makes the magician know what card a person will pick, before they pick it. Impressive stuff, powered by very simple methods.

I won't give away the methods here – you can find them easily if you are so inclined. Suffice to say that they do not require any special prop. You can do the string trick using only pieces of string, the coin vanish using only a coin, and the card routine using only a pack of cards and a piece of paper with a drawing on it of the card your friend will pick.

One early autumn afternoon, I walked into my study with strings, a coin, a deck of cards and a mirror in front of which to practise, and started. In a feel-good movie, this is where the soundtrack would kick in, providing a suitably uplifting accompaniment to my progress towards mastery. In the event, my progress was neither impressively good nor impressively bad. It was violently average. (My soundtrack, if you are interested at all, was Fairport Convention's *What We Did on Our Holidays*.) The card trick was foolproof enough for me to learn reasonably easily. The string one was more difficult, the coin vanish even more so.

After two weeks I felt ready for my first road test, and I asked Paola to give me some feedback on my performance. Was it wonderful enough already? I began by messing up the coin trick. Even before I had properly started, Paola noticed me carrying out a move that is necessary for the trick to work – and which the audience is not supposed to spot. I had no good explanation so the whole thing was dead in the water. I moved on to the card routine, which I managed, more or less, but I messed up again with the string, making a clumsy move that revealed the method.

'You need more practice,' said Paola, kindly.

I certainly did. The next day I marched into my study with

coin and cards and strings and a new resolution. I decided that, for that day at least, it was not practice in the strict sense I needed, but rather, to study some more. I spent my allotted magic hour looking at videos on my computer. The day after that, I carefully selected and bought a new book on magic, which surely held better secrets than the ones I knew.

On the third day, it dawned on me I was never going to practise again. To put it simply, I couldn't be bothered.

Seeing how my favourite magical effects were achieved gave me a satisfying 'ah-ha' moment, but this came from a sense of understanding rather than a sense of wonder. It was still pleasant, and without any doubt still valuable, but not what I was after. *Methods* were not what I was after. Methods are quintessentially rational: I was chasing something more ancestral than that.

It made sense: the blight of adulthood is that we know too many tricks. I did *not* need to grasp even more of those. How could I have thought that learning how to create the illusion of a vanishing coin would be inherently more magical than learning how to create the illusion of a monster on the wall? The underlying process was identical. I was simply making myself more disenchanted than ever.

I had to take the opposite path. I was after a form of philosophical judo that would allow me to use the tricks of life to re-enchant my world. What I wanted was to learn how to look at myself with a magician's eye and use what I knew to fool myself into wonder. I shouldn't try to be smarter, not in a conventional sense; I had to become a better sucker.

I asked a friend for help.

※

Ferdinando Buscema is an internationally renowned Italian magician. His work has been praised by the likes of Mihaly Csikszentmihalyi, the psychologist who invented the concept of 'flow', and Kary Mullis, the Nobel prize-winning biochemist. He has been a friend for many years, after we bonded (I promise I am not making this up) over our shared interest in all things wonderful. He was not surprised to learn that my foray into the magical arts had not borne fruit.

When I told him of my misadventures, Ferdinando commented, 'When I'm performing, the last thing I want to feel is a sense of wonder. What I want to do is *give* a gift of wonder to my audience. But I cannot feel any myself, not in that specific moment.' He explained that he needs to be entirely in control of himself, very aware of the technicalities of methods and effects, and of the rapport between himself and the audience, for the show to be a success. Professionals like Ferdinando train wonder out of themselves, as far as magic is concerned, to make it happen for others. When the spotlights go out, the music fades and the public go home, the nitty-gritty of their craft is every bit as gritty as for any other craft.

'And I'll tell you more. I love it when another magician

manages to amaze me, but it doesn't happen that often, these days. I know the basics, the *perimeter*, of what's going on, even when I am not sure about the details.'

That was beautifully put. It made me think that is exactly how we all live: we know the perimeter of adulthood, even when we are not sure about the details, and that makes us very difficult to amaze. I asked Ferdinando, 'What is it that you do, then? To give your gift of wonder to your audience.'

'It is tricky to articulate,' he replied, 'and honestly, I would rather do it only to an extent. As Wittgenstein put it, *what we cannot speak about, we must pass over in silence.* There is a role for theory in magic, but after a certain level, thinking too much becomes a waste of time. Magic starts and ends in the perform-ance. It lives in the moment.'

I was getting frustrated, as often happens to laypeople talking to specialists. 'Yes, but *how* do you make it happen?'

I was making yet another mistake, as I realized later: I was looking for a quick fix. During my journey, I would learn the apparently simple truth that a journey takes *time*; it entails detours and pauses. Our sense of wonder is powerful yet subtle, and it quickly vanishes when you stalk it too openly. I had to learn a difficult lesson – the value of patience and sideways glances. But these were early days.

'There is no one answer, a straight path. I need to practise the method until it is perfect, seamless, but that is only the beginning. Everyone can learn a trick, if they put in the hours.

Gestures and words are important, and the way they come together. But you have some numbers that only have music, with not a single word, and they're great. There is the personality of the magician to consider, and so many other factors. It all needs to come together in the moment, but you can't tell *how* it comes together.'

It was all maddeningly vague. I had seen Ferdinando perform a few years earlier. During a quiet dinner with friends, on a tiny table in a Soho restaurant, he had happily smashed the laws of physics to smithereens.

'What about the audience?' I asked. 'What about us, the people who receive the gift?'

'The audiences at magic shows are tough. They don't want to be fooled, and they put their shields up. They won't willingly suspend their disbelief for me, not in a thousand years. What I do is, I *force* their disbelief with a crowbar. *You guys have to believe* whether you like it or not, because a wondrous thing is happening there in front of you, under your eyes, and you just can't deny it. Magicians are like stand-up comedians, in a sense. When comedians tell a joke, and the joke is good, and they are good, you laugh. You don't *decide* to laugh, you don't go along with them because you wanted to do so, you just laugh, you can't help yourself. Maybe not at the first joke or the second, but comedians know what they're doing. They string together one joke after the other, until they sweep you away. The impact is immediate. It's the same for us. We create a show, an experience for you, and we string together one number after the other until you can't help yourself. When the magician is good, the performance becomes a privileged door to wonder.'

And yet this awesome power must have some limits. In order to go home with a gift, you still need to accept it. You might not need to 'suspend' your disbelief as such, but you shouldn't actively sabotage it either. And we tend to do that a lot.

At every magic show I have seen, whether it's a performance at a market stall or a sumptuous theatrical extravaganza, there's a guy in the audience who, just seconds after the number begins, says: *I know how this is done.* I once heard a bloke scoff because, as he mansplained to his girlfriend, he could see perfectly well the magnets involved in a 'Balducci levitation' – an effect in which no magnets are involved. There is always a guy, and it is possible *you* have been that guy. Such guys are quite vocal about their (usually mistaken, Ferdinando assured me) understanding of how the trick is done.

'They are seeking for reassurance,' Ferdinando said, 'which is not what magic is for. I show them that there might be aspects of our reality they don't get. I'm telling them, look, you didn't understand all there is to understand about the world. And some people like this. Some, though, take it as an affront, as if I am insulting them personally. It makes them,' he paused for a moment, like the consummate performer he was, 'afraid.'

It makes them afraid.

When I listened to our recorded conversation the next day, I realized that I had never questioned Max Weber's notion that disenchantment is a direct consequence of modern science and technology. Science made us stronger, the theory goes, leaving us with no use for fairy tales. Weber's narrative is convincing in its neatness. But rather than a by-product of our culture, disenchantment could in fact be an armoured wall we have built around it. The world is an incredible magician, and we are an audience too afraid to accept its gift.

'Egocentrics make the worst audiences,' Ferdinando said. 'And self-assured people are the easiest.'

Disenchantment happened when we put ourselves at the centre of the world. We have become more egocentric, and less self-assured. A part of us never stopped believing that there are shadow creatures in our room. Once upon a time, myth, religion and fairy tales provided a context for that belief, an irrational context in modern terms, yes, but still a context, still useful, and still, from a practical point of view, *real*. That context made monsters bearable. Without it, we can't deal with them any more. Our ancestral instincts tell us the monsters are still there, but our culture has made it impossible for us to have faith that there are any heroes to fight them, and we are left to fend for ourselves. So, we *decided* not to believe. We fooled ourselves into thinking that we have traded in our heroes in return for scrapping our monsters. But we have been ripped off: while the heroes have all gone, the monsters still remain in our room. Left on our own, we cannot cope with their presence, and we pretend that we can't see them any more.

We are told that modernity dispelled our sense of wonder because it made us stronger – so strong, in fact, that we do not need wonder any more. The opposite is true. Modernity made us *more vulnerable* in some respects, and we had to renounce wonder because we couldn't handle it any more.

Be honest. When you find yourself in the dark, alone, are you never, ever afraid, not even a little bit? You tell yourself that your fear is irrational, that monsters do not exist, that it is burglars who represent the real threat to your life and property, and that your front door is locked and alarmed against them. But before all that sensible thinking took place, something brief and powerful happened within you. You do not have to admit it out loud, but you know that sometimes you are tired enough or worried enough – or drunk enough – to entertain the possibility that some monsters are *not* imaginary. It is ridiculous, yes – and yet. Just occasionally, even if only for a fleeting moment, wondrous terrors arise from the depths of our soul.

The same thing happened to you at that market stall, when you saw that miracle, a young woman reading a stranger's mind. You forgot you don't believe in real magic, for a moment, a moment only.

Magic comes together in the moment, and no one can quite

say how. There was something important here. Ferdinando had pointed me in a new direction.

And there I would find my spark, at last.

✳

The magician Ken Weber says that an effect can feel either like a puzzle, or a trick, or an *extraordinary moment*. When it feels like a puzzle, you and I assume that we could do what the magician just did. We don't know precisely how he knew that a random chap would pick an Ace of Clubs from a shuffled deck, but we do know there is a method and it can't be that laborious. This is disenchantment in a pristine form, the polar opposite of what a magician is trying to achieve.

A magic trick is a display of consummate skill: the magician accomplishes something that *looks* immensely difficult (although whether it is or not is another matter). On seeing the elephant vanish in a puff of smoke, or a chained and straitjacketed Harry Houdini wriggle his way out of a water tank, the response on the spectator's part is to think: 'How on earth is such a thing possible? I *certainly* couldn't do that.' This is what most magic is about, and it is exhilarating and a lot of fun.

But then there are the extraordinary moments, the moments of wonder that leave you dumbfounded, still able to *feel*, yes, but not to *think*. 'The viewer,' Ken Weber says, 'gasps for air rather than grasps for a method.' Puzzles are boring, tricks are entertaining, extraordinary moments are true gifts.

As such, they are mysterious. Some effects lend themselves to extraordinary moments better than others, but you can achieve an extraordinary moment with very simple effects. And also, you can come up with a complex procedure that reaches, at best, the stage of a trick: as Ferdinando said, many elements need to come together for wonder to happen.

Ken Weber takes the example of David Blaine, who, with a deadpan delivery, very few words, an unassuming style, and mostly with effects that any good magician could perform with their eyes closed, often manages to create extraordinary moments. Look at Mr Blaine stopping random people in the streets. Suddenly he is levitating, here, where no cables could possibly pull him up, and the people jump, and you jump too. Extraordinary moments make you forget that a method exists, they make you forget that magic is not real. Disenchantment is not an option, because the disenchanted part of yourself gets clubbed on the head. You can't figure out what is happening, can't frame it within the boundaries of what you know and make it familiar, dull, safe. In the words of Jim Steinmeyer, 'the purpose of the magician's performance is, for a brief period, to reinvest life with a sense of mystery and wonder and strangeness. That is a great need and it is taken away from most of us at a very early age.'

Note the word he uses: *mystery.* An extraordinary moment has a power of its own. Sure, you can go and look for the trick if you are one of those people, but that will not diminish the experience itself, in the same way that learning the truth about Father Christmas at an older age didn't spoil the memory of those childhood Christmases. When you go through an extraordinary moment as an adult, you are as enchanted as you were when you found an empty glass, crumbs, and presents under the tree. It is a different sense of wonder, more mature and probably shorter lasting, but its intensity is the same. It is a fleeting state, which makes it even more precious. An extraordinary moment leaves you bursting with enthusiasm. It ignites something within you. There might be only one extraordinary moment, a few seconds long, in a ninety-minute show, but those few seconds are all the show is about. Those few seconds, as Eugene Burger put it, are the mystery.

Not only *a* mystery, but mystery itself.

✳

Eugene Burger again, the philosopher-magician, the secret rock star. In a community not lacking sophisticated thinkers, Burger was the most sophisticated of all. He had a theory supporting his every single word, and he transformed humble routines into metaphors of life and death. His ideas still constitute a benchmark for other magicians, or an orthodoxy against which they react. And he didn't even get into the game until he was almost forty.

Watching Burger perform on video, listening to his interviews and talking to those who have seen him live, it is difficult not to think that there was something priestly about him, though he was always very clear that what he did was create illusions. In an interview with Erik Davis and Maja D'Aoust, he described his calling to magic in subtly religious terms. When he was eight, Burger saw a magician perform in a theatre, and he decided on the spot that magic would be his life. Then *real life* happened, he went to college, where he studied philosophy and divinity, found a job, and let his passion slip into the background. Until, at the age of thirty-nine, he remembered his early resolution and took the leap. Bringing together manual dexterity, original thinking and an academic background, Burger became that rare thing, a successful hybrid between theoretician and practitioner of a craft – an Umberto Eco of magic, if you like.

At some point during the interview with D'Aoust and Davis, Burger said that, broadly speaking, there are two philosophies of modern magic. Think about the standard gesture of 'passing the hoop over a floating object' to show that no hidden wire cables are involved (as if!). Some magicians swear you must always do that, because magic must appeal to the intellect. You show your audience your pack of cards, you let them touch your hoop, you do everything it takes to convince them that they cannot possibly figure out the method. So you'd better pass the hoop.

Not at all, other magicians answer back. You should never set the audience the intellectual challenge of working out what the method is. Your mission as a performer is to send them a subtler invitation: you make them forget that a method exists at all. By passing the hoop 'you are inviting people to think of methods and enter into a different frame of mind'. So better not to pass the hoop.

Burger was, essentially, an adherent of this second school. He accepted that magicians sometimes feel they have good reason to pass the hoop, but he was concerned that *passing the hoop takes you out of that state of wonderment*. Sense of wonder, Burger said, 'is an experience of the present moment'. The audience should not think about the method at all, because the method should not be the point.

Magic is an 'invitation to just take a vacation from your rational mind for a while' – not because our rational mind is useless (it is not), but because 'we don't need it all the time'. The magician should not make the audience believe that what they see on stage is difficult; rather, she should make them feel it is utterly impossible. The best magic creates extraordinary moments, in which we stop being rational and allow ourselves to be enchanted. After enjoying this short holiday, we can go home and be sensible again.

This was Burger's central idea. He often expressed it in terms of the difference between a *problem* and a *mystery*, borrowing his language from the French existentialist Gabriel Marcel. Such a difference is easily explained. A problem is something you can solve. You might not know the solution, and you might never find it, but you are entirely sure that there *is* a solution. Problems clearly belong to the sphere of disenchantment.

A mystery is a lot stranger than that. A mystery cannot be solved, and not because it is too difficult. The point of a mystery is not its solution; the point of it is *the effect it has on you*. You see a mystery and you say to yourself, *wow*.

Marcel uses the example of a person who is ill. A doctor would be likely to regard the illness as a physical – bodily – problem, whereas a priest might say that it is the manifestation of a spiritual problem. Different though these approaches may be, they both treat the illness as a *problem* that we can definitely solve once we understand how cause and effect have worked in this particular case. Which is not a bad way to treat it, of course.

But the ill person might feel there is more to it than that. Her illness is, in Marcel's terms, a 'presence', not quantifiable, not definable in traditional scientific or religious terms, but still there, strongly felt, entirely real. Someone with a psychotherapeutic background might be able to give an interpretation of that feeling, but, Marcel would argue, that would be yet another way of not acknowledging the feeling for what it is, of simplifying a profound mystery by dressing it up as a problem.

The shadows on the wall of your bedroom are a presence. The mind-reading magician at the market stall is a presence. You feel, for an extraordinary moment, that there is *more* to them than you can ever dream of explaining. They are presenting you with a mystery. Scary in one case, elating in the other, but always wondrous.

This notion of 'mystery' might sound like dangerously New Age-ish hogwash, and our instinctive reaction might be to steer it back towards the safe haven of a definition in terms of a 'very, very difficult problem'. The basic promise of modern science is, after all, that there are no questions that cannot be answered. Which might well be true, but even so, there are questions whose whole raison d'être *is that they are not to be answered*. Rather, these questions *do* something for you and to you. They give you an opportunity to grow not necessarily in knowledge, but in wisdom. When a Zen teacher asks what is the sound of one hand clapping, he does not intend you to come back to him with an essay on the subject. Our world behaves a lot like Zen teachers. It gives us dark and luminous mysteries, awakening in us an inchoate feeling that cannot be elucidated either by science or spirituality, but which sets both of them in motion. That feeling is our sense of wonder.

Wonder is *beyond* reason and *before* it: it is the emotion we feel when we find ourselves face to face with a mystery. So, *mystery* is our first key. Before setting off on our journey, we will find the spark that will jump-start our tired old motorbike *by relearning how to recognize mysteries as such*. Children are good at this because they still don't know that everything is supposed to be a problem waiting for a solution. It is a tougher call for us jaded adults.

Magicians can help us once again, for they reveal the simple and profound truth that mysteries are not always grandiose. When we think of wonder, we tend to conjure up visions of magnificent natural landscapes, of towering mountain peaks and raging oceans haunted by white leviathans. And yet mysteries can be very small. Magicians re-enchant us using everyday props (or props that *look* as if they are everyday props, which is even better). If a magician conjoins and then separates two hoops that look – shall we say – rather unusual, your first thought will be that these hoops are special, they are not your regular hoops, so there is nothing strange or miraculous about their conjoining and separation. But if the hoops are just plain steel ones, well, *that* is strange, isn't it?

Magic works through what is already at hand, already around you and already *within* you.

Eugene Burger was an adept at close-up magic, working on the same old tricks with cards and coins and strings. It was his crystal-clear understanding of the necessity of mystery that made all the difference to his art. When he cut the strings and joined them together again, he made you look at them with a different set of eyes.

This is what magic can give us. Not a better understanding of the tricks of life, or even a better understanding of psychology in the strict sense, but rather, a new outlook on our humdrum daily routine. Magic teaches us that we can make it wonderful, with some training and some work.

We are surrounded by mysteries, at every twist and turn of life, but we have forgotten how to look at them. We can learn again. Enchantment never left the world: it is we humans who shut our eyes and closed our ears. The good news is that an appreciation of mystery is such an important part of us that we can bury it within ourselves, and bury it deep, but we can never ever make it go away. We haven't used up our sense of wonder. It is still within us, within you. With the workout at the end of this chapter, we start the process of unearthing and polishing it.

✳

The more time I spent immersed in theatrical magic, the more I realized the extent to which it occupies a zone of creative tension between science, whose discoveries magicians turn into fodder for a show, and spirituality, whose feelings magicians want to awaken. There is a technical dimension to magic, but it would be disingenuous to deny that there is a spiritual one as well: the very word *magic*, as we have seen, comes from the earliest days of the history of religion. A lot of magicians are sceptics and atheists, but rare is the magician who never thought about the spiritual implications of his illusions.

Spirituality and science, then. Now that I had found my spark, it was time to start the real journey, to explore these two crucial strands.

So I set out on a quest to meet witches, scientists and other priests.

THE WORKOUT

Before beginning the workout, please buy a notebook: this is going to be your Book of Wonder. It can be a cheap notepad or one of those elegant Castelli ones made in Italy, it does not matter. But please use an actual *physical* notebook as your Book of Wonder, rather than an app or a word processor. Digital technologies make noise in our mind, below the threshold of consciousness, and we want to keep that threshold free for new thoughts and ideas.

Some exercises in the workout will require you to write down your reflections: you should record these in the Book of Wonder.

Every time you do an exercise of any kind, make a note in your Book of Wonder. Write down what exercise you did, and a few words about how it went. Was it easy? Was it hard? Did your mind push back against it? Did you think it was pointless? Write down as many reflections as you can in the time you have, without censoring them: no one else is going to read your Book of Wonder, so don't be afraid to sound silly.

If possible, write in your Book of Wonder immediately after doing an exercise. If this is not possible, write as soon as you can. Do not let a night's sleep intervene between when you do the exercise and when you write your notes.

Please bear in mind that the workout will be much less effective if you do not keep your Book of Wonder up to date. Updating it need not take any more than five minutes, if five minutes is all you have.

In our first workout, we are going to get acquainted with the idea that mystery is a doorway to wonder.

1. The Effect We Want

Write down in your Book of Wonder three or more ways in which wonder might help you. Would you like to re-enchant your relationship? Do you want to be more creative? Are you stuck in a career you don't particularly enjoy? Do you want your life to be more enchanted as a whole?

2. The Suppression of Why

For three days, refrain from asking *why*. For example, if you find you have missed a call from your parents, you might immediately start hypothesizing about what they wanted. When that happens, try to push the thought away gently. If you don't manage to do that, find a good reason to cancel the explanation you just gave. For example: Mum cannot be calling to say she is ill, because you saw her yesterday and she was fine. Do not look for alternative explanations; just cancel the ones your mind is instinctively producing.

You will probably find that you are reaching out for explanations all the time: you tell yourself that there is a traffic jam because people can't drive, that you didn't like the film because of the main actor. Just refuse to engage with that part of your mind, temporarily.

If you have the opportunity, take a marker pen with you, and every time you notice yourself thinking in terms of causes or explanations, make a small mark on your arm. How many marks do you have by the end of the day?

3. The Estrangement Gambit

This is a very simple meditation. Pick a time to do it every day, for three days in a row: it is probably easier in the morning or the evening, but that depends on you. Whatever time you choose, stick to it.

For five minutes, look at your hand. Just this. Set a timer, so you won't have to worry about keeping track of time. You will get bored, you will feel silly, you will grasp for some metaphysical enlightenment. Do not worry about these thoughts – just keep looking at your hand. When I say 'looking', I mean *physically* looking. What colour is your hand? What signs can you see on it? Is it different today compared to yesterday? What is it about it that you never noticed before? What kind of questions does it make you ask?

Keep your Book of Wonder and your pen close at hand. For this exercise in particular, and for other meditations we are going to do, it is crucial to take notes as soon as the meditation finishes.

The Second Key

The Shadow

If you get into definitions, the
world starts ending

I n the year 1900, William Butler Yeats and Aleister Crowley went into (magical) battle. Yeats was thirty-five, Crowley ten years his junior. They were both members of the same group of magicians, The Hermetic Order of the Golden Dawn.

The Golden Dawn had nothing to do with the modern Greek far-right movement with a similar name. It was a coterie of intellectuals and bohemians, based on some ancient ciphered documents that would turn out to be utterly fake. The Order's mastermind, Samuel Liddell MacGregor Mathers, was a magician from Hackney, London, well-educated and for the most part self-taught, who faked a Highland heritage as well. To be sure, when I say 'magician' here, I am referring to individuals who were very different from the illusionists we met in the last chapter: these men and women were *occultists*.

Yeats and Crowley met through their common acquaintances in the occult scene, but they were never friends. Crowley was (among other things) a poet, convinced he was destined for greatness, and when the chance arose for him to show his verses to the famous W. B. Yeats, he jumped at it. Yeats, however, was not impressed – and Crowley was offended. The younger man decided that Yeats must be jealous of his talent; for his part, Yeats thought that Crowley had embraced black magic.

Other troubles were brewing elsewhere within the Order. Years earlier MacGregor Mathers had moved to Paris; now people in London were casting doubt on the authenticity of the ciphered documents and, consequently, on Mathers' moral standing. It didn't help matters that Mathers had taken to the young, brazen Crowley, while almost everybody else wanted nothing to do with him. A perfect storm was in the offing.

By now, Yeats was convinced that Crowley was sticking pins into wax images of his enemies, a grave act of magical aggression. Crowley would say, years later, that Yeats in turn was attacking him and his London house, where 'weird and terrible figures were often seen'. Yeats himself would admit to lesser magical mischief: some magicians in his circle used their psychic powers to convince one of Crowley's lovers to dump him – for her own safety, of course.

Things came to a head when Mathers, in Paris, promoted Crowley to a higher rank within the Order, but the London branch of the Order refused to give Crowley some documents he was now entitled to. The London magicians were spurning Mathers' authority. Rebellion was afoot, England was lost! But Mathers and Crowley would not go down without a fight.

Thus the Battle of Blythe Road began. A set of rooms at the top of a shop at 36 Blythe Road, Hammersmith, paid for by the actress and occultist Florence Farr, was the 'Temple' where Yeats and his friends met. On 17 April 1900 Crowley surreptitiously changed the locks, making access impossible. Florence Farr called a police constable, who wasn't quite sure what to do with these feuding magicians. The landlord was nowhere to be seen, so the constable decided not to do anything at all and said he couldn't help. The premises remained locked. Crowley had drawn the first blood.

The battle rumbled on. On 19 April, Yeats and another member of the Order, E. A. Hunter, finally managed to get hold of the landlord, who decreed that since Farr was paying the rent, as far as he was concerned the place was hers. Satisfied, the constable allowed Farr and her cronies to force the locks open.

Crowley had big plans for the day: he would judge the rebels in a way befitting a magical Order. He donned full Highland dress (in deference to MacGregor Mathers' made-up ancestry), a dagger and a mask (to make it clear that he was acting as an impersonal bringer of justice), and marched over to the Temple, where Yeats was waiting for him. No great magical showdown was forthcoming, however: landlord and constable kept calm and carried on in the face of this black-masked, tartan-clad apparition, and simply refused to let him in. The kilted and sporraned Crowley was obliged to retreat.

Undeterred, he brought the battle to court, where it quickly became clear he didn't have a case. Crowley ended up paying

£5 in legal costs and that was that. Not with a bang but with a whimper, the Battle of Blythe Road was over.

※

There is more to this story than comedy gold. The Hermetic Order of the Golden Dawn was created in 1888, the year Jack the Ripper became a celebrity. Wonder, ineffable and aimless, was being crushed under the weight of big business, rapid technological advancements, and a news cycle quicker than the world had ever seen. Wonder thrives in conditions of ambiguity, and this was a time of growing certainties.

While the usual suspects – poets and artists, mostly – mourned the disappearance of wonder, society at large celebrated it. Indulging in wonder was increasingly considered to be a waste of time. The age of dreamers was over; this was the age of the *doers*. In Oxford parlance, the hearties run the Empire, with no place left for the aesthetes.

And yet Victorian London, the city at the heart of this revolution, was a hotbed of magical orders, battling wizards, and strange rituals conducted in suburban homes. You had factories and banks, yes, but you also had Crowley, a Cambridge-educated fellow, donning an Osiris mask in Hammersmith. Up to that moment, magic had all but disappeared from British life, but then, when one would least expect to see it, up it popped in London: all of a sudden people were making up 'ancient' magical documents, performing rituals, conjuring spirits.

The players of the occult underground were a sharp bunch, and they weren't (all, or exclusively) crooks. Crowley's persona as a vaudeville villain was just one of his many faces: he was also an excellent mountaineer and chess player, an erudite conversationalist, a good poet (at times) and a sincere mystic. Among other things, Yeats wrote a whole book on the existence of fairies. As for the Golden Dawn, with all its squabbles, it was a socially radical group in which women and men met as equals, in an age when women did not yet have the right to vote.

It would be easy to dismiss the occult underground as a backward-looking reaction to a world suddenly made barren of shadows and spirits, a sweet and fundamentally doomed one. It might be. But why call it a reaction and not a *resistance* movement? Yeats, Crowley and their motley crew were waging a beautiful guerrilla war against plain common sense, the same plain common sense that argued women were not intelligent enough to vote. They had a point, which we shouldn't dismiss too quickly. We should be suspicious of *common* sense. We want all our senses to be extraordinary.

The insurgents didn't win, but they managed to pass on the flame. Their descendants are still around. London is still a hotbed of magical orders, battling wizards, and strange rituals held in suburban homes. The guerrilla war goes on.

And these insurgents developed some handy skills.

Theatrical magicians had taught me a lesson about the importance of accepting the *mystery* as something that cannot be solved – not because it is too hard a problem, but because it is not a problem at all. No amount of science will 'solve' a mystery, in the same way that no amount of hammer blows will paint a room.

The word *mystery* has an interesting story behind it, steeped in spirituality. It comes from the ancient Greek *mustērion*, which indicated a secret revealed after initiation into a sacred cult. As the scholar of religion Karen Armstrong puts it, the mystery 'was not something that you thought (or failed to think!) but something that you did'. To join a 'mystery cult', the would-be initiate had to go through an exhausting sequence of rituals requiring fasting, processions, hymns and other – more obscure – elements, whose details were kept secret.

This ritual was *the only way* the mystery could be communicated. In practice, the ritual *was* the mystery. Words alone were not enough to pass it on, because the *mustērion* was not a specific piece of information. In all likelihood, some piece of information was part of it, but so were the pilgrimage, poetry, music and incense. The *mustērion* was not an abstract *idea*, but a transformative *performance*, facilitated by the priests.

The most celebrated of the cults of ancient Greece was the Eleusinian Mysteries, whose roots may have extended back to the Mycenaean era, around the twelfth century BC. At the core of these mysteries was the myth of the abduction of Persephone by Hades, god of the Underworld. At initiations, novices to the Mysteries would *live* this myth with their own body, in a ritual representation of death and resurrection. As far as we know, the ritual was intensely corporeal, and would involve all the senses through music, incense and other tools. The priests were *making* the mystery with the initiates. And considering that the mystery cult in Eleusis survived for a thousand years and more – from the age of Homer to the fourth century AD – they must have been on to something.

Our clear-minded understanding of the world has given us many marvels, but if we want to learn how to capture the myriad miracles of life, we need to be able to switch it off every now and then, to go back to a frame of mind in which ambiguous symbols are as important as rational theories. We need to learn how to *make* the mystery for ourselves.

To learn how to do that, I decided to pick the brains of a High Priestess.

The Fitzroy Tavern, on the corner of Charlotte Street and Windmill Street, is one of those London pubs where history talks, especially after you buy history a couple of pints. The district of Fitzrovia takes its name from it. It used to be a favourite hangout of London's bohemians, its patrons including Dylan Thomas and Aleister Crowley (him again). It was here I had lunch with a witch and her dog.

I was not frightened. Witches do not scare me much, and neither do dogs. Besides, Christina Oakley Harrington and I go way back. We met when I first moved to London, in 2008. Searching for some unusual books, I stepped into her shop, Treadwell's, which in those days was in Covent Garden. So I knew Christina, and I knew Rambo, a good-hearted mongrel rescue terrier who, despite Christina's and her partner's best attempts, stubbornly refused to have his name changed to Rimbaud.

Christina has a PhD in History, and before opening her bookshop she was a university lecturer with scholarly publications to her name. She still occasionally lectures at conferences on her specialist topics, occultism and feminism. As a former academic, a public speaker and the owner of a business in central London, she has all the markings of a sensible person. She also happens to be a Wiccan High Priestess.

Now, hold on a moment. At the mention of the word 'Wicca' your mind will summon up *The Craft* and other teenage Nineties movies, and Goth bric-a-brac, but before it became a sweetly bonkers teenage staple, Wicca was born as a religion in the spirit of the ancient mystery cults. It was, in fact, the first new religion home-brewed in England.

This strand of Wicca, the original one, is a secret oral tradition you can only learn in person: you *learn* Wicca by *doing* it. It is not much advertised and not much written about, but it is practised more or less worldwide, albeit, as far as I can make out, by very small numbers of people.

Wicca became a sensation in the Fifties, when a retired

colonial civil servant, Gerald Gardner, published *Witchcraft Today*, in which he posed as an anthropologist revealing the existence of a tiny secret cult, whose rituals had been transmitted orally across the generations from the Stone Age and whose adherents were the 'witches' of folklore. Gardner, like Mathers and countless other occultists, was being creative with the truth. This religion did actually exist, but rather than being an age-old hand-me-down, it had been concocted by Gardner himself and a group of countercultural friends scattered across London, Hertfordshire and the New Forest.

Be that as it may, the publication of *Witchcraft Today* got the new religion going. Gardner was widely interviewed by newspapers and on television shows. People wrote to him asking for more information, and some of them went on to be initiated, and initiated others in turn. Some of the new Wiccans went abroad, taking their mysteries with them, and people from abroad travelled to England to be initiated. And so it is that a mystery religion, closely guarding its secrets, spread across the world.

*

With its moon goddess and horned god, Wicca can seem more than a little surreal. But it feels less so when you are in a pub in Fitzrovia with a High Priestess and a mongrel terrier called Rambo. Witches are people and their pets are pets, and having lunch with them doesn't feel any different from having lunch with any other friend and their dog. I was after practical wisdom, ideas and actions that could be adapted to use in a secular context. It wouldn't be the first time that happened – mindfulness, now praised by Western doctors and offered as a therapy by the NHS, started life as an Eastern spiritual practice. With a bit of luck, I could find one of my keys to wonder in Christina's very British tradition.

Christina wouldn't reveal to me anything specific about what she does, but she agreed to talk about the broad contours of her life. And these would be remarkable enough even without Wicca. She comes from an Anglo-American family. Her father worked for the UN in developing countries, and she grew up in Nigeria, in West Africa, where she attended her first trance possession ritual at the age of six. At eight, she witnessed her first execution. She spent time in Pinochet's Chile, she visited Buddhist temples in Burma – all this before hitting fifteen, when she moved back to America to go to high school. The impact of her first encounter with the Western world was devastating: she felt, in her own words, 'spiritually deprived'. In the USA she lived in a wealthy suburb, which made her 'die inside'. She needed more than big houses and tree-lined streets to be happy. She needed more than *things*. She explored Buddhism, which she had experienced first-hand in Burma, but it was not a tradition with which she felt comfortable.

At twenty-three, she was still looking. That was when a friend made an offhand comment about Wicca, and gave Christina a copy of *Drawing Down the Moon*, a study of neopaganism written by Margot Adler, journalist, Wiccan High Priestess and granddaughter of the celebrated psychiatrist Alfred Adler.

The book inspired Christina: finally, she could put a name to what she wanted. She decided to look for *real* witches. Her journeys took her to Europe, where Wicca originated. She hitchhiked in Scotland, ended up on a tiny Orkney island, made contact via letter with a bona fide English Wiccan and finally, after a serious bout of illness that convinced her to leave the small Orcadian cottage where she was living and studying, she arrived in London, where she found 'it'. A coven of witches. She started her training, she was initiated, and went on to become High Priestess of her own coven. Amidst all this, she studied for and was awarded her doctorate, as well as starting her own business, which is now a thriving bookshop a stone's throw from the Fitzroy Tavern.

A 'coven' is a group of up to thirteen witches. Each coven is independent, with no central authority to answer to, even though most covens are informally in touch with each other. In the majority of cases a coven is led by a High Priestess and a High Priest, but the High Priestess comes unambiguously first. She is, however, *primus inter pares*, first among equals: she is the centre of the group, but this does not give her any moral authority over the others. As one of the very first High Priestesses put it, if she exceeded her role, people would 'vote with their feet' and leave.

A coven is basically a group of friends – though one that practises rituals in a rigorous way, within the guidelines of a specific tradition. Gaining access to a coven can be a rather laborious affair, and even then, you won't necessarily like its members and they won't necessarily like you, as can happen when any individual encounters a long-established group of friends. No reputable coven will take in a new person before an adjustment period, which lasts never less than 'a year and a day' and often more. Wicca does not require any exchange of money or favours, but it does require *time*.

In sum: there is a discreet international network of people, from all walks of life, organized in small groups, handing down an oral tradition based on a modern interpretation of ancient pagan religion, in which women have been leading the show since the Fifties. If I couldn't find any wonder there, I was doomed.

My opening question to Christina was pretty basic: what on earth is a 'High Priestess'?

She took her time before answering, sipping her sparkling water and nibbling at her vegetarian curry. 'I'm going to answer circuitously,' she said, 'because if you get into definitions, the world starts ending.' She patted Rambo's head and went on. 'I became an initiated witch at the age of twenty-six. I felt I knew that this was what I wanted to do for the whole of my life. That was twenty-eight years ago. Over time I went from being in a coven, where I did my apprenticeship, to having a coven of my own, and passing on the tradition. And when somebody is the head of a coven, *High Priestess* is the term given to them. It is a very grand term, but the grandness, at its best, applies to our aspirations. It is an archetype, an ideal. It means that I pass on the tradition that was passed to me, that I practise in a coven, and that I do the Work.'

'Which is...?'

'The Work is to be a friend of the mystery,' she said. On seeing my expression, she laughed, and tried to explain. 'Becoming a witch was my way of marrying the mystery. It was me saying, *I will be faithful to the unknown, I will not let that fall by the wayside. I will never walk away from the unknown, the mysterious, that thing that makes me tremble and allures me in equal measure.* The Work is to be faithful to that. The Work is also to bring that into the world.' She laughed again, at her own words this time. 'It sounds very noble, and strange. But yes, the Work is to bring that into the world. That which is unseen, that which is...' she paused, searching for the words, '...maybe on the other side, and remains largely unknowable. I made this promise, that I wouldn't shut in myself the door on the mysterious. The door on the *sacred* that is found in the darkness behind candlelight; or in the cave.' She paused once more. 'I kind of see myself as somebody who has their foot in the door to keep it from slamming shut.'

Christina loved what she did, she was aware of how odd it sounded and she was entirely unapologetic about both oddness and love. She didn't try to justify or explain or cajole – she simply stated what she thought. Or, better, what she felt.

That thing that makes me tremble and allures me in equal measure.

I was on the right track.

✳

Rudolf Otto was a Christian theologian with an interest in other religions. In 1917 he published a book called *Das Heilige*, *The Idea of the Holy*. The book tried to answer the question: what exactly do we mean when we say that something is 'holy'? What is a 'sacred' thing? And why is it sacred? This is a useful question for us wonder-seekers to ask, and we do not need to subscribe to any supernatural belief to understand why.

Say that you are walking in the woods, on your own, on a Sunday morning. Nothing strenuous, just an easy circuit you found in a book of local walks. It is one of those early warm days in May that make you feel young again, and the scent of blooming wild flowers lulls you into a contented mood. Right now, your life is not complicated or troublesome or messy. Right now, all is good.

You sit on the soft moss growing on the serpentine root of an oak tree. You take from your pack a cereal bar and your water bottle. You drink the water, you eat the bar, you put the wrapper in a pocket and decide to move on. You rest your hand on the root to push yourself up on your feet – and you touch a spot with no moss, and you notice the pleasant roughness of the wood. You don't stand up immediately. You keep your hand on the root.

You look at the oak. It must have been alive and growing on this spot for two hundred years and more. Your hand is still connected to the root, and now your hand tingles, as if an echo of all that energy, all that *life*, is running through you, from wood to flesh. You know it is not possible, you know it must be only suggestion and that there is a perfectly viable physiological explanation for that tingle, but that is beside the point. Your hand still tingles. This oak was here before the Second World War and even before the First, it was here before W. B. Yeats and Aleister Crowley were waging their magical war. Decade after decade the oak stood, and all those years, all those decades and centuries, all those days and hours and minutes in which so much happened, are here, under your palm, physically present with you.

You feel dizzy; a hint of vertigo. A part of you would like (will you dare to admit it?) to hug the oak. Another part of you is uneasy. This oak is a very old, very powerful living being. Much older and much more powerful than you. You are new and vulnerable and small and also, to tell the truth, a bit useless – the oak produces oxygen, something precious for the rest of the planet, while... what is it that you do for a living again?

Suddenly the woods seem very vast indeed, and empty of human presence.

You are afraid, a little bit. Why? It is a bright sunny day, and this isn't exactly an impenetrable fairy-tale forest. There is nothing to be afraid of. You shake your head and decide to move on, and you are so ashamed of this strange, childish moment that you never mention it to anybody. Maybe, in time, you forget about it altogether; or you don't think about it, which is the same.

This is a small experience of the holy, or *the sacred*. It is fuelled by a sense of wonder and generates one in turn. You can be the staunchest atheist and still go through an experience like this. It has nothing to do with what you think and everything to do with what you *feel*. Organized religions come later, as a response to that feeling, like a poem can be a response to falling in love, but organized religions *are not* the feeling itself.

Otto used the beautiful word *numinous* to describe the particular sense of wonder you feel when you are in the presence of something sacred. And, in turn, something is 'sacred' *because* it evokes that feeling. In the same way as you call a person your beloved because he makes you feel love, you also say that a place is sacred because it makes you feel the numinous.

Otto was convinced that the 'numinous' had to do with the supernatural – namely, with his god. Whether we agree with him or not, does not matter. To us, the feeling is vastly more important than its source. It is our privilege to interpret the feeling as supernatural, or psychological, or in-between, and to change our mind as we change in time. What is definitely real is the feeling itself, and so are its benefits. The numinous is one of the forms our sense of wonder takes.

Numinous. Try saying it aloud, feel the word roll off your tongue. It is one of those words that sound what they mean. The numinous is like that, something that can be evoked and never taught. The word comes from the Latin *numen*, meaning 'divine will' or 'divine presence'. If you want to 'help another to an understanding of it', says Otto, all you can do is bring that friend to a point where 'the numinous in him perforce begins to stir'. The potential for that feeling is always within you, but it must be 'awakened' rather than explained. To *communicate* the numinous, you will have to make people feel it, or remember about it. Reason is not the right tool for the task. It does not take a scholar, it takes a magician.

The numinous is a *mysterium tremendum et fascinans*, a mystery both frightening and attractive. You hanker after it and you are afraid of it. That curious thing you saw at dusk when you were nine, that thing that could have been an animal or a plant or something else entirely, that thing you wanted to touch, and at the same time recoil from, and you were never quite able to describe; you dismiss it now, you say it was *nothing*. But it didn't feel like nothing back then.

One of the reasons that children have such a sharp sense of wonder is that they haven't yet mastered language, and they are not under the illusion that language can master everything under the sky. There are a lot of things they can't express and it is quite natural for them to believe that some things cannot be expressed at all. Both ingredients of the numinous – fear and longing – are much stronger with them. They don't know who and what they are yet, they don't have a stable place in the world, and thus their world is a numinous network of fear and longing, always reverberating. An object of wonder.

But the truth is, even when we grow to adulthood we don't know who and what we are either. We just pretend we do. We don't know whether the face we show to our best friends and partner(s) is our real face, we don't know whether we have a real face at all. We know even less about ourselves than we do about the rest of the world, and if we suffer from 'impostor syndrome' it is because we are indeed, in many ways, impostors. We don't know how to go through life. We just wing it.

This thought is so anxiety-provoking that we end up buying wholesale certainties and off-the-peg identities. I am a respectable professional with a wild streak! I am a patriot! I am committed to social justice! I am a writer of books! I am this and I am that, and my truths are better than yours. We need to say this out loud and say it often, we need to scream it when we are drunk and to bang on about it on Twitter, because we know it is not true. All those certainties are not exactly lies, and not even masks – but clothes that we wear. They protect us, they warm us, they can be comfortable, useful and even beautiful; but beneath them, we are naked, and raw. We need to rediscover that rawness.

The same goes for the external world. We dress the world with those same clothes, and the world as well is still raw beneath them. An oak is an alien being, a living entity with its own agenda, which communicates with its environment, which is massively stronger and more resilient than any of us, which has the potential to outlive you, me, and a good number of our reincarnations (if reincarnation turned out to be a reality). When you feel *this* for a moment, you are peeking behind the veil with which you initially covered the oak. When you feel the strangeness of this, viscerally, rather than just understanding it intellectually, then you feel the oak's numinous presence. It is a feeling both frightening and alluring, a *mysterium tremendum et fascinans*, and it is attractive *because* it is frightening, and it is frightening *because* it is attractive. When you look down a wild cliff, and for a moment you think, *what would it feel like to jump.* This is the numinous.

This is what Christina is faithful to.

✳

'I can't define it,' she said, 'or explain it, but I can expand on it. The mystery is like... a black hole that is full, a plenary void, a night in a bedroom that is completely dark and closed and intimate and feels wonderful and scary all at once. It feels as close as... as a mother's breast in the dark, and also terrifying, like looking up at the night sky and thinking you could just fall off the Earth and fall into space. For ever.'

I wanted to go deeper. Religions sometimes have a tendency to first hint at things that are impossible to define, and then define exactly what those things are and what they are not; the 'true' mysteries and the 'phoney' ones. Otto wrote a 230-page book about the numinous, which is not a small number of pages to devote to a topic that in theory can't be spoken about.

When I mentioned this, Christina laughed again. 'I know what you mean,' she said. 'Wicca is less about what you *believe* than what you *do*. It does have a theology of a sort, to quote an old friend, and that theology is painted in broad brushstrokes, and the broad brushstrokes are broadly drawn, so that the details are not artificially fitted in.'

'You lost me there,' I said.

She nodded. 'Ok, let me put it this way: Wiccans believe that human beings have a sense of the sacred. We don't really have much of a "we believe in", but we do believe *that*. We believe that our conscious part is a small part of ourselves. It is an important part, but there is another one, which is a vast terrain we touch upon in dreams, a terrain of untapped creativity, of *a body that knows*. We also believe that the female principle, which we call the goddess, is hugely neglected. If somebody would really press me, I would say we believe in magic, in the goddess, and in ritual as a tool to connect with those realms.'

'So you *do* believe in a goddess.'

'And a god as well, but these are just… words we use,' Christina said. 'My tradition has always refused to define them. We use words, movements, rituals: we are not a text-based religion. We don't have our Tertullian, our Augustine. I could say the goddess is the female force of nature, and also a being.'

'You mean, an actual being?'

She shrugged. 'Maybe. Somebody could say, *the goddess is a principle*, somebody else could say, *it is female essentialism*, and somebody else could say, *she is an actual spirit who actually has a personality and I know what colours she likes*. Wicca itself doesn't do that. It is centred on *practice*. It just gives you a set of experiences, from which you draw your own conclusions.'

I didn't have the impression that Christina was avoiding the answer. I had the impression she was saying exactly what she meant to say. I tried to corner her, asking, 'Have you ever seen anything bizarre in a ritual?'

'My entire life is bizarre, when looked at from the outside. I transform my kitchen into an incense-making workshop, with piles of frankincense, and essential oils in jars, and smoke billowing and setting off the smoke detector, and two friends trying to disable the smoke detector before the neighbour knocks at the door. My partner coming in, and saying, *why are there twenty-eight jars in the kitchen, and what is this pile of herbs that looks like bad marijuana?* And I love that that is my life, I love that that is happening in central London.'

'I get your point.'

'But it doesn't answer your question.'

'Not exactly, no.'

She sighed, resigned. It dawned on me that she must be asked to answer this question pretty much every day of her life. We like to believe we are intellectually subtle and sophisticated, but when everything is said and done, we all wish for a touch of Hogwarts.

'Sometimes I see things, you know. Not anything that would blow anybody's socks off. I have experiences that are hugely amazing to me, but if I described them to you now, they would feel like a bit of a waking dream. For example, the person who taught me Wicca came to me shortly after she died. I felt her presence in a ritual, very strongly, at the edge of our circle. It was not in my imagination, but I wouldn't want to die on the hill of defending that to an atheist. It is a conversation I don't want to have. All I would say is, in witchcraft rituals I feel profoundly transported and profoundly moved. Things happen there which are real, on a mythic level. I have a mythic parallel life, and that gives meaning to my *whole* life, and never ceases to amaze me, and nourish me.' She paused again, looking me straight in the eye. 'Look,' she said, before delivering some of the strangest lines I have ever heard, 'I have seen a chicken sacrificed at six, I trekked in the desert when I was thirteen, I have seen monks levitate in Burma. My mum studied with them, and I saw her levitate too. Not much,' she added, as if that made the whole affair a bit humdrum, 'just a couple of inches or so. When I say that I have experiences in my rituals in London, experiences that transport me and make me want to do this for the rest of my life, *that* is the landscape I am comparing them to.'

I have been listening to the recording of our conversation quite a lot, and I have been taking plenty of notes. This is the part that struck a chord with me. The exotic and the mundane, travel and self-exploration, the spectacularly strange and the gently meaningful: Christina was telling me that she got to a point where those different 'landscapes' are one and the same for her. She can be as amazed in her kitchen as she was when, as a girl, she journeyed to a Buddhist temple to see levitating monks. It is a crucial point – a crossroads we need to reach ourselves.

You may find the idea of flying monks appealing or you may find it absurd. Either way, I'd like you to forget about it. I appreciate this may be difficult, because the image is hard to dislodge from your mind. But our journey is not about the paranormal; our journey is about the normal, redefined. In Christina's story there is a nugget far more precious than the possible levitation itself.

It is the way she told it. When Christina related the levitation episode, she dropped it in casually, with no fuss, showing little or no interest in it. Make no mistake, she believes the levitation was genuine (she trusts her mother). But *she actually doesn't care* about gravity-defying monks and mums. Witnessing human levitation is to her not inherently more prodigious than making incense in her kitchen. This is an astonishing quality she has: she can – quite literally – find the magic in the everyday.

A magic so powerful, so *intense*, as to overshadow miraculous feats in faraway temples.

We want that.

Flying monks, like theatrical magicians, offer us a visual miracle, a precious gift of wonder, regardless of how it is achieved. Learning the world view of a High Priestess may help us to find wonder not just in things that are obviously extraordinary but also in things that are quietly so. Thus can apparently mundane aspects of our daily lives take on a magical light. An enchanted world is not a place where we don't see different things, but we see things differently.

Our sense of wonder sharpens when we stop chasing the spectacularly strange to focus on the gently meaningful. Think how much more intense and pleasurable your life will be when you stumble upon a numinous experience in your own home. Whatever we think of the thorny relationship between monks and gravity, we all have kitchens, and it is those we need to enchant.

By using – yes – magic.

✳

Witches cultivate to an impressive extent what the poet John Keats called 'negative capability': the skill of *not* asking questions. True artists, such as Shakespeare, he said, should know how to accept 'being in uncertainties, mysteries, doubts without any irritable reaching after fact and reason'. This goes against the grain of everything we were taught: when you want to understand something better, you ask a question; when you want to show interest, you ask a question; when you want to gain a deeper level of self-knowledge, even then, you ask a question. The principle that *asking questions* should be our default mode is rarely itself under question. The only alternative, after all, is bleak ignorance.

Questions are the spotlights our mind uses to dispel the shadows. As such, they are immensely useful – and yet a human being cannot live in perpetual light. In order to flourish we need to sleep, and dream, and you can't do that in a neon-lit office. Keeping the spotlights on 24/7 cripples our sense of wonder and does serious harm to our well-being: it is in the darkness that our subconscious stirs, it is in the shadows that our best ideas grow. We need to make space for that darkness in our life.

There are times when asking questions is the right thing to do (the journey we are taking in this book, is, after all, based on questions asked), while at other times it is better to embark on a different form of exploration. Witches ask questions – Christina is adamant that most of them love science, and it is certainly true of those I have met (when they have a cold, they swallow paracetamol). But they also know how to change gear. They can turn off the light and enter into a state of mind that makes the numinous more likely to happen – that lets them appreciate the strangeness of life. We have been taught that the light of reason is all there is; witches, without renouncing that very precious light, teach us also to embrace the shadows, the flickering daydreams, the things half-seen and half-imagined.

The problem is, the spotlights inside us have been switched on throughout our lives, and the outside world today is full of noise at an unprecedented level. After spending a day on social media, email, messaging apps, even when we switch off our physical devices (assuming we do so at all), their ghostly presence remains in our mind. The feeling of hardened glass lingers on our fingertips, and the last thing we see in our mind's eye before falling asleep is not a kindly old teacher of magic, but a white F on a blue background.

The magical insurgents discovered early on that they couldn't wish reality away: Victorian London, with its smoke and clangour and stink, was there, indisputably real, whether they liked it or not. Changing gear required more than a decision; it required a conscious effort. We are in the same position. To find shadows and silence, so as to let the numinous stir within us, we need to *make* shadows and silence anew. The technique the insurgents developed to do that is called *ritual*.

Wicca has no set belief, no promises about the afterlife. Practice matters, whereas faith does not. You can think what you want about the ultimate nature of gods and spirits, or the fate of your soul after death; but when a ritual with your coven is in the calendar, you have to show up. 'Like a musician keeps time with a metronome,' Christina said, 'we do that with rituals. Come hell or high water, whether the timing is convenient or inconvenient, we show up. The aim of a ritual is to put you in a space where your inner door to mysteries can open. What happens in rituals is beautiful, poetic, candlelit, always familiar but always unknown.'

Witches meet in the woods, or in private spaces, and they 'close up the outside world'. Wherever they are, they make sure they are not going to be interrupted or disturbed. They need to be fully engaged with what they are doing, in body and mind, and the smallest of distractions could break the spell (it's tricky opening an inner door if you're worried you are going to bump into someone walking their dog).

Rituals are held in a circle, which is 'the shape that we form around the campfire', the oldest way in which humans come together. Without giving me any specifics, Christina said that during a ritual 'we dance, we sing, we speak words of praise and poetry. We drum, we have moments of ecstasy and moments of stillness, engaging all senses. The exact details of what we do are not very old, but all the important components you find in tribal initiatory traditions from Sumatra to northern Liberia, to the Inuit. Look for the circle, look for the drum, look for the calling of the spirits, look for what in that language is considered the most beautiful poetry, look for the moments of ecstasy, look for the moments of stillness, look for the experts who have gone through a secret initiation.'

Secrecy is important: rituals are like Las Vegas, and what

happens there, stays there. 'Things that happen in the private sphere,' Christina said as we were leaving, 'have a lovely intimacy about them. They live in the same place of remembered dreams, things that are not out there to be debated and discussed. They live in the place of our mythic self, where the doors are switched open to the realms of the gods.' Those are the last words in the interview; we said goodbye, and went our own ways.

Christina's words made me think of those famous lines of John Milton: 'the mind is its own place and in itself / can make a Heaven of Hell, a Hell of Heaven'. Wiccans seem to think along similar lines, and though they do not believe in Heaven and Hell as such, they work to make their mind a different place: a mythical wilderness where gods still walk.

To learn the tricks of their trade, we need to make one more move and realize that *mythical* does not mean *fake*. A myth is a different sort of truth, as the ancient Greeks were aware. For them, there were two ways of understanding the world and our place in it. One was called *logos*, and it was about logic and clear-mindedness – about shedding light, if you like. It was about asking well-defined questions in the search for well-defined answers, and then trying to understand whether the answers were correct. In time, this way of thinking would give birth to modern science.

But there was also a second way, which has been all but forgotten in the West. It was called *mythos*, and it was about ambiguous feelings and personal meanings that couldn't be explained, only more or less pointed at – it was about shadows. It was celebrated by priests and *aedi*, the Greek bards, and was prominent at mystery rituals. It involved tales of gods and heroes and sacred performance, it was about art, poetry and, of course, mystery. *Logos* formulates theories, *mythos* tells stories.

If *logos* is the reassuring, competent parent who has a law degree and helps you to find a good, well-paid job with prospects, *mythos* is the unreliable uncle who shows you how to break the ice with girls. *Logos* is there to help you understand objective truths, *mythos* is there to help you deal with those parts of your life that will always remain profoundly mysterious. *Logos* is the map you use to find your way in the woods, *mythos* is the lines of poetry that inspired you to walk in those woods in the first place. *Logos* is not boring and *mythos* is not fanciful. For a full life, you need both. Otherwise you're going to get lost in the woods; or you're not even going to bother to visit them.

When Christina mentions her *mythical life* and her *mythical self*, she is not referring to 'unreal' things, but rather, to things that are real in a *mythos* kind of way. She refuses debate because debating her spiritual life would be both wrong and pointless. Debate, with its coherent arguments and counter-arguments, is how you abandon *mythos* and slip into *logos*.

The secret to a healthy inner life is balance. Today we insult *mythos* by making it synonymous with 'fake'. Even those who defend positions that are scientifically indefensible – say, that we shouldn't vaccinate our children – appeal to *logos*, in a far-fetched way. Religious fundamentalists appeal to a *logos*-based view of their faith, in which stories must be considered literally true – because the only other option would be to consider them utterly fake. No one wants to be tainted with the accusation of being in the thrall of naive, filthy *mythos*.

Over and over again we are told that *logos* (for the smart and the well-adjusted) is wholesome and useful, while *mythos* (for deluded hippies) is pointless at best and more often harmful. But that is like saying that, because you look good in the elegant tailor-made suit you go to work in, you should wear it all the time – when you go to sleep, when you go to the gym, and even when you go for a swim. Sounds uncomfortable, doesn't it? Applying *logos* to our whole life is likewise uncomfortable. We need to recreate within ourselves a bridge towards *mythos*.

We can do that through *ritual*.

Ritual focuses on words and actions that are *meaningful* rather than *useful*. It gives us a context in which what we say and what we do resonates with larger truths about what we wish for and what we fear – truths we cannot fully articulate in a clean, logical way. It gives us a way to think with our body, to think with our friends, to think with our dreams. It nurtures our most creative intuitions.

Witches dance in ways that are not so different from the ways party-goers dance in a club, but the witches' dance is enchanted, *because it takes place in a magic circle*. Because it is made into a ritual. Witches want to live in modern cities and fully engage with them, and at the same time they want to cultivate an ancestral mindset that harks back to a time before cities, an age of wild shamans and things in caves. An age of wonder found in shadows. In those shadows, in *mythos*, dancing with your friends is also a prayer, an illness is also a demon, a lake is also a god. This system of echoes and mirrors within mirrors, this dazzling world view in which some things are real, others are fake, and others yet are mythic, is what they create in their mind through ritual. And by doing so they transform their kitchens into mythical sites, dreamier than a distant temple where people levitate. Hogwarts is not a place you go to, it is a place you *make up*. This is what both W. B. Yeats and Aleister Crowley were striving for with their poetry and their magic – if there is, at this point, any difference.

✳

We cannot decide to have a numinous experience any more than we can decide to fall in love. But we certainly can do something to open our heart to love, and similarly we can open ourselves to the numinous. We can create the conditions for it to happen. It seems an odd endeavour only because our society prizes love and talks about it incessantly, while by and large it ignores the out-of-fashion and incommunicable numinous. Even churches look at it with embarrassment, as if it were a drunken grandfather crashing a very polite party. We start at a disadvantage here.

The numinous is shy. It cannot be chased, only lured, and the more we hunt it, the further it flees. All we can do is turn off the light, burn a candle, and invite it in. We open the door and we wait, in the silence, in the shadows.

THE WORKOUT

In our second workout, we are going to learn how to embed *mythos* in our life.

1. The Transfiguration of the Everyday

Write down three or more dull things that you often do, or that you are going to do soon, or that you have recently done. For example: a long meeting, dinner with the in-laws, standing in a queue. Make notes on why you find that particular activity so dull.

Then talk to a friend about these dull activities. With her, find reasons why they are not so dull after all. The difficult bit here is that you are *not* looking for ways to make those activities less dull; you are looking for reasons why they might not be that dull. Reasons you did not see in the first place.

I cannot promise that this will make everything you do fun and interesting, but it will show you how to cultivate a deeper, more enchanted perspective, in ways that make sense for you.

2. The Candlelit Week

For a week, use electric lights as little as you can. When evening comes and you are home, rather than turning on the light, turn on candles. Make notes on how this makes you feel, and what impact it has, if any, on your relationship with darkness, on your mood and on your creativity.

3. The *Mythos* of You

Create, and write down in your Book of Wonder, a mythic reason to explain the loss of wonder in grown-ups, and the dangers that loss entails. For example: a jealous god steals wonder from early teenagers and keeps it in a jar. Has anyone ever stolen theirs back? How can you steal back yours?

4. The Ritual

Based on the *mythos* you wrote, create a small ritual for yourself, and repeat it over a period of time that you set in advance – a week, or ten days, or even a month. For example, if your *mythos* says that a god stole wonder and kept it in a jar, your ritual might consist in drinking every evening a sip of water from a jar you bought only for this reason, and that you filled with water on the first day. You keep the ritual going until the jar is empty. Make the moment in which you sip the water a meaningful, sacred moment. Approach the water as if it really was *your wonder made liquid*.

Whatever your ritual is, keep it a secret: do not reveal it to anybody, not even to your partner or closest friends. It is only for you. When you are creating the ritual, consider the necessity of secrecy (if you are not often home alone, it might be difficult to have a secret ritual entailing a perfumed bath every day for one month).

Write down the ritual in your Book of Wonder, and give it a name. Also, make a note every time you do the ritual.

5. Fear of the Dark

This can be an upsetting exercise; please skip it if you are particularly anxious, prone to fear, or you just feel it is too much for you at this moment of your life.

We pretend that we stopped being afraid of the dark. When that happens, it is because we refuse to imagine what the dark could hide. Fear and attraction are both features of the numinous, and we need to reconnect with both.

Sit somewhere in your house, alone, in darkness. Do not put a blindfold on; just find a room that is as close as possible to completely dark.

Listen to the silence: is there a scratching on the wall? Focus on the shapes in the dark: why are they moving? And is that a strange smell that you sense? A cold hand brushing against your shoulder? Think of the things that made you afraid when you were little: are they still with you, unseen, unheard?

Do this for five or ten minutes, depending on how long it takes for you to become unnerved. Repeat it three times, letting at least a day pass between each iteration. Every time, write down your thoughts immediately after you turn on the light. What was it that made you afraid – and how is that connected to what attracts you?

If the exercise causes you anxiety, stop it at once.

The Third Key
The Light

*Too much of a good thing
can be wonderful*

I n my early twenties I visited a *Wunderkammer*, a chamber
of wonders.

Such a chamber, also referred to in English as a 'cabinet
of curiosities', does what it says on the tin: it is a collection of
wondrous curios. Picture the scene. You enter a candlelit room
overflowing with oddities stacked from floor to ceiling in no
perceivable order, looming over you on all sides. On your right,
a human-shaped root sits side by side with the remnants of a
creature that might or might not exist. On your left, an elabor-
ately carved wooden clock rests below a tiny ivory ship. You
will find crammed in a square metre more objects than you
have in your entire home, and each of them is (or purports to
be) unique.

When modern science was getting started, between the late
sixteenth and early seventeenth centuries, it was common for
people of note to keep such a *Wunderkammer*, which could be
as small as a cabinet or big enough to occupy a suite of rooms
in a palace, depending on the owner's wealth and inclinations.
Natural 'wonders' merged seamlessly with artefacts. A wealthy

collector might juxtapose a real, stuffed, brightly coloured bird of paradise with an automaton in the form of a duck that appeared to eat grain, digest it and then defecate it. And those fearsome talons, labelled 'griffin claws' – were they perchance the claws of an actual griffin?

The thread connecting the exhibits was that they were all in some way interesting, strange – and new. The *Wunderkammer* gave visible form to the cutting-edge spirit of science, with its insatiable curiosity about everything beneath and beyond the sky, and its thirst to catalogue, to understand, and to *know*.

In our enlightened times, that kind of *Wunderkammer* is no more. Some descendants linger, in the form of commercial museums big and small. Ripley's Believe It or Not! is a chain with branches worldwide; the Viktor Wynd Museum of Curiosities, Fine Art and Natural History occupies a basement in Hackney, London.

The one I visited was a travelling *Wunderkammer* that stayed in Florence for several weeks. As soon as I read in an article that the exhibition included a *mummified siren*, I knew I had to go. Yes, I was perfectly aware that the siren was fake. Even so, someone had taken the trouble to *create a siren*.

I was living in Rome back then, a student and young writer with more dreams than skills, exquisitely broke. A round trip to Florence, a ticket to the show: the sad truth was, it was an expensive undertaking. I counted my *lire* and found very few. After some accounting, I realized that if I dialled my social life down to zero for a while, I could make it. Drinks or sirens? It was a no-brainer.

On a November morning I packed my lunch, got on a train, and travelled all the way to Florence. The journey, although not a long one, felt interminable: it had not been possible to book a ticket over the phone (online bookings lay some way in the future), so I fretted I would find the show sold out for the day and would never get to see it.

After taking one or two wrong turns, thanks to my non-existent sense of direction (smartphones too were yet to come), I managed to locate the little building that hosted the *Wunderkammer*. I was immensely relieved to discover that the show hadn't sold out. I bought my ticket and, at last, was admitted into the holy place.

It was not at all what I had expected.

There were all the right exhibits, the ones I had read about. Odd plants, check. Stuffed animals, check. There were shamanic masks and mysterious etchings, and the *pièce de résistance*, the mummified siren. It was brown, and wrinkly, and looked passably siren-like if you weren't too strict about mythology (it was half-woman and half-fish, but originally the sirens were supposed to be half-woman and half-*bird*). It was okay.

Only okay.

I realized with horror that I was getting bored. I dragged out the visit, hoping against hope that *something* would strike my eye, grab my heart, and squeeze out a tiny drop of wonder.

I was eager to be amazed, willing to be bewildered. I took another look at the siren. Maybe I had missed something, and if I tried a little harder, I would be left astounded by...

It just didn't happen. Finally, I had to give up, admit that I had wasted my money, and trudge back to the station, defeated. I couldn't even afford to buy a consoling glass of wine.

I have visited other *Wunderkammern* since then. I enjoyed them all the more for lowering my expectations. They didn't fill me with wonder, but then again, they weren't trying to. They aimed to entertain, and to make people smile. They were never going to inspire a real sense of wonder. And nor could they, because even though they are offering us more or less the same selection of items as the *Wunderkammern* of past centuries, *we*, the spectators, have changed beyond recognition.

A *Wunderkammer* was a model of the world; it was, in a sense, the world. Lost in its sweeping collection of marvels, visitors participated at a visceral level in the cultural revolution that was going on. Between shelves and cabinets, they would discover the miracles of the natural world, and understand that there were more things in heaven and earth, way, way more, than in anybody's philosophy. Yes, griffins could be real, and sirens too, and it was possible to build automata, and to stuff birds of paradise. And if that was feasible, what else might be? The *Wunderkammer* opened up a world of possibilities, of unanswered questions.

In the sixteenth and seventeenth centuries – the era of the

Scientific Revolution – science was asking a whole lot of new questions no one had ever thought of asking before. It was revealing the world to be a *Wunderkammer*. Were the stars fixed in their positions, as everybody had believed for centuries without number, or did they perhaps move? Why do apples fall? The questioning of the old certainties was creating a climate of doubt, which found its expression in the *Wunderkammern*.

That climate is long gone. I told myself that knowing that the siren was a fake wouldn't make any difference, but of course it did. I knew that in all likelihood sirens do not exist, and I also knew that making a mummified one does not require a huge amount of skill. I knew that a mandrake root looked like a person only because of a perceptual phenomenon called *pareidolia*, by which we see familiar patterns where none exist. Rather than astonishing me, the accumulation of oddities in that modern-day Florentine *Wunderkammer* made me feel that oddities were cheap and easy to come by.

Overwhelmed by scientific information, at times we might feel the same. A new star was discovered yesterday, but a new star was discovered last month as well. That's what new stars do, they get discovered. If a sense of wonder is connected to a sense of the mysterious, then science, which has no patience with the mysterious, seems bound to kill wonder. We might be led to believe that science – humanity's adulthood – has sanitized the world, making of it not a *Wunderkammer* but, at best, a museum with a gaudy gift shop attached. John Keats, in his poem 'Lamia', asked, 'Do not all charms fly / At the mere touch of cold philosophy?'

It is a good question.

✳

An Experiment on a Bird in the Air Pump, painted in the 1760s by Joseph Wright of Derby, is a splendid work of art. I discovered it during my first visit to London, towards the end of a hard day's sightseeing. After trekking around town since morning, I had reached a point of saturation in which all the sights I had seen merged into a psychedelic kaleidoscope of shapes and colours. The only reason I stopped in front of Wright's painting, in the National Gallery, was that there was a wizard in it, and even in a state of exhaustion I could never say no to a wizard.

I moved a little closer, and realized it was not a wizard I was looking at.

The painting represents a scientist performing an experiment for a rapt audience. He is a severe man with a mane of white hair, clad in a red robe with black hemming that would be the pride of any wizard. He takes centre stage, light coming from below, his robe a fiery column in a dark room. The scene is candlelit, which adds to the impression that magic is afoot. With one hand the wizard-scientist is beckoning to us, inviting us into his world, while with the other he lightly touches a crank handle on the top of an exquisitely shaped glass jar, which in turn sits on a wooden pillar. In the jar is a bird.

The bird is going to die.

The glass jar and the pillar form an 'air pump', a mechanical contrivance invented by the German scientist Otto von Guericke in the seventeenth century. In a moment, the scientist, or 'natural philosopher' as he would have been called in 1768 when the painting was executed, will create a vacuum within the sealed jar, and the bird, with no air left, will convulse, and die.

Calling this an 'experiment' is generous: the natural philosopher knows perfectly well that the bird is going to die. It would be more honest to say that he is performing a trick.

The audience forms a circle around him. A young woman shields her eyes, while a little girl courageously looks at the bird, upset, but still prepared to watch. A patronizing older man explains the goings-on to both of them. Another man is lost in contemplation, while a younger one looks on attentively. There are other characters; they are all expecting something to happen, something unusual but not mysterious. They know as well as the scientist does that the bird is doomed, and they know – or are learning – why. This is the opposite of the 'mystery' we have learned from magicians and witches, and of the 'negative capability' praised by Keats, the ability *not* to ask questions. In this painting, everyone is asking questions, to receive robust, no-nonsense answers.

And yet, not one character is jaded. A powerful awe pervades their faces, the room, the ill-fated bird. Nothing suggests that science is disenchanting the world; quite the opposite, the scientist is casting a spell over the room. Looking at *An Experiment on a Bird in the Air Pump*, we might feel that, if we could only accept his invitation and find a way into the painting, he would lead us to a secret kingdom of endless miracles, no less astonishing for being 'scientific'.

Wright's scientist – part scholar, part showman – was an 'itinerant professor', a well-known breed in eighteenth-century England. These professors would travel from town to town, like actors in a touring theatre company, to give lectures, perform spectacular experiments, sell books and gadgets – and then move on. Some of them even went on tour abroad: the blind lecturer Henry Moyes, a Scot, toured the United States for two years between 1784 and 1786, impressing audiences from Boston to New York to Charleston with his wit, his knowledge and his round-rimmed dark glasses.

The very idea of science was young and fresh, and it opened a space for private entrepreneurs. Moyes and his ilk were creating a new form of entertainment, while at the same time teaching real science to real people. A contemporary journalist praised them for being 'midwives of other people's discoveries'. They awed their audiences with scientific miracles and inspired some to carry out experiments of their own, thus creating new touring opportunities for aspiring scientist-showmen. Science was offering a different kind of magic, alluring and terrifying.

Our third key lies concealed deep in the roots of modern

science. In order to unearth it, we will first turn to a mercenary-soldier-turned-philosopher, named René Descartes.

✳

Were Princess Elisabeth of Bohemia alive today, she would rightly be recognized as a first-rate intellectual. But she was born to the 'Winter King' Frederick V and his wife, Elizabeth, daughter of King James I of England (VI of Scotland), in 1618, when it was a pipe dream for a woman to achieve intellectual recognition. She was gifted, though, very much so, and came from scholarly inclined parents, who spent most of their time and money surrounding themselves with books and philosophers. Good scholars rarely make good politicians, and Elisabeth's parents managed to hold on to power in Bohemia for one meagre year. Still, they made sure that their clever daughter received an excellent education – and she would certainly make the most of it.

In the 1640s, Elisabeth entered into a correspondence with the French thinker René Descartes. He was one of the philosophers that were shaping the Enlightenment – that is, the era that did away with the notion that some questions cannot be answered. During the Enlightenment, our modern notion of 'rationality' was born.

In their letters, Elisabeth and René discussed all sorts of matters at length. Descartes recognized the princess as 'the keenest sort of intellect', though she posed as a clueless damsel in cultural distress, who looked up to Descartes 'as someone who can help her to remedy the weakness of her own mind'. Elisabeth was an accomplished thinker in her own right, and her pose was a disingenuous one. No mere muse, she was not too shy to challenge Descartes, criticizing him, pushing him to think harder. She convinced Descartes to mine their correspondence to produce a treatise on passions.

This Descartes did, and in 1649 he came up with *Les passions de l'âme* (*Passions of the Soul*), in which he uses the cold light of reason to understand its apparent polar opposite, the passions (what we would call the 'emotions' today). He began by turning his attention to the emotion of wonder.

Up to that moment it had been accepted that our emotional life was based on two basic impulses, that is, whether we were attracted to something, say a happy puppy, or repulsed by something, say a decomposing badger. Every other feeling was a variation on this theme. Descartes didn't stray too far from this template, and five out of six of the 'fundamental' passions he listed (love, hatred, desire, joy, sadness) fit it perfectly. But there is another passion, he said, which comes before you decide whether something is good for you or not. It is the passion that grabs you when you encounter something entirely new – when you witness a curious experiment, when you meet a good-looking stranger, when you embrace a new experience. In the moment before you decide whether that as yet unknown thing is good or bad, you feel a sense of wonder (in French, *admiration*).

You feel it when you are faced, all of a sudden, with something you did not expect. A tree is nothing remarkable, but a walking tree, *that* would fire up your sense of wonder. Father Christmas was so impressive to me as a child because, as far as I knew, sledges were not supposed to fly, elderly men were not supposed to come down the chimney, and giving away stuff was not something that trustworthy individuals generally did. I didn't believe such things were possible until my older brothers assured me that on Christmas Eve, and only on Christmas Eve, they were. This discovery enchanted my Decembers.

Think back to an experience of wonder you had. You will probably find that it had to do with something you had not noticed before, and not necessarily because it was something new. You have seen a full moon a hundred times and more, but when you saw it that night on the beach, *then*, it filled you with awe; *then*, you noticed the gentle strength of her light for the first time.

Wonder comes when you notice something, or something happens, that you did not expect. Coming first, when no other passion has arrived yet, wonder sets the stage for them all. Without wonder you would feel no other emotions, because something that does not make you wonder won't grab your attention at all.

Descartes' era was brimming with bright new things. Natural philosophers, astronomers, alchemists and other intellectual adventurers were inventing science, which was then *far* from being common sense. The Sun rotating around the Earth was common sense. But the idea that the Earth might be rotating around the Sun? That was weird and dangerous, that was wild and wondrous.

Science was opening up new, counter-intuitive ways of thinking, ways that shouldn't work and yet did. Itinerant professors made a living out of demonstrating impossible things – they could kill a bird without touching it! Since the dawn of humanity, the power to smite down hapless mortals with invisible fire had been the preserve of gods. And yet the new philosophers proclaimed that mortals need never be hapless again: they had stolen the fire from the heavens and now it was *them* doing the smiting.

When people emerged from these professors' lectures, they were *roused*. The professors were using a sense of wonder to teach science, and in so doing they were nurturing a sense of wonder in their audiences, showing them a host of new, unexpected things. It was a perfect match – for a while.

It didn't last long. By the early nineteenth century, John Keats was already mourning the end of enchantment. Science had become commonplace, wonder-phobic. As Keats put it, 'Philosophy will clip an Angel's wings, / Conquer all mysteries by rule and line / Empty the haunted air, and gnomèd mine.' In the century in which Keats lived most of his short life, so many angels were having their wings clipped that, as we have seen, an insurgency of magicians started fighting to save at least a few of them. Keats fought on the front line.

Yet on rereading his poem 'Lamia', I am left uneasy. On the one hand, I can relate to the sentiment. On the other, however, blaming science is a dangerous game. Science might have chased gnomes out of mines, but it also saved miners' lives, and though it made charms fly, it also made *us* fly. Not to mention that Keats died in Rome at twenty-five, of tuberculosis, and with a little more science, he might have lived.

We know this; so we are tempted to believe that life is a matter of choosing between a short, dysfunctional life of enchantment, or a life that is long, successful and quite dull. It is once again the core choice our society sets up for us – are you a dreamer or a doer? A binary choice, apparently simple, as all the best traps are.

We started our journey because we refused to fall into it. Others made the rules for us and decided they are the only rules possible. We should not obey; we can make rules of our own. Magicians and witches set us on our path, and now scientists will show us the next move.

But first, let's leave Descartes behind.

※

Descartes said: 'it's only dull and stupid folk who are not naturally disposed for wonder.' The 'dull and stupid' do not understand that trees are not supposed to walk, so if they happen to see one ambling around, they shrug it off and carry on. Nothing can astound them. We tend to believe that the unflappable ones are wise. But no, said Descartes – they are just dense.

The problem is that life, left to its own devices, makes us all dull and stupid. When you are little, you run outside excitedly when it snows, but then, when you are grown up, you grumble about the snow that makes your train run late. I know for a fact that you are dull and stupid. So am I. We are on this journey because we refuse to die that way.

This is where we must part company with Descartes. He noticed that wonder 'seems to diminish with use', because with the passing of time fewer things are new to us, and more and more things become *déjà vu* and *déjà entendu*. But he was convinced that first, this was inevitable, and second, this was a good thing. Wonder must come, leave useful memories, and then go.

Descartes expressed himself like a tough-talking boss who tells you that enjoying the magic is fine only as long as you stop early. Let your jaw go slack, kid, but then shut it and get to work. You live in a clockwork world and you'd better get on with it. For Descartes, the sole function of our sense of wonder is to spur us on to understand the world better and master it with a stronger grip. That's it. Wonder on its own is worthless. Those who don't have a sense for it are 'dull and stupid', true, but having too much of it is a 'disease whose victims seek out rarities simply in order to wonder at them and not in order to know them'. Even worse, 'things of no importance are as likely to grab their attention as things that would actually be useful to investigate'.

You hear the echo of his words in those of the teacher who kept telling you to stop looking out of the window and *focus on what really matters*. Do not become 'too full of wonder', he admonished, with Descartes. Don't build castles in the air. It's bad for you.

This might seem wise: too much of a good thing is a bad thing, they say. Is that true, though? Descartes took it for granted that everything comes in definable measures, like the amount of water you drink from a single cup, or the miles you cover in a day. He believed – superstitiously, for he had no reason to do so – in a purely mechanical universe, in which everything was a pump, a cog, a quantity either known or soon to be known. So, you should keep track of how much wonder you feel, until the moment you say, 'I'm good, thanks', as you would say to the guy buying the next round at the pub.

Everything is quantifiable, measurable, everything is a matter of economics. All life (and human relationships) can be reduced to a zero-sum game. It is a waste of time to just sit and contemplate a hare in springtime; you contemplate just enough, then you hunt the hare and slice it open, to understand how it *works*. There are things of consequence and things of no consequence, the useful and the useless, and sober Descartes knows which is which.

The Light · 115

Well, let's not be sober: let's jump on the table and sing bawdy songs. Too much of a good thing, as I read once on a graffiti in Glastonbury, can be wonderful. Let's kill the idea that our sense of wonder is a humble servant whose job is to prepare the place for the better things to come.

I am not implying that we shouldn't study a hare's biology. There is a lot of pleasure to be gained from that, a lot of wonder, and a lot of wisdom too. I am saying that life is not a zero-sum game, it is not a sum of binary choices, of yes or no, here or there. Unfortunately, we inherited Descartes' view: wonder is a young people's game, and in order to grow up we *have to* give it away. This is a widespread superstition in which we should stop believing.

Rather, we might let our sense of wonder breathe and speak and grow. It will change organically on its own, becoming at times the curiosity to understand a tree, at times the inspiration to write a poem. Rather than decide where to go from wonder, rather than fretting over being in control of it, let's trust wonder and see where *it* leads *us*. You might discover that what you wanted to do all along was, indeed, to study a hare's biology; or just to sit under the canopy of a beech tree. You thought you wanted to be an artist and instead you discovered you were keen to go to law school; you thought you wanted to get a PhD in mathematics but you found that life as a schoolteacher was more rewarding.

Descartes left us with the gloomy prophecy that we will

lose our sense of wonder as we grow older. It is a self-fulfilling prophecy, which only comes true if we believe it to be so. Rather than the first move of your emotional life, you could think of wonder as its bass note, booming into prominence sometimes, then fading in the background only to rise again, always playing. It is not something that happens *first* but something that happens *always*. Listen to it and you will realize that 'things of no importance' do not exist in this bizarre universe of ours, only things you didn't look at closely enough, because you were too 'dull and stupid' to realize how new they could be. Descartes too was dull and stupid in some respects. We will find our third key when we learn to look *more carefully*.

We began our journey by locating a first spark of wonder within us, with the help of magicians. When that spark lit a flickering candle, we danced with witches in the shadows it cast. Now we are going to set our world ablaze, and to do that, we are not going to hide from the light of reason any more. Rather, we are going to embrace it – to the utmost extent.

✳

The world is not a second older than you. Are you seventy-four? Then your world is seventy-four years old. Depending on your knowledge of history, you have a vague or a slightly less vague idea of some of the stuff that happened before you were born, and a vaguer idea about what might happen after you die, and yet every idea you have had, every experience you have been through, every thought you have ever thought, *the entire lifespan of the world from your point of view* is contained within those seventy-four years. Do you seriously believe that you can run out of new experiences in seventy-four years?

Think about this: 66 million years ago, dinosaurs became extinct. Before that, they walked the Earth for around 177 million years. This is such an enormous span of time that it is almost impossible for us to conceive it. To get a better idea, just think of this – our entire species, *Homo sapiens*, has been kicking around for a mere 200,000 years or thereabouts, and we are already self-destructing: I wouldn't bet on our making it to our one-millionth birthday. Dinosaurs were on this planet far – immeasurably far – longer than us. No scholar believes that dinosaurs ever managed to create the advanced technology it takes to self-destruct. Maybe they were too stupid, or maybe they were too smart.

And now this: there is a jellyfish in the Mediterranean, called *Turritopsis dohrnii*, that is as immortal as Tolkien's elves. It can be killed, but if it manages to keep a low profile, it can live for ever, by regularly reverting to an earlier stage of development, literally rejuvenating itself. The jellyfish you killed last summer in Puglia could have been swimming with Cleopatra.

And now this: peregrine falcons, which can dive faster than a Ferrari 488, have left their wild lairs and come to squat in London. They nest on roofs and niches high above the streets and find prey in abundance. Londoners rarely get to see them only because Londoners rarely bother to look up. They are too busy looking at their mobile phones.

And now this: when you look at the stars, you are looking at the past. Starlight takes many, many years to reach our planet, and when you lay your eyes on a star burning seventy-four light years away from us, you are looking at the star as it was when you were born, if you are seventy-four. Meanwhile it might have ceased to exist, or it might have turned into cheese, and even with the most advanced telescope, you couldn't possibly know. Moreover, each star is set at a different distance from our planet, so the light of each star comes from a different time. The night sky is a patchwork of ages woven in light.

And think about this, too: the matter that makes your legs, your head, your chest, was created in the Big Bang, at the beginning of the universe. After you die, it will go on to make other things – animals, planets, stars, tentacled aliens. For a pitifully brief time, that matter came together in a very specific way to generate a conscious being, *you*, a being that would allow that matter to *think*. Before you were born and after you die, the matter just went on being and it will go on and on, like Lego bricks that sometimes take the shape of a house, sometimes of a car. How come that when those bricks took the form of *you*, they suddenly could think, and in such a sophisticated way that they were capable of creating, well, *actual* Lego bricks? No one knows.

Our universe is weird. A human lifespan is not enough to

make it seem less weird, even marginally so. For that matter, the amassed knowledge of the puny 200,000 years our species has been here is not enough to make it seem less weird, even marginally so. If anything, the more we learn, the weirder the universe seems. Respectable physicists argue that parallel universes might exist; respectable neuroscientists argue that you don't feel an emotion as a *reaction* to an event, but as a *prediction* based on past experiences and cultural expectations.

The problem remains, the universe might be forever strange, but we still get disenchanted as we grow older. If that is not because we inevitably run out of new experiences to reignite our sense of wonder, then why is it?

This is the question I asked myself in the cold, rainy winter weeks I spent shuttling between my study and the library, surrounding myself with books and articles on the history of science, the philosophy of science and the lives of scientists – and chatting with my scientifically inclined friends and acquaintances.

The peregrine falcons of London brought me a possible answer.

✳

I learned about the falcons from an article in the *Guardian*, which I read on the Tube. I couldn't stop thinking about it as I walked from Piccadilly Circus Tube station to the library. The article is by an urban birdwatcher, David Lindo, whose motto is 'Look up'. His words resonated with me. In a novel I wrote more than ten years ago, *Pan*, I made the same point: we city-dwellers should look up more. Lindo says that, by not looking up, we are missing a lot: including the fact that peregrine falcons have arrived on London's rooftops. There are wonders above our heads we could enjoy if only we bothered to use our necks a little more.

I read the article, I felt validated, understood, and nodded vigorously. I got to the library, left my umbrella and my coat in the cloakroom, and set to work, internally smirking at those lesser mortals, corporate drones and suchlike, who never look up.

As I sat down in the hushed atmosphere of a panelled room, I realized that, while I was thinking about an article on the importance of looking up – an article I was going to quote in the book I was researching – I had, in fact, never actually looked up. My attention had been divided between juggling the umbrella and a bag full of books, and trying not to get run over by cars and tourists. I hadn't thought of checking the sky for peregrines. I was a lesser mortal myself.

I had excellent reasons for not looking up: I had a lot of work to do and not enough time to do it. Nonetheless, I felt like a bad person and the worst kind of writer – one who doesn't put his money where his mouth is. A liar, in fact.

Then I realized that in my predicament was the answer I had been looking for.

The older we get, the more relentlessly we focus on what

we must do, and the trade-off is that we cannot focus much on what *we would like to do*. As an infant, I was looked after: there were no duties to perform – I could enjoy (for the one and only time in my life) the luxury of unlimited free time and a quiet mind-space. Then, slowly, social interactions started and I had to make friends. And, on top of that, there was homework to be done. In a while, I needed to muster the courage to ask girls out. Then came essays, then bills to pay, then a career, then health checks, responsibilities stacking one on top of the other. The tower of things we have to do grows taller by the day, but the day's length remains the same.

To make our lives manageable, we find shortcuts. We focus on the things we know how to do, the paths already mapped, so that we don't have to map a new path every time. It makes sense. When you must regularly get to the other side of a mountain, it is more convenient to dig a tunnel once than to climb up and down every time. There is nothing wrong with that, as long as you never forget that by going through the tunnel you won't get to meet deer and pick blackberries and stumble upon sweet secret glades.

But you take the tunnel day in day out, and you *do* forget. You forget that you could climb the mountain any time you wanted to. You forget that taking the tunnel is a strategy, not a necessity; a habit, not a destiny.

✳

Peregrine falcons soar above children and adults alike, but only children look up. Growing up is a process of making and wearing our own blinkers. A spectacularly strange world unfolds around us; we train ourselves not to see it, so that we can continue blithely on our way. It is not that we run out of new things to see, it is that we stop seeking them out.

We deserve compassion for that. Probably some New Age guru would say that you must rip off your blinkers, *now!*, and let your soul joyously fly with the falcons. This makes for a good sound bite – but it is terrible advice. Humans get used to things: this is one of our most significant traits. We put on our blinkers and carry on in the face of illness, carnage, stress, loss of limbs and loved ones. The cars that could run me over in Piccadilly were real enough and so were my deadlines, and for the time being I needed to be blind to the falcons so that I could see the cars and the deadlines. Ripping our blinkers off would leave us defenceless, like children, who are free and safe only insofar as adults take care of them.

The trouble begins when we stop seeing the blinkers *as blinkers*, clever survival devices that we can take on and off, and start seeing them as 'the way it is'. In other words, when we start believing too much in what we think we know. It does not matter what kind of blinkers we have, it does not matter whether we believe in gnomèd mines or in a purely mechanical universe. Every world view, every belief, every 'reality tunnel', to borrow an expression from the cult novelist and self-styled 'agnostic mystic' Robert Anton Wilson, becomes disenchanting when you convince yourself that is all there is. Even ghosts get boring when ghosts are all you think about.

A sense of wonder does not come from a specific way of seeing the world; it comes from your ability to *shift* whatever way you have of seeing the world.

Children don't yet have a fixed world view, they shift it all the time, so they wonder a lot. And they love science. A chemistry set is an evergreen present; looking at a flea through the lens of a toy microscope never did any harm to anyone's sense of wonder.

We won't even try to set aside the blinkers. Rather, we will learn how to make a thousand of them, all different from one another, so we can look at the world in a thousand different ways, and continuously rejuvenate our world view, like immortal jellyfish. Good science helps us with that.

❋

When science erupted on to the scene, it came with punk-rock braggadocio. It wanted to unblock tunnels with loud explosions, be loud and brazen. It was born as a reaction to the dominant mode of thought, that said that any person worth their salt was supposed to do little else than obey their betters and admire God's work. In a different way from our own, the world into which science came was disenchanted: nothing new was to be discovered, nothing new was to be understood. 'And there is nothing left remarkable / Beneath the visiting moon', to use Shakespeare's words. Miracles and prodigies could show you the greatness of God, but then, you already knew God was great. Miracles were not meant to rock your world, but to confirm its ultimate nature.

The early scientists – Copernicus, Kepler, Galileo – mostly believed in God, and yet they said, *look, we can lift the lid off His cauldron and look inside.* They were not casting themselves as enemies of spirituality. Their faith was much more than perfunctory: Isaac Newton devoted his last years to biblical scholarship. They were rejuvenating spirituality, seeking to remove blinkers that were preventing people from seeing the full glory of God's creation.

Then as today, though, scientists also needed something less elevated than enthusiasm and courage: they needed hard cash. They had to convince wealthy patrons to finance their research, and, as a rule, wealthy patrons wanted something back. Scientists started arguing that their research was principally *useful*, that it created things of practical benefit – like better weapons, for example. The strategy worked all too well, and too many people (unfortunately, even some scientists among them) started believing in the delusional idea that science must be *for* something. Science came to be valued for the technology it helped to produce, and for the money it helped to make. Before you knew it, science and capitalism were marching in step. Science existed in order to make things in order to make money. Human beings existed in order to make things in order to make money.

This was exactly the kind of 'philosophy' that John Keats was denouncing in 'Lamia'. And with good reason: if science's only job was to cleanse the mines of gnomes so as to make miners work harder, science would be indeed a force of despair. But science is a way of seeing the world, and while at its worst it is cold and disenchanting, it is at its best exactly the opposite.

To the best kind of scientist, the world is forever full of questions, and the scientific method is a way to scramble for temporary answers. As the writer Philip Ball puts it, science began when philosophers started asking questions about things that had until then seemed entirely obvious – such as the revolution of the Sun around the Earth. Scientists were mocked by those who had far too much common sense to entertain such fanciful theories (the definition of common sense changes, the unquestioning certainty of its enforcers does not).

The difficulty lies in that the blinkers you have been wearing have come to define what the world is *for you*. You only see other people, the planet, the universe, elephants and jellyfish, as filtered through those blinkers. Your entire life experience has been shaped by looking through those blinkers, and you see only those things that they allow you to see. If you had never seen a giraffe, never read about a giraffe, and never talked to anyone who has seen a giraffe, it would be virtually impossible for you to realize just what long-necked splendours you were missing. You don't know what you don't know.

Early scientists understood this problem. The remarkable

thing they did, the thing that changed history, was to find a quite elegant, simple solution. It goes like this: when you are in doubt, ask questions, and when you are not in doubt, *ask questions anyway*. (Yes, I know, witches taught us precisely the opposite lesson; but please, trust me for now and we'll get there.)

If you found yourself in a completely dark room, you would, naturally, wish to find the exit. You would grope your way around, not expecting to encounter anything specific but preparing yourself to negotiate whatever you might stumble upon. The same goes for scientific questions. Because we don't know what it is that our blinkers are hiding, we question everything without fear of appearing naive. With this simple move, the tremendous strangeness of the world reveals itself again.

Let me provide an example.

※

Let's look at a word: *dog*.

OK? Good.

The word evoked an image in your mind. You automatically associated the word with the image, even though, when you think about it, in and of itself the word does not 'mean' the image. It does not mean a thing. Words are shapes made of straight and curvy lines. They do not 'communicate' by means of some special, intuitively graspable power; they are doodles.

Words have meanings because you and I decided that some specific doodles are not doodles at all, but 'letters' that represent units of spoken sound. We also decided we can assemble these letters to form larger doodles that we call 'words'; and we decided that 'words' represent objects, memories, experiences of beauty and of sorrow.

Your mind translated the doodle 'dog' into its meaning, 'a diverse range of four-legged animals with a bizarre love for, and loyalty towards, *Homo sapiens*'. But try looking at the word itself, as a series of scribbles on paper or screen, without immediately rushing to translate it into a mental image. I will type the word here again, so that you don't have to search for it: *dog*. Now, try to look at it as a meaningless doodle.

It is hard, isn't it? The meaning of the simplest word is something that we *create*, but once we have created it, it binds us. The moment your eyes rest on the doodle-dog, images of canines start crowding your mind.

Everything we know (about the world and ourselves) is like this. Every piece of knowledge we have only exists within an immensely sophisticated network of rules. Within these networks, what we know seems obvious, banal, even. But only when we accept the rules without question.

By contrast, when we look at things in close-up, what we thought we knew becomes out-and-out strange: a simple action like reading a word reveals endless layers of complexity (in our lightning-quick tour around the meaning of the word 'dog', we did not touch on the question of how words sound). Get close enough to a solid-looking wall, and you will find that a wall is not actually as solid as it looks. Look closely at a crow (yes, the glossy black bird of the family Corvidae), and you will see that it knows how to use tools. Look at trees as closely as a dendrologist does, and you discover that they communicate with each other using an 'internet' of underground networks of fungus. All is strange. The world has always been, and ever will be, the ultimate *Wunderkammer*.

Children intuitively grasp this strangeness. Then society trains that intuition out of them, out of us, by teaching us the rules, forcibly so if need be: if you don't do exactly as you are told, you will get a bad mark; if you want to get a grant, you need to pursue *this* line of research, not that one. You might think that you wonder less than you did as a child because you know more, but in a sense, it is because you know *less*: you have lost touch with the real weirdness of the world, while you were trained to believe in the false reality of banality.

But the world remains weird, and banality remains false.

※

In 1660, shortly after the Restoration of the English monarchy, King Charles II gave his blessing to a new scientific institution, the Royal Society. It was dedicated to asking questions and finding answers, and one of the ways it did this was by carrying out experiments. The Society had a programme of 'public' experiments, whose curator was a 'natural philosopher', from a modest background, called Robert Hooke. His role meant that he had to know how to do research, but also how to put on a good show: he was the David Attenborough of his time. He was the first to use the word 'cell' in biology, borrowing it from the word used for monks' sleeping quarters: when he looked into sliced cork with a microscope, he noticed structures that, to his eyes, could be best described as similar to those found in monasteries. In his *Micrographia: or Some Physiological Descriptions of Minute Bodies Made by Magnifying Glasses with Observations and Inquiries Thereupon*, Hooke revealed the magnified flea as a fearsome armoured monster, bristling with spikes – but also as a recognizable animal, with head, body and limbs.

In the heyday of the Scientific Revolution, microscopes and telescopes were revealing things so strange and extraordinary that they seemed to go beyond the bounds of human understanding, and the best that early scientists could do to explain their findings to people, and in some measure to themselves, was to use analogies. Not much has changed: quantum physicists today use analogies to try to explain their findings to us, and in some measure to themselves (Schrödinger's cat is not an actual cat). The closer we look at our universe, the stranger it turns out to be. We try to normalize it as much as we can in order to pretend that we get it.

As Philip Ball has pointed out, the technology of lenses had been available for centuries, but it was only with the beginning of modern science that people realized that, by changing point of view so radically, they were seeing new things, rather than simply seeing better what they already knew. It was a different mindset, rather than a more advanced technology, that ushered in an age of discoveries and made the world a stranger place. Everybody could look into a microscope; it took a scientist to ask, *what if these things we see through a microscope can point us to as yet unknown features of nature?* Sensible people were certain that their senses were all they needed to understand nature. Gizmos that amplified them were just a bit of fun. *Or are they?* scientists asked. Scientists were not very sensible, and where others saw obviousness, they saw doubt.

The adventures of scientists, their colourful lives and the risks they take (whether Galileo facing the Inquisition, or Marie Curie dying from the effects of radiation) are born of their passionate spirit of inquiry. Scientists doubt everything, even their senses, even common sense, *especially* common sense. The motto of the Royal Society is *Nullius in verba*, which means 'Take nobody's word for it'. Like children sitting in the back on a long car journey, scientists keep asking questions, never tiring, never stopping.

And not just any questions. The neuroscientist Stuart Firestein says that the best questions are the ones that make us, not less, but *more* ignorant, by giving us a glimpse of what we don't know. The scientific use of the telescope was a watershed moment because for millennia we had thought that we knew what was going on in the heavens, and then suddenly, we didn't any more. By answering a tiny question about the rotation of celestial bodies, Copernicus and Galileo were opening up a million more. In Firestein's words, 'science produces ignorance, possibly at a faster rate than it produces knowledge'. Ideally, science shows you a little bit of what you don't know: it broadens your world to include a magical menagerie of immortal jellyfish and city-dwelling falcons.

✳

We can apply the same thinking to our non-scientific lives, to make ourselves more ignorant. Let's start with a very simple question: how did we get here?

I don't mean in any grandiose, meaning-of-life kind of sense. Just, how did we get here, you and me? I take it that you – a 'you' that exists in my future, while I am tapping these words on a laptop perched on a ramshackle bureau – bought this book, or someone bought it for you. You might have stolen it, or borrowed it, or picked it up from a skip outside a neighbour's house, but let's say, for the sake of my mortgage, that cash was exchanged. You and I are not face to face, this much is obvious. I might well be dead by now (*your* 'now'). And yet, in a way, we are meeting one another. How did we come to do this?

Let's see. I can speak for myself: I am alive (for the time being), it is early morning, I had a breakfast of yogurt, honey and abundant coffee, and then I shuffled to my office to work. Before that, I found a publisher who wanted me to write this book and gave me some money to get started, and before that

I found an agent who found me a publisher. Before that, my girlfriend at the time suggested we could spend four months in London. Four months became ten years and counting, during which time she became my wife. Before that I wrote a few books in Italian, learning the ropes of the craft of writing; and before that I met my girlfriend, one childhood summer many years ago. And we can travel even further back in time until we get to a gentle day in May 1981 (or so I am told), when I was born in a southern Italian town to a ridiculously loving family. An interplay of decisions and chance brought me from there to here, from southern Italy to London, from crying and wetting myself to writing a book on a topic that interests you, in a language that you understand.

What about you? How did you end up here, with me? Whatever mind-bending series of coincidences brought you to read these pages, you, too, will have started your life in a manner very similar to myself, wailing and helpless.

But we haven't yet answered the original question. The chain of events that brought us here to meet (more or less) started before we were born. Before being a baby, you were a foetus, and before you were anything at all, there was an ovum and a spermatozoon, and before those met, there were two people who might even have been in love. Keep hopping from one *before* to the next, picking them up like rocks in the stream of time. From parents to grandparents to ancestors, from global conflicts to the first signs of language, the further back we travel, the more your path and mine will diverge, only to come together again, intimately, in a land we know as Africa, where our species, *Homo sapiens*, originated around 200,000 years ago.

The story of you and me does not begin there either. Before *Homo sapiens* there were other species, and before those species there were other forms of life, and before them there was probably a single cell, from which all life on Earth originated (you and I, your dog, my cat, the octopus you had for dinner that unforgettable night in Crete, the crunchy Greek salad you ordered as a side). And before that, there were majestic cosmic forces shaping a star and a planet, just at the right distance from one another to give birth to life, and before that there were cosmic forces even *more* majestic that shaped what we sometimes call the 'laws' of physics, laws that seem miraculously fine-tuned to allow a star and a planet to give birth to life. And before that there was no 'before' because time and space themselves did not exist, and when we reach that beautiful and terrifying point, the magic of words fails us.

A lot of effort went into me writing this book, and you reading it.

Just a few years ago we were a bunch of apes hanging out on the savannah. From an evolutionary perspective, it was a blink of an eye, and in a very real sense *we are still a bunch of apes*. Nothing changed there. You and I were born naked beasts with a hard-wired desire to eat and fuck and avoid pain, animals trapped on a not-so-big planet with other animals, which are, for the most part, better endowed in a physical sense than we are. We are poor runners, pitiful climbers, abysmal fighters, and our fangs and talons are rubbish. We are the nerds of Planet Earth.

And yet one way or another we managed to leave our caves and visit the moon, and now we are making plans to travel further, towards Mars and beyond. We have come a long way, and if we can prevent idiots with too much power from blowing us to smithereens, we still have a long way to go.

What happened in the little less than 14 billion years that passed from the Big Bang to now is extraordinary. But it is even more extraordinary that a bunch of apes are figuring it out.

✳

Descartes was not alone among his contemporaries in his belief that wonder was only good to start off the journey, not see it through. Scientists were re-enchanting the world by revealing its strangeness, and yet their endgame was to make wonder cease, to answer all questions and master nature. This is an unfortunate view; and it is even more unfortunate that it has somehow survived to this day. This is science gone too far, some might say. I disagree. This is science that hasn't gone far enough.

A scientist's training is long and demanding. After spending twenty years shuttling between a university and a lab, working late hours for very little financial reward, you can be forgiven for thinking that your specific way of doing things is the best way there is. It is a handy delusion you use to keep yourself sane. Because of the way science works in practice, because of the byzantine twists and turns of grants and academic careers, scientists need to build their own tunnels, in the same way we all do, in order to get on with life, pay their bills, raise children and put them through university. Exactly like anybody else, they can end up forgetting that those tunnels are shortcuts through reality and not reality itself. They stop questioning what they think they know. They learn that they must look up, and they do so, but then they *always* look up, and never sideways.

We tend to believe that scientists are the ultimate grown-ups, that they have everything sorted out. But they are not, and they have not. They are people like us, and they are winging it, like us. They are prone to the same mistakes we are prone to, the same delusions of grandeur. The good ones are aware that this problem is inescapable, and they keep applying science's clever trick – they keep asking questions, and all the more so when the answer seems obvious. Is immortality possible? Do animals have consciousness? What about plants? Sooner or later those questions will lead them to strange, unexpected places they have never seen before. To the stars and beyond.

Scientists and witches use opposite methods to reach the same point, a point where their dearest certainties hold no water. We are going to steal both methods. Life needs to breathe in, breathe out, and we shall alternate between moments when we stop asking questions and moments when we push questions to their extreme limits. We will switch between strategies, so that neither becomes just another deception, just another cage. Breathing in with mystery, breathing out with questioning, your world will be forever new, forever unexpected.

THE WORKOUT

1. The Familiar Unknown

Select an object you use every day, such as your phone, your fridge, your car. Write down in your Book of Wonder what you *know for certain* about how it works, what you *perhaps know*, and what you *definitely do not know*. For example, if it is your phone: how does a signal reach it? How come it can connect to the Internet? What makes a touch screen possible? What is electricity? How is it produced, and how does it reach your home? How does it charge your phone's battery?

After writing down your list, research all three areas – what you know for sure, what you perhaps know, what you don't know. It does not need to be a scholarly, in-depth research, but it needs to question even the things you are entirely sure you know.

How much new information did you find out? How many things did you discover you had taken for granted, without *really* knowing them?

How many more things do you take for granted every day?

2. The Reversal of Obviousness

Write down in your Book of Wonder a very obvious statement. For example: *Cats like to play*. Then question it. For example:

aren't there individual differences among cats? How can you be sure that the behaviour you define as 'play' is, indeed, play? Write down all the things you need to take for granted in order for that statement to hold true. For example:

Most cats are similar, I know exactly what 'play' is, humans and animals 'play' in similar ways, I have observed enough cats to know what I am saying, cats exist… and so on.

How many of those statements are demonstrably true, when subjected to rational analysis? How many of them could you demonstrate yourself, and how many are beliefs you hold for no good reason?

3. The Rational Moves

Thinking is an undervalued activity. What little thinking we do, we do while on our commute, while doing the dishes, while listening to music. It is very unusual to just sit down and think, without doing anything else. Because of this, our mind has very little training in what it is designed to do.

So we shall do just that. Every day for a week, sit down and think for seven minutes, making a chain of logical statements. Start from something you are absolutely certain of: for example, that you are sitting in your room. Then think of something you can safely deduce from what you just thought. For example, that if you are sitting in your room, then you must have a chair.

Be careful, and question this second statement thoroughly. For example, could you not be sitting on the floor?

When you come up with a second statement that satisfies you, move on to the next one. Continue the same chain for the seven days of the exercise, picking up every time from where you left off the last time.

You might notice that it becomes extremely difficult to keep focusing on the chain of thoughts. You will be tempted to check your phone, to stand up and make tea, and you will notice your thoughts drifting away. When this happens, gently bring yourself back to the exercise.

Each time, make notes in your Book of Wonder as soon as the seven minutes are up.

On the last day, look back at your journey – how far did you travel from your first statement?

4. The Daily Problems

Every day for a week, write down in your Book of Wonder three things you don't know. For example: how the human brain works, how birds navigate during migration, why we age. It does not matter how banal or oddball the things are – it is your list and nobody is going to look at it and judge you for it.

At the end of the week, look at the twenty-one problems you have listed. How many of them make you curious enough to go and look for an answer?

The Fourth Key

The Wild

Nature is a misty place where
soul and world, inside and outside,
meet, and become one

When I finally admitted, 'Okay, we are lost,' I still thought it was funny.

Paola did too. It was the month of May and the sun was shining. Everywhere I looked, I could see that luminous frail green that survives only for a handful of days, when the sap has just begun to stir within trees and shrubs, making them yawn and stretch, not quite awakening them just yet. It gets stronger by the hour – and darker. That shade of green does not exist in southern Italy: I had never seen it before moving to England. It makes me wistful. It is destined for an early death, to fade away and yield to less subtle hues. I was wandering along, thinking these thoughts and thinking how clever I was to be thinking them, which is probably why we got lost.

Another reason we got lost was Paola. My wife and I complement each other in many ways. For example, while I am inclined towards the big picture, she is fascinated by detail. I tend to like people, she likes certain individuals. She has been patiently teaching me the importance of the small, the local, the contingent. I have learned from her, but she is still more talented than me. Come springtime, a walk to a café with Paola can be excruciatingly slow: she will stop for every flower born in a crack of the asphalt and every new leaf, for every robin and every blackbird, and will comment on the lovely way a fern I hadn't noticed curls its fresh blades. In the woods, her fondness for small marvels makes her stray from the path. It is my job to keep us on track, but on this occasion I had followed her, absorbed in contemplation. I was looking at the forest, she was looking at the trees; no one was looking at the path.

'Are you sure?' she asked.

'Have you been on this bridleway before?'

She glanced at the oaks, at the rocks, at the shrubs. 'No,' she said.

I brandished the walk I had printed off the Internet. 'We are supposed to be on our way back, on a path we walked earlier this morning.'

'We are not.'

'Exactly.'

Paola said, 'You have a compass.'

'Yeah,' I admitted, in my most noncommittal voice.

'But?'

'But I left it in the car. Besides, it'd be kind of useless. We have no idea where we are, so we don't know what direction we need to walk in to get back to our starting point.'

'Are you for real?'

I waved the printout once again. 'If we had stuck to the route without taking detours, we'd know where we are.'

'The sun was on our left this morning.'

'Wasn't it on our right?'

She looked again at the woods, as if she was seeking their advice. 'We could always double back.'

'Agreed. I think I know where we took a wrong turn.'

We turned off the bridleway to follow a narrower side path, a barely visible strip among ferns, which then gave way to a larger path running beside a stream. Both of us remembered the stream; neither of us remembered how we had got there the first time. 'But I was sure…' I mumbled.

The sun was still high in the sky, and we were not worried yet.

We sat by the stream, and drank from our bottles. Paola teased me good-naturedly for not checking the compass.

'*You* are the one who kept leaving the path,' I said, to defend myself.

'*I* allow myself to get sidetracked because I trust *you* to keep *us* on the right track.'

'Blame it on the fairies, then. They're planning to snatch us and take us to Faerie.'

'I wouldn't mind visiting Faerie.'

'Me too.' And it seemed perfectly possible that we were there already. The stream in the woods felt very remote. The only sounds we could hear were the trickling of water, the crackling of leaves and the singing of birds.

I took out my phone. I hadn't had a signal for a while, since before getting lost. I still had no signal.

'Mine's dead,' Paola said. Her phone is always out of juice, not because she uses it often but because she charges it so rarely.

'Any ideas about what we should do next?' I asked.

'We keep walking until we hit either a road, a spot we recognize, or one where we have a signal. If we do find a signal, we call the rangers.'

'That would be embarrassing.'

'Better than dying out here.'

'As soon as we find a signal, we use Google Maps to get an idea of where we are, and then walk to the nearest road.'

We were having a great time. We were in the New Forest, rather than the depths of Tolkien's Mirkwood, and the possibility of actual death was far lower than on a packed Tube train in central London. The woods of the New Forest might look dark and deep to city-dwellers like Paola and me, but they are tame, and empty of predators. We had a good three hours of light left, and my phone had enough charge. Our being lost was real, and yet it was also make-believe, because we were not actually in danger: the worst that could happen was being lectured by a forest ranger dragged away from his comfy chair. We left the stream and kept walking, with that congenial feeling you have when you can pretend that you are on an adventure, but without the raging torrents, sheer precipices and orc attacks that a proper adventure entails.

After an hour or so we still didn't have the faintest idea where we were. We had crossed the bridleway again, and then walked into heathland, and then, somehow, ended up in a different part of the forest, with fewer oak trees and more beeches. We hadn't met a single human being; perhaps we were indeed in Faerie. I checked my phone at intervals, but never found any signal. And the phone was running out of charge faster than I expected. I had forgotten that when they can't find a steady signal, phones stretch desperately in search of one, eating up their charge like locusts. I checked my phone again.

'No joy?' asked Paola, the cheerfulness gone from her voice.

'Nope.'

We kept walking, pretending there was a principle behind our choice of paths. We went deeper and deeper into the woods, getting more lost with every step. Woods are bigger on the inside: the fantasy writer Robert Holdstock, in his novel *Mythago Wood*, created a complete mythological world set in a three-square-mile piece of woodland, within which magical realms are hidden. But you don't need magic to get lost in a patch of Hampshire woodland three miles square. You can wander for hours without finding a way out, although you probably won't be in much danger.

We *certainly* weren't in danger. So why was I beginning to feel afraid?

The shadows grew longer, the air cooler. The breeze had become a light wind. Paola and I pulled our ponchos out of our backpacks: they wouldn't be much use if it got cold, but they offered some protection from the wind. We were not having fun any more. The prospect of spending the night in the woods, without a sleeping bag, without a fire, without so much as a flashlight, loomed larger. We had agreed to forget Google Maps, and to call the rangers at the first opportunity, but we still couldn't find a signal. And my phone's battery was draining fast.

We might stumble upon a road at any moment, but we might also not.

What was the worst that could happen? A night spent on the forest floor; and then, tomorrow, we would encounter other walkers. Or perhaps the owner of the B&B where we were staying would notice that our beds had not been slept in and would work out that those stupid Londoners had got themselves lost. The night would be cold, but not dangerously so. We would keep walking as long as we could, then wrap ourselves in our picnic blanket, and get a few hours of sleep. It wouldn't be that bad. It wouldn't be that good either.

'Is this the road?' Paola said.

I stopped in my tracks. I had heard the noise as well: a hollow murmur.

'No,' she said, before I could answer. 'It's the wind.'

The wind in the woods has a different voice from the sound it makes in the city – it is like a wail from deep in an old person's throat.

We were in a place where sounds come not from cars, trains and buses, but from wind, leaves, branches and beasts – from things not human creeping at the edges of our vision, and out of sight. We were utterly lost.

Yet the objective situation didn't justify what I felt – a rising fear that blocked my stomach, froze my chest, and filled my head with an anger directed not exactly at myself, or at Paola, but at the present moment in its entirety. We were the only humans for miles around. Who knew how many miles? Truth to tell it couldn't be *that many* miles, but by now primal fears had hijacked my rationality. I knew we were not far from civilization, but I could not see any trace of civilization: all I saw, and heard, and smelt, was a deep forest, which might go on for ever. I was scared. Why was that?

It dawned on me that I was not used to such a complete lack of *structure*.

I had spent all my life surrounded by human inventions, both physical (roads, walls, computers) and social (laws, cash, manners). If I broke a leg in Greenwich, there were other humans who would help me, ambulances that would come and get me. If I were lost in Paris I could ask for directions. If I were hungry in Rome I could buy food, if it started raining in Milan I could enter a bar and wait for it to pass. Human inventions had enveloped me completely since the moment I was born. The backdrop of my life had been a film set composed of reassuringly familiar objects: buildings, roads, clocks, signs.

Even in rural southern Italy I was never far from a house, a farm, a second cousin who would come and get me.

Here in the woods, Paola and I were alone – or, to put it more precisely, we were not with humans. We had fallen off the human grid, and we were utterly powerless without it. If we had a map with us, or if our phones were working, we would still be anchored to the world. But, as things stood, we were not on a point on a map in a place owned by humans; we were in a nameless wood with more beech than oak where night was falling fast. The time signalled by my watch didn't matter; what mattered was whether it was dark or not. This place existed on its own, with us or without us. It *was* Faerie.

The moment I realized that – and all these thoughts passed through my mind very quickly – a strange elation spread from my head to my feet. The fear was still there, and yet I also felt, on top of it, relief. I was *free*. Paola and I could jump and scream and only birds would think we were two idiots. The coordinates of a map are the bars of a cage and we had escaped. We could tear our clothes off and start making love in the centre of the path and nobody would care. We were in the wild. We *were* wild. I absolutely loved it.

The well-trained voice in my mind that always wants to spoil the fun was yelling at me that these thoughts were ridiculous, that it took a special kind of fool to consider the New Forest 'wild' in any sense, that the path we were on was human-made, that my backpack was a human invention. I was still firmly tethered to the film set. If I had *really* lost my way, if I were, say, floating in outer space, I would not feel free, I would feel *terrified*.

That voice did not spoil the fun. That strong feeling of being in the wild, of *being* wild, finally liberated, remained with me.

The trees came alive all around me, and so did the grass, and the flowers that were closing their petals for the night. As we continued randomly on our way, pretending that we were choosing particular paths for a particular reason, the forest was moving around us, changing its nature, becoming not just a voiceless place we were walking through, but a talkative *companion* we were walking with. The forest was as real as we were. It did not exist for our sake, but for its own. It was breathing, sovereign, independent. It was a presence.

The hollow murmur returned.

This time, it was the road.

✳

Viktor Frankl, the Austrian psychiatrist who survived Auschwitz and Dachau, wrote a book inspired by his experiences there. *Man's Search for Meaning* is a manual offering guidance on how to cope with life's darker challenges, including hopelessness and a loss of sense of direction. In the camps, Frankl observed the sometimes counter-intuitive psychological strategies prisoners used to get by, and he reasoned that if such strategies worked there, they could also help us with more humdrum daily struggles. One of the things he found was that prisoners developed a sense of meaningful connection between their inner life and the natural world.

There are those who believe that an inner life is a luxury for people who have too much time on their hands, or who aren't tough and resourceful enough to face up to real life. Searching for wonder, prizing beauty, striving for a deeper meaning to our existence – these are trivialities we shouldn't waste our time on. High-achieving, go-getting individuals don't have time for trees, birds and wild flowers – they have eyes only for spreadsheets. Life is tough, so you need to be tougher. And being tougher means getting on with life, without seeking refuge in woolly notions of 'inner life' or – even worse – 'spirituality'.

Not true, Frankl whispers. During his time at Auschwitz and elsewhere, he observed that the brutality of daily existence in a concentration camp made inner life *more*, rather than less, intense. The prisoners who survived longest were the ones who treasured that intensity. Frankl describes a personal, almost mystical, experience in which he came to understand that 'the salvation of man is in love and through love'. Even in the worst situation possible, Frankl realized, even when you are on your knees, you can still 'achieve fulfilment' by contemplating a mental image of the person you love. Frankl had been separated from his wife, Tilly, in the final weeks of the war, and he knew that he might never see her again (indeed, she died of typhus at Bergen-Belsen after having been forced to work in conditions of 'terrible, indescribable suffering'). Yet the simple and unassailable fact of their love, the fact that she had existed and that there had been an unbreakable bond between them, was enough to sustain him, even in the face of death.

Despite becoming more introspective, the prisoners did not shut themselves off from the world outside. The 'intensification' of their inner lives actually led them to a deeper appreciation of art and nature. People who had been taken from their homes, separated from their families, starved and beaten, still managed to find pleasure in small things. It was common for prisoners toiling in the woods to take a moment to look at the sunset; and in their huts they would organize 'a kind of cabaret' as entertainment.

Frankl recalls how once, while working in a trench at dawn, under grey skies, he was lost in memories of his wife. He felt a strong sense that she was there with him, within physical reach, and when this sense was at its height, a bird flew close to him, perched on the ground, and looked at him.

A human being stripped bare took refuge in the only place left available, inside himself, and the paradoxical discovery he made there was *a way out of himself* through a connection with the natural world. He encountered a network of connections in which birds echoed his own thoughts, and the distinction between 'external' and 'internal' fell away. The bird is a common symbol for the soul, but Frankl met a real bird, not a symbol. To ask whether its appearance was a coincidence or a message would be to miss the point: its appearance was a mystery, in the sense we explored with the First and Second Key.

In this connection between inner and outer worlds Frankl was witnessing the workings of nature in their purest form. The word 'nature' has two opposite meanings. On the one hand, 'nature' is the external, material world, which you can touch and smell and walk in at the weekend; doctors say that it is good for you. But on the other, 'nature' denotes the way you are inside, the innermost essence of every person, animal and rock, an essence that is not necessarily material. 'It is her nature,' you say, proud of a friend who is generous with her time and money; while astronomers and theologians investigate the 'nature' of stars and gods.

Which makes the idea of 'going into nature' problematic. We believe that 'going into nature' is a matter of going outside, of taking a walk in the fields and woods; or, even worse, that the real point of 'going into nature' is 'to meet ourselves', that an encounter with nature is a journey of personal discovery (thereby making of nature just another tool from the therapeutic toolkit, alongside shiatsu, moxibustion and aromatherapy). The first view denies the dignity of our soul, the second the dignity of our world. We get closer to a sense of wonder when we understand how intimately connected our soul and the world are.

When you are in a forest, you are part of the forest, as much as the trees and the deer and the mushrooms. You are not in nature, you are *with* nature, *you are nature yourself.* Nature is a misty place where soul and world, inside and outside, *meet,* and become one, with no barriers left between them. The language of magic describes it as well as the language of science. But we have been talking far too much. When we shut up and start listening to nature's own voice, we will find the path to our fourth key.

After studying with magicians, witches and scientists, our next step is to learn how to listen not to humans but to other voices from the natural world, and learn lessons from them.

✳

Nature is supposed to fill you with wonder. But does it? Does it *really*? The starry sky, the boundless sea, the full moon over a field on a sweet summer's night – are these things marvellous to you? Travel guides, Sunday colour supplements and National Park websites urge us to plunge headlong into nature. Once you are in the woods, contemplating a carpet of bluebells, you will, surely, gorge on wonder. But then you go into the woods, and all you find there is mud and nettles, and the bluebells are, well, all right, kind of, but they are only flowers, after all, and you can't wait for the walk to be over and the pub to be in sight. Those mystical communions, those numinous experiences, are nowhere to be found. You might feel guilty about that; you might worry that there is something wrong with you. Or maybe you are just not the nature type?

There is nothing wrong with you, and you definitely are the nature type, because you are a creature of flesh and blood, and as such you *are* nature. The problem lies elsewhere. The notion that all you have to do is step outside and the world will acquire a magic light again is just another example of our culture's obsession with quick fixes – a pill to ease the pain, a spray of Roundup to kill the weeds in the garden, a get-rich-quick scheme. We have been wrecking our relationship with the wild for several centuries now, and we cannot fix it by booking a B&B or taking a Sunday stroll.

Back in the days when wonder came easily to me, it came even more easily when I was in nature. I remember one experience very clearly. I was eleven, and camping in some deep woods in Basilicata, a region of southern Italy even more rural than Puglia, with the Boy Scouts. I had been tasked with organizing the activities for the day, and I had decided on a simple game. I hid in the woods, leaving some clues behind, and the other Scouts had to find me. It was a glorified game of hide-and-seek.

Nobody found me. This was not because I was a master of camouflage, but because nobody could give a stuff about the game. As I discovered when I eventually wandered back to the campsite several hours later, the others had been messing around, having fun in the woods, playing other games, picking wild strawberries and not bothering to look for me.

That gave me a lot of time to spend in the spot I had chosen as my hiding place, four or five hours with nothing to do. It was a secluded spot just off a path, with a fallen trunk covered in soft moss, on which I sat. The canopy was thick, and it filtered the harsh sunlight of the southern summer. By the time the light reached the brown bark of the forest floor, it was still bright and warming, but less intensely so.

The first hour or so was nice, then it got better. For no external reason that I could discern, I felt a rising excitement, not dissimilar from what I would feel years later when I got lost with Paola in Hampshire. The excitement kept rising and rising, until it peaked, and I remember, as if it was yesterday, that I was hit by the certainty that everything, everything in this world, was beautiful and sacred. I felt I had to act in accordance with that feeling and I did it the only way I knew then: I fell on my knees and prayed. My inner life and the natural world were in close communion.

I am very far from being a Catholic these days, and I find the idea of falling on my knees for anything or anybody rather repulsive. But I was raised in a culture that considered the resurrection of Jesus to be a historical event, and heaven and hell hard facts of life. Back then, Catholicism was all that I had to explain to myself the numinous feeling that had overcome me, and I made do with it. I was the same boy who read science fiction for hours on end, who found time to read *The Lord of the Rings* twice, and who joined a stargazing club. I was not jaded yet, not by human life, not by the natural world.

To find wonder in nature will require changes deeper than

those offered by an occasional walk. Throughout our life we have taken our relationship with nature for granted, always asking, never giving back, and when you take a relationship for granted, you ruin it. To get a second chance we must understand what we did wrong, and how to apologize.

✳

Nonno Arcangelo, my paternal grandfather, was a dedicated listener to the natural world. He was a peasant who could read and write, just about. A well-respected *mastro innestatore*, 'master grafter', he spent his life working in southern vineyards, where the heat, the colours, the scents have a particular intensity. His son, my father, was a civil servant, the first professional in his family, very proud of what he had achieved, and also very proud of his heritage. He had been working in the fields since he was a boy and continued to do so throughout his university years. He had time to learn from Nonno Arcangelo. My father could tend fruit trees in such a way that come summer they would be overflowing with apricots and peaches, he could gather wild herbs, he could hunt and fish (though he was lousy at both). I showed an interest in nature that my brothers never had, and when I was little he had started to teach me the basics, taking me into the garden with him, wringing chicken's necks with me. But he developed early-onset Alzheimer's, and died young, and peasant skills were one of the things he did not have a chance to hand down.

There is a fundamental difference between my father and me. He was of the first generation of our family who knew *more* than the previous one, and I was of the first who knew *less*. He knew how to live with nature and also how to negotiate the modern world; I knew only the latter. A combination of historical change and personal bad luck severed an ancestral connection with the land that had lasted for millennia. This combination is quite typical of the last century or so.

I don't mean to romanticize the peasant's life. I have seen it too close to believe that it is a blessed existence spent in communion with a bountiful land. It is a tough way of living, much harsher than mine, and I wouldn't in a million years want to swap my early-twenty-first-century urban life for the rural life of a mid-twentieth-century Italian peasant. I am grateful to those who came before for giving me the chance not to break my back in the fields day in, day out.

But there is a downside. Reasonably competent as I am in urban society, I am useless in the muddy, bloody, non-human world. I could not build a wall, prune a vine or coppice a hazel; I would have no idea how to set about hunting quail or butchering a pig. I am like one of those insects that specialize in doing one thing and one thing only – in my case, moving in a human-made setting. Such insects thrive as long as absolutely everything stays the same, but when you change the smallest aspect of their environment, they die. I can feed myself in an urban setting, but leave me in a deer-filled forest for a week, and you will see my bleached bones.

Nonno Arcangelo could not articulate his connection to the land, because he did not need to. That connection was a self-evident fact, necessary to his own survival: I don't think he had any notion of 'nature' resembling ours. He had to know what kind of weather was coming and how to act accordingly, what parasites were attacking his vineyard and how to dispatch them for good. He had to know how to get through winter when the harvest was poor. He and his family depended on nature as much as they depended on other people. There was a seamless connectedness between his relationship with the land and that of, say, a goat: they both got their food from the same source. And there was a connectedness between his relationship with the friends he played cards with and with the vineyards he grafted: he listened to the vineyards as much as he listened to his friends. He lived in a quietly harmonious cosmos.

By and large, we have removed ourselves from that cosmos. We depend on supermarkets to satisfy our hunger, on a regular salary to pay for a roof over our head. Our most intense relationships are with banks, offices, air-conditioned shops, all human-made objects, rather than grazing animals, olive groves and hailstorms that might damage our crops. We are all specialized insects. Most people I know have never seen an animal being killed; to them (and to me, unless I make an effort to recall hazy memories of my grandfather's world) a 'chicken' is born dead, clean and wrapped in cling film. We say that the flavour of game is an acquired taste, but to my father as a boy it was the way meat tasted, because if he wanted to eat something that was alive, he had to kill the quail or the rabbit himself. There is no denying that the world we have built allows us to do a thousand marvellous things – to advance medical research, to send peasant children to university, to study philosophy. But we have forgotten that most of the world was not built by us. To admit this is not to belittle what we have created.

All humans, from all cultures, posit a boundary of sorts between themselves and what they call 'nature'. Nonno Arcangelo was of course very well aware that he was not a goat and that there was a difference between a human friend and a vineyard. This boundary though is permeable, ever-shifting, for human life and the natural world are intimately connected to one another. That is still the case and it cannot be otherwise, but we don't see it any more, and the soft, penetrable boundary has become a high wall, with razor wire on top and armed guards policing it. We believe that there is no relationship at all between goats and us, except for the fact that we eat their meat. That they are animals, and we are not.

Native American tribes of the Pacific Northwest welcome the first salmon of the season with all the pomp of a state visit. The salmon is caught, presented to the tribe, spoken to with as much dignity and respect as if it were a political leader – even sung to. After personally addressing the salmon, a priest shares the salmon's meat with the rest of the tribe, being very careful not to damage the skeleton, which he gives back to the river at the end of the ceremony. It is important that the skeleton is not damaged, because from that skeleton the salmon will return to life, and he will go back to his hidden home, where he will be human once again. According to their tradition, all salmon are also human, belonging to a tribe that lives elsewhere, and when the season is right, they transform themselves into fish so as to feed the other tribes. You must, therefore, show gratitude to the salmon, and not offend him, or he might not return.

The American scholar Lewis Hyde describes this ceremony as an example of 'a gift relationship with nature'. These tribes do not set themselves apart from the wild world of fish and river: they believe (they know) that the salmon is very much like them. Their society and their economy are based upon gifts given and gifts received, so it makes perfect sense for them to extend the courtesy to salmon. They treat 'nature' the same way they treat each other.

We have forgotten that we are of the same nature as the salmon. The word 'animal' is an insult to us, a slur we slap on our enemies to 'dehumanize' them. But animals are exactly what we are (the word ultimately derives from the Latin *animalis*, meaning 'having breath'). Ideally, 'you are an animal' should be a compliment we pay to other humans; the right answer would be, 'thank you, yes, you too'. The story of the salmon becoming human (or, better, of the human becoming salmon) encapsulates a profound truth about our place in the world – that we are an animal among animals, a truth that science has confirmed and society has brushed under the carpet. We will never become better listeners to the natural world without recognizing this. Our brain is an animal brain, our nervous system is an animal nervous system, we have animal instincts, fears and hormones, and animal needs for comfort. Some animals have longer lifespans than us; some live more sensuous lives. We are far more intelligent than any other animal on this planet, true, but, to be honest, we decided what is 'intelligence' and what it is for, so the argument by which intelligence gives us a superior status is too circular to be of any value.

You can believe that there is something special about us humans (I do, on good days), but that does not change the fact that we are just another organic part of the same world of salmon and vineyard, rather than external masters hovering above it, with rights of life and death over its denizens. As the American poet and ecologist Gary Snyder has put it, 'nature is not a place to visit, it is *home*'. When Paola and I got lost in the forest, I had a glimpse of home. It made me long to find my way back there.

✳

Most people satisfy their desire to return to nature by means of travel (another name for tourism). A multi-billion pound industry has developed around this very basic longing. After all, if nature is 'out there', it makes sense to go out there looking for nature.

Or not. Travel is pleasant, and it can teach us a lot, but it is unlikely to take us to the place Gary Snyder described as home: you can trek in Yellowstone, swim off Phuket, or fly in a hot-air balloon, and you will have a splendid time, but you will still be *visiting*. You will still take yourself with you, and as your balloon drifts gently across the sky you will be plotting your counter-attack to the crafty move that Pedro from Finance is surely planning right at this moment. I have met many obsessive travellers whose Instagram feeds are more interesting than their conversation.

The American author Annie Dillard wrote, in *Pilgrim at Tinker Creek*, a travelogue about her immediate neighbourhood, celebrating the immense amount of wonder that you can experience without ever buying a plane ticket – provided that you engage with the natural world surrounding you wherever you are: she lovingly describes the changes in the seasons, and the richness and complexity of the flora and fauna in the fields, woods and streams of a valley in Virginia's Blue Ridge Mountains. 'The lover can see, and the knowledgeable,' Dillard says. When you love a person, you notice the unique way one corner of her lips goes down just before going up in a smile. When you know a person, you notice how she passes a hand through her hair, on the right side. This noticing reinforces your love and your knowledge, and the pleasure of it never palls.

As a little girl, Dillard would hide pennies by the sidewalk and draw arrows on the ground as a sort of map, so that strangers could find them. It was a way of enchanting the strangers' world, throwing a pebble of surprise into their life. Dillard suggests that we should 'cultivate a healthy poverty and simplicity'. Our home towns, villages and streets are full of hidden pennies, which we will never see unless we take the trouble to look for them and to stoop and pick them up. And it would be healthy for us to stop thinking that the richest pickings are in some other neighbourhood, or in some more distant, more exotic place.

Self-consciousness, Dillard says, is the enemy: with our attention turned on ourselves, on our past and future, we forget to be with nature in the present. She calls self-consciousness 'the curse of the city and all that sophistication implies'. It is a curse we are all victim of, today more than in 1974 when Dillard published *Pilgrim at Tinker Creek*. Our phones, our tablets, our earbuds, our smartwatches, are all instruments of self-consciousness. They create around us a bubble of predictability, which moves with us and will surround us whether we are shooting photographs of wildlife in the Congo or planting bulbs in our back garden. We take photographs to relax, we plant bulbs to have summer colours – everything is about *us*. By hiding pennies for strangers, by creating a new map for them, a random situation of no consequence, young Dillard was bursting their bubble.

Getting lost in the (tame, tiny, two-hours-from-London)

woods of the New Forest burst my bubble. As long as I knew my position on the map, I considered the woods on my own terms: I opened the map and *hey presto!* – the woods came out of it as the cardboard cutouts of a pop-up book. It was very nice to see that particular oak or that bend of the stream, sure, but I didn't think in terms of oak and stream, I thought in terms of which leg of the walk I was on. If a friend had asked me 'where are you?', I would have confidently answered 'here', with a finger pointed at the printout, not at the grass underfoot.

But a 'here' on a map is not the same as a 'here' in the world. When I contemplated the green of the forest, and Paola the individual shapes and colours of the trees, as we each focused on the natural world in our own characteristic way, we lost our position on the map. In doing so, we stumbled upon home.

Be mindful of your GPS the next time you use it: you might notice that in your mind you are moving on its map rather than in the world, that when you say 'I am here', you mean the point where you see the cartoon car or character or blue dot representing you on the screen. The things we have built have trained us so well they have convinced us that we *are* the blue dot, that we have more in common with coloured pixels than with a goshawk on the hunt. That the pixels are 'here'.

'Here' is actually a physical place in the physical world, in which you are with your physical body; where the wild things are, where home is.

To get there, we need to change the map we use.

The writer Robert Macfarlane once went on a journey of exploration of the wild places of the British Isles, his aim being to fight 'the prejudice induced by a powerful map'. The 'prejudice' is the idea that there is no wildness left in Britain and Ireland, and the 'powerful map' is the road atlas (or the digital version contained in a satnav). Everything that is not a road finds no space in a road atlas, for obvious reasons. Using the atlas as our only guide, we gradually forget that the things not marked there ('the fells, the caves, the tors, the woods, the moors, the river valleys and the marshes') still exist. The fact that we have little use for them does not make them any less real. They have little use for us too.

A road atlas is one example of a 'grid map', that is, a map based on Cartesian coordinates. To put it very crudely, a grid map is made of horizontal and vertical lines, which cross each other to create, exactly, a grid. That grid makes it easy to locate any point with a good degree of accuracy: all you need to do is identify its horizontal and vertical coordinates, and you can then pinpoint its position on the map. If you have ever used a London A–Z, you know how this works; satnavs work the same way, although you cannot see the grid when you are using it.

Remember Descartes, who believed that wonder is useful only as long as you quickly move on from it? It is no coincidence that Descartes gives his name to the coordinates that form grids: grid maps concern themselves with geometry rather than our senses, with ideas rather than bodies. Grid maps are about getting measurable results. There is no space in them for anecdote, emotion, personal reminiscence. Following Descartes, they want you to *move on* from a contemplation of the territory, so that you can accomplish things. They make the world more manageable, and smaller. They are another technology of self-consciousness.

Grid maps are probably the only kind of maps you have seen. Consider the effect this has on you. As we found out with our third key, once you start using a word to label a thing, it becomes nearly impossible to think of the word without thinking of the thing, and vice versa. In the last chapter I used as an example the word 'dog': when you see the word printed on paper, you immediately think of humans' closest allies, and when you hear a real dog barking in the real world, the word 'dog' immediately comes to you. The made-up word and the real thing are one and the same in your mind. So far, so good.

Just as the word becomes the dog, so the grid map becomes the place – in fact, it becomes all places. Every time we visit a new city, every time we drive through a new part of the country, every time we go abroad on one of those trips they sell us with the promise that it will change our life, we think of those new territories in terms of the same grid. Even the maps used in the fantasy role-playing game *Dungeons & Dragons* – maps of places that do not exist – are based upon it. The grid is such a pervasive fiction that we literally cannot *imagine* a place without it. It becomes the only way by which we understand place: it becomes place itself.

In both the experiences of wonder I shared with you – when I was little and fell on my knees to pray, and when I was older and got lost – I had forgotten to be self-conscious and I had peeked behind the grid to see a much vaster reality, a *mysterium tremendum et fascinans.*

But we do not want to fall on our knees any more – and getting lost on purpose would not work. Purposefully ignoring something is the best way to make it matter more than ever. So, what do we do to open ourselves to that vaster reality?

Macfarlane offers us a possible answer. He reminds us that there is a second kind of map, which he calls a 'story map' and which 'represent[s] a place as it is perceived by an individual or by a culture moving through it'. A story map is idiosyncratic, mutable, concerned with our senses. It can be a literal story, a drawing, a wooden sculpture, but in all cases, it takes into full account the emotional resonance of human beings and the places where they happen to be, of experiences, feelings, myths and fables. It tells you to avoid the river that is home to an evil spirit who kidnaps people your age, then follow the shape of the big rock where your uncle and aunt got married and walk on to that old tree that looks like the mountain where you were born – mind, I don't mean the tree that smells like roasted cabbage, no, the other one. A story map is art more than science.

The aboriginal peoples of Australia would orient themselves using 'song lines', mythical stories they would sing while walking along particular tracks and which would lead them along the track and then back to their starting point. Bushes and rocks inspire the narrative, humans lend their voices, together they tell the story. A story map brings together time and space, history and myth, memory and hope, and ultimately, human being and nature. A story map is specific and concrete: you cannot project the same structure on your garden and on a Cambodian forest. Using story maps to move through the world keeps you grounded in the world as it is, in the present, in the specific nature of the place where you are right now. Story maps break the curse of self-consciousness: they force us to burst our bubble once and for all and pay attention to where we are.

Macfarlane's entire opus so far is, in a sense, about the creation of modern story maps, a quest to bring magic back to the land. It is an inspiration to create story maps of our own. Do not think that your daily journeys are too humdrum to be mapped through stories. They only seem humdrum because you haven't mapped them yet. Here is a map you could use to get back to the station from my house, after dinner:

As you face the spot where children meet to learn about their future, look at the direction the sun rises, and walk for the time it takes to hum the beginning of U2's Sunday Bloody Sunday. When the chorus arrives, turn towards the broken nutshells discarded by squirrels, and continue past the point with the funny smell. Go closer to the shadowy corner where Martin says there are spirits (I am not sure I believe in spirits the same way he does, but who knows), and keep going until you get to the corner where your friend tripped up three years ago. Now you only have to follow the slope downhill, reciting Walter de La Mare's The Little Green Orchard at a leisurely pace. When the poem is over, there you go, the station is there.

Grid maps capture the wild with a handy net, while story maps make the wild speak. When you are using a grid map, you locate yourself through a set of numbers. You *are* a set of numbers on the map.

When you are using a story map, you locate yourself through that specific house which had a barking dog who frightened you when you were little, that streetlight under which your first girlfriend kissed you, the neighbour who reminds you bizarrely of Gandalf; and in that map, you are a character in a vibrant relationship with other characters. Relationships make you strong, while on your own, you are not much. A grid map can take you anywhere, but a story map can take you home.

Grid maps are a consequence of the wider superstition by which nature would be an advanced mechanism that we can disassemble, examine and then put back together. This superstition, a by-product of the Enlightenment, is shared by many atheists and theists alike. They both agree that the universe is like a watch; however, while theists believe this means there must be a watchmaker, atheists believe we can explain every cog and lever without the need for a creator.

But there is a certain arrogance to the belief that the watch, a thing that we ourselves invented not long ago, is a model for everything that exists. Why exactly should the universe be like a watch? Why not like a salmon, or an oak tree, living beings that are part of the universe regardless of us? Why not like a human being?

A mechanistic interpretation of nature is just another useful fiction, and we must learn to step away from it. It is handy to focus at times on the mechanics of the world (grid maps are great at doing what they do), but when we convince ourselves that those mechanics *are* the world, we lose our way home. In a universe where everything but you is an object, you are like a cranky billionaire living alone in a fortified palace: wealthy, yes, but lonely.

Buying more knick-knacks will not make you feel better. All too often, we humans look at the natural world and see there not family to be loved but a resource to be exploited. The travel industry connives in this by advertising and selling nature as a commodity. We extract oil from the land, and gas, and now we also want wonder on tap.

The expression 'recharging one's batteries' sums it up. It sounds commendable: you take a walk in the woods to *regain strength and energy.* Your doctor recommends it highly. You will be restored; you will be more productive when you return to work. But by thinking in this way, you are not engaging with the woods on their own terms. Rather, you are ordering them to serve you, in the next four hours *s'il vous plait,* you are a busy person and you don't have all day.

This is what the philosopher Martin Buber called an I-It attitude. He said that we can approach the world and everything within it (people and trees equally) with two different attitudes, which he called 'I-It' and 'I-Thou'. When we consider a person as *It*, we consider that person as an object. That person matters to us insofar as she can do things for us. This is not necessarily mean-spirited: to give an example, we might be in distress, and we might ask a friend to lend us a hand. But certainly I-It is never a true relationship. You may be reading this book because you hope I may have practical guidance to offer you. I am *It* to you. Ours cannot be a relationship, because you cannot have a relationship with *It*.

In an I-Thou relationship, however, you value me, the woods, the universe, *for what we are.* When you open yourself to whatever you encounter, without asking favours, without trying to get *anything at all* from that relationship, it is then that you establish a relationship. You don't come at me with a set of questions: you silence your voice and listen to mine. You don't go to the woods to 'recharge the batteries', you go there because the woods are nice. 'All real living is meeting,' Buber says, and you can only meet *Thou*, never *It*. To let that happen, you have to accept that the woods do not exist for your own benefit. They do pretty well on their own.

The reliance on grid maps made us take for granted that nature is *It*; by using story maps as well, we realize that nature has always been *Thou*. Self-consciousness crumbles away, nature comes alive and we come alive to nature. When the world is *Thou*, it is unpredictable and full of surprises; it becomes wild again – and very vast indeed.

✳

In 2003, the psychologists Dacher Keltner and Jonathan Haidt published a seminal paper on awe, which they say is 'central to the experience of religion, politics, nature, and art'. Awe has two recurring features: vastness and accommodation.

The experience of awe begins when we perceive something much, much bigger than ourselves. That something could be a person who radiates charisma (triggering the feelings we experience in the presence of someone we love deeply); or it could be a work of art, a scientific theory, or an element of the natural world seen in all its wild glory. Whatever the cause, you experience a life-changing moment in which you realize – to paraphrase Hamlet's words to Horatio – that there are more things under the sky than you dreamt of in your philosophy.

This vastness is too much for you. It overflows, and shakes the core of your world. You thought you cared only about your career, but after you met that girl... now, you are not so sure any more. You thought you were an atheist, but how can a lake so pristine be the result of a game of chance? You thought you were a Christian, but how can you hold on to the idea of a God after solving such a perfect equation as the one on your notepad, which explains the birth of a star without any need for supernatural intervention? An experience of vastness is that extreme place that both witches and scientists strive to reach. Once you are there, nothing is certain any more.

When vastness turns your world upside down, you have to find a way of accommodating it in your life, of finding a space for it – even at the cost of changing your life entirely. This is the phase that Keltner and Haidt call 'accommodation'. They warn us to be careful – we might not succeed in accommodating vastness in our lives. Witches advise against 'gnostic burnout', which happens when you concentrate on your spiritual practice to the point that you have problems in the mundane world. Quite a few scientific geniuses ended up with mental health issues.

A failure to accommodate vastness won't always lead to dire consequences, but it will be terrifying. We humans like certainties, and vastness wipes clean the slate of our certainties. It is again the idea of a *mysterium tremendum et fascinans*, translated from the language of theology to that of psychology.

As a culture we have managed to accommodate vastness a bit too neatly: we have been ingenious enough to reduce the sky and the earth to maps that fit your pocket. The entire planet is contained within the grid of latitude and longitude.

Story maps accommodate vastness in a way that is less effective but more interesting. By their very lack of reliability, they might lead you along new paths and into new territories – some of them stranger than your strangest dreams.

To find our next key, we will let story maps lead us all the way to Faerie.

THE WORKOUT

1. The Acquaintance with a Tree

Find a tree in your neighbourhood. Every day for a week or more, spend a few minutes with it. Try not to think of it in terms of its taxonomy, as an 'oak' or a 'birch'. Think of it as that particular tree, as you would do with a friend. How tall is it? Notice its bark, its roots, its leaves, the insects and other animals living on it. Listen to it every day: put your ear against its trunk, and listen for at least a minute to the noises coming from within.

By the end of the week (or longer, if you need it), you should have come to consider that tree as an individual being. Did this happen? If not, why?

Make notes in your Book of Wonder.

2. The Rewilding of the Neighbourhood

For a week, make an effort to notice the wildlife that you can find in unlikely places in your neighbourhood: flowers blooming from cracks in the asphalt, squirrels living close to a station. Make notes in your Book of Wonder about the wildlife surrounding you where you live.

3. The Story Map

Over the course of a week, make a note of the feelings and sensations you experience and of the colours you perceive during your commute to work. Record the spots that awaken memories, and those that make you dream about the future.

Then write in your Book of Wonder a story map of your commute to work. In the example I gave in the chapter, the primary school close to my house became 'the spot where children meet to learn about their future'. Think of each step as an element of a quest, a part of a larger story, and describe it accordingly.

Finally, the next time you go to work, keep that story in mind, looking at your commute through its lens.

What does it change? Make a note in your Book of Wonder.

4. No Pictures Taken

This is not a real exercise; rather, it is a habit that you might want to get into. Every time you are planning an outdoor walk, decide in advance a small number of photographs that you will be allowed to take (for a four-hour walk, two will be plenty), *and then stick strictly to that number.* This will help you to engage with the world outside with one less filter between the world and yourself.

The Lore

✦ ✦ ✦ ✦

You feel awe, dread or confusion, you
could even be sick; reality crumbles
beneath your feet and you fall over.
And you encounter a fairy.

The village of Woolpit, Suffolk, would be unremarkable (although not charmless) were it not for the green children. They appeared on a summer's day during the reign of King Stephen, in the twelfth century, at harvest time. They came out of one of the wolf-pits after which the village was named. There were two of them, a boy and a girl. They looked lost – and as surprised to be there as the good people of Woolpit were to find them. Their skin was green, and their clothes were of strange hues that did not belong to Suffolk. The villagers asked them where they came from and about their parents, but the children did not speak any English. They spoke a language nobody had ever heard spoken before.

Wealthy Sir Richard de Calne of Wykes took them in; they were children, after all, lonely and afraid. Sir Richard tried to feed them, but they refused everything he offered, as if they did not recognize it as food at all. They went for days without eating, until they saw some raw broad beans, which they wolfed down. They ate only beans for a while, but gradually developed a taste for other foods; as they did so, their skin turned the colour of ours.

The girl seemed to fare quite well in the village; the boy did not. He fell ill and died, leaving the girl alone.

In time, the girl learned to speak English. She said that the boy had been her brother, and that they came from a land of perpetual twilight, bounded on one side by a river. Sources offer differing versions of how they came to Suffolk. One says that they were herding their father's cattle when they heard a loud noise, and suddenly found themselves in Woolpit; according to another, they followed their father's cattle into a cave, and then through an underground maze, which brought them to the wolf-pit. But these were descriptions, not explanations. The girl didn't know by what magic she had come to this foreign land, and she did not know how to go back home. She never found out.

The girl settled among us, as much as she could. She was mischievous, and – the sources hint – too forward in her ways, never fully adjusting to ours. But she worked for Sir Richard, and got married, and led a normal life, and nothing else is known of her.

※

In our search for our fourth key, we saw that psychologists consider *vastness* to be a fundamental feature of awe. Children are surrounded by vastness, although they don't realize it: an enormous number of future possibilities are open to them. Will they study humanities or sciences? Will they be passionately engaged with politics, and, if so, will they tend in a conservative or radical direction? Or will they be apolitical? Will they have girlfriends or boyfriends – or both? Or neither? Will they be compulsive travellers, criss-crossing the globe, or will they rarely stray far from their birthplace?

As we grow up, we become smaller: we have to make choices that narrow the possibilities open to us. Life becomes less vast. With every choice we make, we close the door on a thousand others. If you decide to go to law school, you will have to let go that old idea of becoming an astronaut. Whatever career path you walk, however satisfying it turns out to be, you will never get to walk the many other shining paths you could have taken.

This is not unhealthy: if you refuse to make a choice, you end up frozen – a rabbit in the headlights. The inevitable choices can make us nostalgic at times, when we look back to our childhood and we muse on all the different ways things could have turned out. This is not unhealthy either, provided it does not become an obsession. It is worthwhile to be aware of the trade-offs we make. In fact, we should be rather more aware of them than we are.

There is, however, an unwanted side effect of our getting smaller, and it is that the world gets smaller with us. With every passing year, we encounter fewer and fewer things that are new and unexpected. All the strategies we have been learning on this journey, all the fragments of wisdom we have been poaching, are intended to stretch our world and make it a little vaster, so as to leave space for wonder to happen. Magicians have taught us to appreciate the mystery, and then witches have taught us how to make it part of our lives. Scientists have showed us the usefulness of ignorance, and, lost in the forest, we have explored some old ways of living with nature, and thus with ourselves. Now we are ready to take a radical step, one that will keep our world full of vastness, never fully accommodated.

To locate our fifth key, we are going away with the fairies.

✳

Thomas of Erceldoune should have known better than to rest under a solitary hawthorn: such trees belong to fairies. It has to be said that Thomas was young and bold, and if he believed in fairies, he was probably eager to meet one. That day, with the sun high in the sky, Thomas sat under a hawthorn tree in the Eildon Hills, in Scotland's border country, a landscape of breathtaking beauty. Thomas was good with words. When he was around other people, they enjoyed his wit and expected his rejoinders to be swift and sharp. On a day like this, it was pleasant, for a change, to step back from what people wanted from him, and just enjoy the breeze and soak up the sunshine.

But when a beautiful woman rode by, Thomas could not help himself. She was richly dressed in green – a very promising colour, as you wear a green dress if you have plans to roll in the grass with someone. Thomas very much wanted to be that someone. The lady was elegant and self-assured, and just too beautiful for him to stay silent.

Thomas called to her, 'Queen of Heaven!' – tongue in cheek, of course (when you are talking to a beautiful woman, a light touch is your best friend).

She answered, gentle but deadpan, 'Not of Heaven, no. I am the Queen of Elfland.'

We don't know whether Thomas believed her or not. But when she dared him to kiss her, he did not refuse.

And of course as soon as he did so, he was in her power. The queen – because she was indeed the Queen of Elfland – took him on her horse and rode away on a bonny road that led to her realm. She told Thomas that he was to serve her for seven years, through good times and bad. But should he utter a word in 'Elfyn-land', he would never return to his own country. The queen also said to Thomas that for serving her, he would receive the gift of a tongue that could never lie.

He accepted his fate, which – to be honest – could have been worse. The Good People can flay you or hold you prisoner until everybody you know is old or dead; but the queen liked Thomas. We do not know the details of what happened to him in Elfland, but, sure enough, seven years later he returned home, in good shape.

He was the same, but not quite.

When Thomas came back, he could not lie any more. People

started calling him 'True Thomas'. He was a better poet than ever, a smoother talker, and being obliged to tell the truth did not hinder him in the least.

And there was something else. Some of the truths Thomas spoke were yet to come: for the queen had given him the ability to see into the future. He made good use of her gift.

He is a good man, Thomas the Rhymer.

＊

Is a world that incorporates fairies *too* vast?

We have learned how important it is to shift our world view, but seriously – fairies?

I am sure you agree that the world is vast enough to contain many things you and I don't know, but that does not mean that it contains *everything*. We must draw the line at fairies.

And yet.

And yet – from time immemorial, level-headed, well-adjusted people have claimed to have encountered fairies. Some describe meetings with other strange beings – visitations from ghosts and poltergeists, conversations with doppelgängers.

On a daily basis, everywhere on the planet, from Brazilian slums to the French countryside, men and women have 'supernatural' experiences. But are such experiences *real*? The sensible answer is to say *no*, the eccentric answer is *yes*. We can do better than either.

Dr Simon Young is a British historian living in Italy, a

university lecturer, and an authority on fairy lore. After 'a brush with mortality' he became interested in fairies, and in 2014 started a project for which the word *amazing* is not, for once, inappropriate. Dr Young created an online 'Fairy Census,' where people could anonymously relate their experiences of meeting fairies, with the assurance that their identity would never be disclosed, so they would be safe from the ridicule of their peers. The version of the Fairy Census I consulted was published in January 2018 and recorded fairy sightings up to 2017. It contains five hundred entries. Five hundred accounts of modern people seeing fairies.

Young is confident that most of the people who have recounted their experiences for the Fairy Census are sincere. He is suspicious of only a small number of accounts, for an intriguing reason: after sifting through hundreds of reports, he noticed that there are 'patterns within impossible experiences', and the accounts that aroused his suspicions do not conform to them. But, as he admits, it would be a slippery slope for him to judge what is kosher and what is not in a Fairy Census.

When we were in touch via email, Young, a kind and patient man, made it immediately clear that he is not out to demonstrate that fairies are real. I didn't doubt that. I had assumed that the point of his research could not be to 'demonstrate' the existence of fairies, but clearly, this was not the view of many of those who wrote to him after he had published the census (online, for free). They wanted a *yes* or a *no*, they demanded absolute certainty. This is not what fairies are about. Fairies are about diehard doubt.

Our fifth key is a lesson in scepticism. While it is all too easy to be sceptical about fairies, it is not so easy to be sceptical about other things – the value of money, what a proper career looks like, how an adult should behave, or, for that matter, the non-existence of fairies. But we should, or those things will end up controlling us, choking our sense of wonder.

Young's work shows that *something is going on*: where there is smoke there is, at least, smoke. Fairies might or might not be literally real, but people have met them. And if five hundred people answered a comparatively obscure online census, available only in English, how many more fairy encounters are happening out there, unrecorded and forgotten?

✳

On a night as black as the bottom of a cave, the young man had taken a shortcut through a small patch of urban woodland in Michigan. We don't know his name, because this story comes from the Census and his name was kept secret, but we know he was in his twenties, and had had no prior experience of the supernatural. He had walked through these woods on many occasions; he knew his way around.

Even though it was not late – between 6 and 9 p.m., as far as we know – the woods were very silent. More so than they should have been. If the young man had been a fairy expert, he would have known that a profound silence can foreshadow a fairy encounter; but he was not, and he did not know.

He heard a voice. More than one. Whispering and laughing. The young man jerked his head up and looked around. He was not alone, but it was not humans he saw. There were shadows in the trees, small and quick, 'darting through the branches', to use his own words.

It was too dark to see clearly, or perhaps the figures didn't want to be seen. The young man suddenly felt lost. Surely he couldn't lose his way in such a small patch of woodland; and yet, he was not sure where he was any more: it had become even darker, and he couldn't see the path.

There was something older than him in the branches, something age-old and ancestral; and perhaps it was an age-old instinct that dictated the young man's response. For reasons he could not fully explain, he reached into his backpack, took out a small bell and tinkled it for a while. Then he left it on a branch as an offering. And now the woods were less dark, and his mind too, and he could see the path. He hurried home without looking back.

He returned the next day to find that the woods were just woods, small, unassuming and tame.

The bell was not there.

*

Throughout the Middle Ages, priests routinely identified fairies with demons, devils and witches. Clerics and elves were enemies – supposedly. Reality was more nuanced: their daily dealings happened in a grey area between hostility and alliance. What matters to us is that for a long time in history, a person who cavorted with fairies might be condemned but would not be ridiculed. Good citizens kept away from fairies, but not from the people who believed in them.

After having read Simon Young's reports, I became curious about what a present-day religious thinker would have to say. So I went and spoke to a theologian, hoping that he would not consider me insane.

I should not have worried. John Milbank is an intellectually imposing figure, very outspoken. While he holds opinions that some might find difficult at times, he is also unfailingly gentle, an empathetic listener, and erudite in a gracious way that allows you to take notes without feeling stupid. As one of Britain's leading theologians, he started a religious and philosophical movement called Radical Orthodoxy, based on the idea that we should return to ancient, numinous ways of understanding the Christian God, grounding them in our contemporary world. He holds unfaltering beliefs, but 'fanciful' is not a word you would ever use to describe him. He is an intellectual power-house with an unapologetic belief in the 'supernatural'. He was exactly the person I needed to talk to.

For scheduling reasons, we didn't manage to meet in person,

and ended up having a chat about wonder, faith and fairies over Skype. Even so, John's voice filled my study. It soon became clear he didn't consider my questions to be insane, and I relaxed a bit, and felt my reality stretch.

We started chatting about nature, where fairies are often encountered. 'People used to have a different relationship with nature,' John said. 'Nature was seen as having a symbolic value. It was like a book to read, and it was communicating something divine to us. It had a meaning. In the modern period, people have become more alienated. When we use the word *nature*, we mean by it something very... reductive.' John echoed my own thoughts, albeit coming from a different perspective. 'We think of nature as *one thing*, while before modernity they thought in terms of *Creation*, where everything is held together by God.'

I asked, 'What do you mean?'

'When they talk of *Natura*, in the Middle Ages, they think of her like a goddess, the immanent presence for God's creation, if you like. It is a *shaping power* rather than just a thing.'

'And fairies are part of it?'

At this, John chuckled. 'It seems like in every culture they have this sense that there are other beings within nature, call them fairies or whatever, beings clearly distinct from God. Why is that? Even today, we still have people who report these things in the United Kingdom, and it would be the same if we looked at Italy, or Siberia, or anywhere else.' John was clearly passionate about the topic; I could almost imagine his voice to be that of a medieval cleric called in to deal with these meddlesome creatures. 'The question we must ask is, is that because people who are closer to nature have an awareness that it is animated? Are they *alert*, or deluded? Do these things not exist, or have many people simply lost a certain sensibility? Why is it that in the past people almost took it for granted that there were these wonderful creatures, and we don't do that any more?'

'What do you think?' I asked.

He measured his words carefully before replying. 'I have a suspicion,' he said, 'that we can't ignore all these reports. Also, a suspicion that we have lost an ability to be aware of certain things. People felt that nature was alive, it was animate, and probably people were aware of more things, in nature, than we are now. Social scientists have come up with all sorts of incredibly convoluted explanations for why people thought these things, but I don't think that those who lived in the past were stupid, I don't think they were self-deluded. They had categories like *unreal* or *pretend*: they knew this stuff.' John did not speak as a rival to fairies: to my ears it sounded as if old enemies were striking a truce against the rising tides of disenchantment.

The idea that nature has a soul, held together by God if you are Christian, or by some other principle if you are not, is very old and very widespread. As we found while looking for our fourth key, it is only with the Scientific Revolution in the West in the sixteenth and seventeenth centuries that we became convinced that the universe was a kind of watch.

Once you swap grids for stories and you start looking at the wild through a new set of eyes, there is a chance that you might peer into something truly exotic, and also that something truly exotic might peer back at you. And yes, I understand – fairies might be too exotic for comfort.

What about aliens, then?

※

Joe Simonton was sixty, and as far as we know he led a peaceful life in his home on the Eagle River, Wisconsin, where he farmed chickens. Late in the morning of 18 April 1961, he was lounging around his house, when he heard a noise. He went outside to discover that a chrome-coloured flying saucer had landed in his back yard.

A door opened in the saucer to reveal three men, who, Simonton would swear later, looked Italian. One of them even had a black suit. They were dark-haired and dark-skinned (as is the case with many of us from southern Italy), and they were thirsty. One of them was holding a jug, and through gestures, he made Joe understand that they would like some water.

Joe believed in hospitality, whatever the circumstances. He went back inside with the jug, and when he got back to the yard, he found that the three Italians from outer space had crowded around a kind of barbecue. They had not invaded his garden: politely, they were grilling inside their ship, on a flameless fire. Simonton gave them the water and asked for some of their food. I think he was more curious than hungry. Fair is fair: the Italians gave him three or four (here sources disagree) of the pancakes they were making. Then they closed the door and their ship took off, never to be seen again.

Joe ate one of the pancakes, but didn't like it much (he said it 'tasted like cardboard'). He then called the US Air Force, who – this being the early 1960s, a time of jittery obsession with flying saucers, fuelled by Cold War paranoia – decided to investigate. Experienced investigators talked to Joe and found him trustworthy. He was sincere, convinced of what he said, and besides, he had nothing to gain from inventing a UFO story, certainly not one so outlandish: when you make up a story that you want people to believe, you are better off glossing over smartly dressed Italians from outer space.

The Air Force sent one of the uneaten pancakes to the US Department of Health, Education, and Welfare. Analysis revealed it to be made of 'hydrogenated fat, starch, buckwheat hulls, soya bean hulls, wheat bran'. In other words, it was a pancake. To hammer the last nail in the UFO coffin, 'bacteria and radiation readings were normal for this material'.

For those of you who were hoping for proof of an alien visitation, this is a disappointing end to the story. For those of you who know UFO stories to be a pile of hokum, it's nice to be vindicated. But in both cases, if you will forgive me for saying so, you are making a curious assumption: that you know for a fact the ingredients of an extraterrestrial pancake.

The world – and the British Isles especially – is rich in different types of fairy. To name but a sprinkling, there are elves, brownies, boggarts, hobs and pixies, from traditions and places as far removed as Germanic folklore, the Anglo-Scottish border and the bleak moorlands of Devon and Cornwall.

Modern folklorists have created meticulous taxonomies that distinguish between a pixie and a brownie, a boggart and an elf, establishing what is what and who is who in Faerie. Such taxonomies are fascinating to read, but a taxonomy is still a taxonomy, and detailed lists of names and descriptions won't take us to Faerie.

In the golden days of the fairy faith, people would not put fairies into neat categories. A boggart was a bit like an elf who was a bit like a demon, and by the way, fairies were not easily distinguished from the dead: the boundaries were ever-shifting.

It seems bizarre to use a 'scientific' procedure to understand something that could never belong to science in any sense. We tend to believe that if something is real, then we can measure and classify it, and on the other hand, if we cannot measure and classify something, then that thing does not exist. Those who want fairies to be real, classify them; those who don't, point at the impossibility of classification as another good reason for cynicism. Both approaches speak of fairies with the language of modernity – i.e. logic and reason. But this is not the language spoken in Faerie.

The adventure of Joe Simonton, he of the extraterrestrial pancakes, is described in *Passport to Magonia*, a book by Jacques Vallée, French-born computer scientist and astronomer-turned-ufologist. Though Vallée has impeccable scientific credentials (he was among those who worked on the first digital map of Mars), his ideas about UFOs are even stranger than you might expect. Aliens, he noted, act a lot like fairies do: in the case of Mr Simonton, for example, they exchanged food, a fairly common occurrence with the Good People.

Vallée thinks that fairies and aliens are different manifestations of the same *something*. It takes different shapes, depending on the people that it is interacting with. This mutable, shape-shifting character is nicely in line with the fairy lore we have been handed down, where fixed classifications did not exist. Once upon a time this *something* would take the form of a lady riding through a wild landscape, while in our technologically advanced society, where horses are out and technology is in, it takes the form of technologically advanced beings. Vallée published *Passport* in 1969, a heady time for psychedelic theories. The book became a subcultural classic, and it has been making ripples ever since.

An English writer, Patrick Harpur, put forward an even dreamier take on Vallée's ideas in his strange masterpiece *Daimonic Reality*.

Harpur, like John Milbank, is convinced that nature is

spiritual. They both draw on the idea that our world has a soul, a *spiritus mundi*. For Harpur, there are some enigmatic inter- mediaries between soul and matter, between the *spiritus mundi* and us. We have been calling them fairies, aliens and whatnot; he gathers them all under the umbrella term of *daimon*.

With daimons, any classification is doomed. Daimons can take the shape of a boggart, a brownie, a phantom black cat, an alien, and we will never be able to explain them or fully understand them, but we can 'mull them over, *mythologize*, in the hope of making some sense of them'. Spirit is matter, matter is spirit, nature is us, we are nature.

Heady stuff. Milbank, Vallée, Harpur, they are all saying, albeit in very different ways, that there is *something* out there, a mysterious *something* we call 'fairies' for want of a better term.

That *something* is the custodian of our fifth key. But don't worry – you will not need to believe that it is real in order to snatch the key from its clutches.

✳

I heard of someone who danced with fairies in Somerset, on a midsummer night. This story comes from Simon Young's Fairy Census, and this time, it is a story that is very easy to believe. It happened at a festival, in a field in which people were drum- ming and dancing.

Two women appeared whom nobody had seen before. There was something about them. It was partly that they were very beautiful, but it was more than that. Their dance was hypnotic – they moved in ways that were entirely human, yet also not so. They did not invite anyone to join their dance, but nor did they create a barrier around themselves. They were happy in their own world.

As if in response to their dance, the drumming became louder and faster, and as if in answer to the drumming, a third figure appeared, a goblin. The women greeted his arrival with cries of delight. He started dancing with them, in a manner more forceful than theirs, but just as happy.

And then a fourth creature came.

Years later, our witness could only call it 'the mudman'. This creature did not have any features to speak of: he was, our witness said, 'just a vaguely humanoid flowing mass of soil, rock, and mud'. The women and the goblin cheered the mudman, dancing frenziedly around him. The mudman was an ancient, ancestral being – this much was clear.

And so it went on, the four creatures frolicking to human music, people moving around them, the drums beating their rhythms all through the night until dawn. But as the first rays of sunlight appeared, the quartet was nowhere to be seen, gone with the moon and the stars.

I said this story is easy to believe. The young man freely admits he had eaten seeds of the plant morning glory (*Ipomoea violacea*), which have a hallucinogenic effect. We can be quite sure that his friends had partaken of the same seeds. So now we understand why they saw the fairy women, and the goblin, and the mudman – don't we?

✳

What you call 'reality' is, at the end of the day, neurochemistry: everything that exists, exists only, from your point of view, as a sophisticated network of chemical reactions and electric impulses within your body. When you die, that network stops functioning and 'reality' ceases to exist for you (there might be a different form of life after death, of course: we just don't know). Drugs are chemicals that you temporarily add to the chemicals you already have in circulation. By changing the composition of your chemicals, you change your perception, and thus your reality.

It does not make any sense to say that an 'altered' neurochemistry shows us a 'wrong' reality. As far as we know, evolution has been driven by chance: it is only by chance that the chemicals in your body work the way they work. By messing with them, we are not doing anything that nature has not been doing since the Big Bang.

It is sensible to say the Somerset party-goer met fairies because he was stoned, but we shouldn't infer from this that fairies are 'only' a hallucination. What if the chemicals had made his perceptions better, rather than worse? Or just different? Maybe the fairies had always been there, and the seeds of morning glory allowed the party-goer to see them at last.

If you resolutely do not believe in fairies, this idea might be hard to accept, in part because of something called Illusory Superiority bias. In a famous experiment, a group of American and Swedish students were asked to rate their driving skills: 93 per cent of the Americans and 69 per cent of the Swedes said that they drove better than average. The irony is there for all to see. But don't laugh too loud, because you and I are just like those students. The bias that makes you think you are better than average is the Illusory Superiority bias. Like bacteria in our gut, we all have it.

It does not matter how high we set the bar of 'average', you and I will always believe that we are above it: we are naturally inclined to think that we know better. *Everybody* is so inclined, which means necessarily that someone must be wrong. I am sure it is not you; all I am saying is, it just might be.

Illusory Superiority is one of many biases we have. The list is long and potentially endless. We instinctively trust a person and we act on our instinct because we know we are a good judge of character, but what we don't know is that we trust that person because he happens to have hair the same colour and cut as a cousin we are close to. Our trust has nothing to do with our supposed observation skills; in fact, probably we are no better than average at judging character.

We believe that our memories are reliable, and that the woman we saw this morning was driving a red car, but the person we saw this morning was not in a car, he was on a green bicycle, and yes, he was a man, not a woman, in his sixties, not his forties. It seems implausible, I know: most of the time you have no reason to doubt your memories, and you go on believing that they are at least vaguely reliable. Quite often they are not, as professionals who have to probe into strangers' memories (police officers, for example) know only too well. We believe we know what is going on in our mind, but we don't. We believe we know what is going on in the world. Try again.

Our biases are not 'mistakes': they are the way we approach the world. The Illusory Superiority bias might get us into trouble, but it also fills us with ideas, enthusiasm and ambition: you need to think you are a little better than average, in order to even contemplate, say, writing a book. We can almost train a bias out of ourselves in a specific field (for example, it is part of a writer's training to learn that when an editor suggests a correction, the editor is right more often than not), but in other areas of life our unaltered biases will cause us to flounder.

Just in case you were wondering, this has everything to do with fairies. Remember what we said about vastness and accommodation? When you feel a sense of vastness, you try to accommodate it, to reduce it somehow to a scale you can understand. Sometimes we have experiences so unusual that we cannot explain them in any way. They bring home to us how *vast and weird is the world*. We cannot live with that. We rush to accommodate the strange new things within our lives, by interpreting them through our biases, both psychological and cultural. Because we have heard stories about fairies, we decide that the odd experience we had was an encounter with a fairy. Or, because we have heard stories about the effect of drugs, we decide it was only a hallucination. Our Illusory Superiority bias conspires to convince us that our interpretation is the only sensible one.

Accommodation is a tricky process. In your zeal to accommodate, you might end up converting to a specific credo, telling audiences at UFO conferences that you have been abducted by aliens. Or, and this is every bit as undesirable, you might decide that nothing truly extraordinary ever happens to anybody.

We can be certain that people's *experiences* of encountering fairies are real. Not necessarily in the way that a watch is real, or the excellent plate of *trofie con crema di gorgonzola* that you had for lunch is real. But then again, a lot of meaningful things are not like a watch or like pasta: love, to name but one.

This is why we trained ourselves to accept the mystery before venturing into Faerie: we had to learn to hold on and not rush to judgement. Faerie has its perils, and overly neat interpretations are one of them. Interpretations feel safe when they are not. This is often true in Faerie: the safest-looking things – fruit, gifts, dances – are very dangerous indeed.

✳

The girl lived in the village of Grange, in County Sligo, a place beautiful and wild, in the shadow of Benbulben. One night the

Good People took her from a field. There had been no warning that fairies were up to mischief, so it was by a stroke of luck that when they came, the girl was not alone. A villager tried to hold on to her, but the Good People managed to snatch the girl anyway, replacing her with a broomstick.

The police constable was called, and was told what had happened. He found himself in something of a predicament. On the one hand he was a local, and he knew that the Good People got up to this sort of thing. On the other hand, he was a police constable, and there were procedures to follow.

He decided to hedge his bets: he would keep one foot in the traditional camp, the other in the bureaucratic. He did a round of the houses, searching for the girl, and as he did so, he asked the villagers to burn all the ragweed they could find in the field from which the girl had been stolen, for the ragweed had magic powers. While the ragweed burned, he would chant a spell.

The villagers set to work, for the girl was well known, and well loved. First they picked the ragweed, then they burned it. The night sky was lit with an orange glow, as the fire burned and the constable chanted the spell, tirelessly, without ever stopping, not even for a sip of ale.

When morning came, it found the villagers exhausted and barely able to stand – and the constable's throat dry and parched.

But the girl had returned.

They found her in the same field where the villagers had gathered. She told how a fairy had carried her away on

The Lore · 207

horseback to a faraway river. The fairy had then whispered in her ear the names of certain people in the village.

They were the names of people who were going to die soon.

This story was told to W. B. Yeats, and recounted by the poet in his collection of poems and mythic tales entitled *The Celtic Twilight*. He explains that the girl had been kidnapped three years before he heard of her story. 'It is better doubtless,' Yeats comments, 'to believe much unreason and a little truth than to deny for denial's sake truth and unreason alike, for when we do this we have not even a rush candle to guide our steps.'

Let's dive into much unreason, then, and see whether we can find some little truth.

✳

Those who strongly disapprove of fairies often invoke cognitive biases, the defects of memory, and other psychological quirks to explain away the encounters that certain individuals have with them. For example, it is exactly because human memory is not reliable that we cannot trust a man when he says that he vividly remembers hearing fairies in the woods. He can honestly believe that, and still be wrong. The US Air Force decided that Joe Simonton had neither lied nor exchanged groceries with extraterrestrials: he must have mistaken a vivid dream for reality. As for the pancakes, he must have baked them himself, possibly in a somnambulist state. It is, perhaps, a slightly convoluted explanation, but less so than an alien barbecue set up by Italians from outer space.

But, just for a moment, just as a game, put yourself in the shoes of Joe Simonton, a man who, as far as he is concerned, received a gift of dodgy-tasting pancakes from aliens. Or in the shoes of the nameless lad who danced with the fairies in Somerset. How do they live, how do they get on with their everyday lives, after having received convincing proof (for them) that aliens visit our planet and fairies dance with mortals? What is it like to have such a certainty, in a world where such certainty is regarded as at best eccentric, at worst as a symptom of a serious mental issue?

Even if you have not been lucky enough to meet a fairy or similar being, there are people like you, people who are mentally sound, who have had such encounters. There are citizens of the twenty-first-century world – people with jobs not unlike yours and living in houses not unlike yours – whose experience of the world includes fairies. You may have neighbours who live next door to Faerie; which means that you too have fairy neighbours. The Fairy Census is proof enough of that.

And once you realize how many people have had these experiences (and are you sure you are not one of them?) and keep them a secret – because, as a culture, we don't have a way to make sense of them – you will realize another thing, which I never cease to find alluring and terrifying.

Those who have met fairies have a rock-solid certainty *that they have had a real encounter*, and yet *you know that this is not possible*, you are certain of that. But how many of *your own* rock-solid certainties are in fact as gossamer-thin as you find theirs?

Are you sure you have come to terms with not getting a first-class degree? Are you *sure* that the first boy you kissed had black hair?

And are you certain that your colleague made that hurtful comment that you think you remember so clearly?

Are you sure you are awake?

When fairies come into play, such questions stop being abstract philosophy. You might well be a no-nonsense person, but other no-nonsense people are just as certain that they have met fairies as you are of being awake now – and, please remember, there is a good chance that you are no more clever or more sensible than they are. Your biases make you think so, and I know how hard it is to suppress them, but please, just as a game – can you try? We cannot stretch our reality without making it uncomfortable.

Fairies are fickle, often cruel. They show us on what shaky grounds our lives rest. As soon as we leave the path at the centre of the forest, the true path, the certain path, the one we take for granted, they come, and snatch us, and take us away with them.

✳

The girl was thirteen. She was with her family in Cornwall, on the first day of their holidays, and she was very excited. She loved coming here, for the freedom from school, for the scenery, and also for the Little People. On a previous trip, her family had told her some of the fairy stories and strange local legends for which Cornwall is famous. She was already too old to believe they were true, but she enjoyed them nonetheless.

When the girl went for a walk with her mother and sister, along a remote path, she dashed ahead of them. She was thrilled, in love with life, and why walk when you can run?

She saw a gnome.

He was sitting close to the track, with a 'nut brown wizened face', a 'mossy brown beard' and 'dark brown shining eyes'. His peaked hat was brown too, his trousers tinted in shades of ochre and brown. He grinned at the girl.

The girl stood speechless. She did not feel any wonder or awe, she only felt confused. She did not believe in gnomes, and yet, here there was one.

The gnome cocked his head, turned his back, and changed into a tree stump.

Only now did the girl find her voice. 'Mum! Look…!' she called, but there was nothing to look at any more. Only an old tree stump.

She mumbled something inconsequential, and they continued on their walk. But the girl was shaken. She knew how it looked: everybody would say that she had mistaken a tree stump for a gnome. But she knew she hadn't. She couldn't explain and she never tried to; until, years later, she found Simon Young's Fairy Census.

The girl had been impressionable, overeager. Her head was full of fairy stories. The encounter lasted only a few seconds. What is more likely – that a thirteen-year-old crossed paths with a gnome who became a tree stump, or that a thirteen-year-old saw a tree stump and briefly thought it was a gnome?

To this day, she swears that she saw a gnome.

✳

What we call 'reality' is a web of connections. For example, for your debit card to exist, an enormous number of connections must be in place: your card can buy you food and books now, but in a post-apocalyptic world in which society had broken down, it would be a useless plastic rectangle. The power of your card is, to use a scholarly term, a 'socially constructed' reality. Which means that it is entirely real, but only as long as we believe in it.

To an extent, everything is a socially constructed reality. Think of a simple and wholesome herb – say, mint. Of course we did not invent the herb, and the herb would do fine without us. In a sense, mint is more fundamentally *real* than money is.

And yet when you and I think of 'mint', we do not have in our mind an image of the plant as it would be if no humans were around; no, we have a highly contextual image of a delicious aromatic herb that we can use to make a sauce to go with lamb and also distil into a syrup that is the basis for a popular Italian summer drink. My image of mint is of my maternal grandfather drinking an old-fashioned mix of milk, ice and mint syrup on a skin-meltingly hot July day, telling stories of his wife (my grandmother), whom I never got to meet; yours might be infused with the aroma of roast lamb for Sunday lunch at your parents' place in Devon. If you and I disappeared today, 'mint' in this sense would disappear with us. A plant would still exist, but it would not be the 'mint' of syrup and sauce.

Social realities require our negative capability, even though they pretend they don't: to make them work, we must accept them without asking questions. If people stopped believing that your debit card is worth something, your card would lose its value, and if people stopped believing that mint is delicious, it wouldn't be delicious any more. The intricate, occasionally frustrating but also often beautiful web of connections that our society created for us, and that we create with our society, is what we call 'reality'. We live inside this web.

As human beings we are the spider weaving the web, and also the fly trapped in its centre. This is a lesson that countless philosophical and spiritual traditions have passed down: don't take the web too seriously, or it will trap you. You made the web yourself. You can, with some effort, undo it, or make it better.

Language, culture, memory, and the drugs that our laws define as either legal or not so – all are tools that we use to weave this web. We consider 'real' a world perceived by someone under the influence of caffeine, and 'not real' a world perceived by someone under the influence of morning glory seeds, for no better reason than we decided one can be bought in a super-market and the other cannot. You join the dots of morning glory, partying and an otherworldly encounter, and the shape that emerges is that of a 'hallucination'. But a shaman would join the same dots and would say it is a 'vision'. Or they could select different dots to join. Perhaps the weather was a factor in the sudden appearance of that strange festival dance? The fact that it was Midsummer, traditionally one of the most enchanted nights of the year, surely needs to be taken into account.

Fairies are 'supernatural' because we have been trained to see 'nature' as a mechanism, a finely tuned watch, and you cannot stick a fairy inside a watch.

But sometimes stuff happens: a malfunction, a tear in the web. It might be you being on different drugs, it might be you having listened to too many fairy tales, it might be a chemical imbalance in your body, it might be just because. What happens is that all of a sudden, a new way of joining the dots dawns on you, something so new and unexpected that you cannot make sense of it. You feel awe, dread or confusion, you could even be sick; reality crumbles beneath your feet and you fall over. And you encounter a fairy.

Back when *Natura* was a goddess and it was taken for granted that she had a soul, fairies were a legitimate shape we could discern in the landscape: seeing a tree stump as a brown gnome was allowed. Fairies were not beyond nature, they were within it. Then again, humans were not beyond nature either.

When we decided we were not part of the landscape, we took fairies with us: we expelled them from the natural world while we were expelling ourselves. From then on, the grid was the only shape allowed.

Our life becomes charmless when we convince ourselves that the dots we know and the shapes we have learned to draw are all there is. Society has worked its hypnosis on us, worn us down. Fairies snap us awake. Fairies are anarchists of the soul.

We can let them teach us to look at the world in radically different ways. When your web gets boring and predictable, you can change it. Money is every bit as absurd as fairies, or if you like, fairies are no more absurd than money. It is an immensely liberating discovery, and for that, a little unnerving.

The fact that even today, even after the triumph of grid maps, fairies are still seen – and that they take ridiculous forms that no one in their right mind could consider 'realistic', such as smartly dressed aliens – shows us that social realities are paper tigers: as long as they hold together, they are formidable, but when the smallest tear appears, they come undone very quickly. The most precious gift a good fairy leaves us is not a belief in her existence, but a radical doubt in the existence of everything else. We can create, to an extent, a different reality. We do not have to please and we do not have to comply. It is radical mojo.

It is the mojo that we are going to learn in the last two steps of our journey.

*

I once saw something. Not exactly a fairy, I don't think so, but not a ghost either, and certainly not an alien. Was it a hallucination? I am not sure any more what that word means. I would say it was almost a monk.

For a long time, I did not think about the almost-monk, until Paola, in our early days together, asked me if I had ever seen anything that was not of this world. We were in a pub in Edinburgh, a city we both love, one with a real sense of strangeness and mystery (in the Old Town especially). 'No,' I answered. And then it dawned on me. 'Except for the monk,' I added.

It had been a cold February afternoon, just after Candlemas. My father had taken me to my family's small holiday house, in a fishing village not far from the town where we spent the winter. He was still well: there was no reason to believe that in just a few years his mind would be gone. I might have been seven or eight, no older than that, and, like most children of that age, I expected that nothing would ever change. Like fortunate children, I didn't want them to.

My father would go to the small house in the fishing village regularly throughout the winter months, to tend to the garden, and more often than not I would go with him. I loved the silence that reigned at that time of year, and the memories of summer that haunted the place.

That afternoon, while my father was busy with various

chores, I wandered around the garden. The sun was high in the sky.

It was then that I saw the almost-monk.

I call him the almost-monk because I do not have a better word than *monk*, but I don't think it was a monk at all. It wore a monk's brown habit, its head was covered by a large, pointed hood, and its arms were folded. Its hands, if it had hands at all, were buried deep within the sleeves. It was moving, not walking, but *sliding*.

I saw it clearly. It was sliding in front of me, just a couple of yards away from me, as clearly visible as everything else in the stark early afternoon light. It slid until it reached the wall dividing our house from our neighbours', and there it disappeared from view.

More than afraid, I was awestruck. I didn't call out to my father (I don't know why: that is another question for you) and I never thought of the almost-monk again until that day in Edinburgh. But I remember some words that came into my mind when I saw it. I thought, *it's him again*.

This is my memory: make of it what you will. I don't remember having seen the almost-monk before, or since, and I wouldn't know where that 'it's him again' came from. The almost-monk's appearance was cartoonish, and the way it slid almost comical. If it was a ghost, it was a very badly drawn one. It might be a memory I made up, it might be a dream that I confused with a waking experience, it might be a figment of my imagination, which was as overactive then as it is today. It might be a spirit. It might be many things.

All of them make my reality flimsier. All of them make me doubt my senses, the shapes I have been trained, like a monkey in a sideshow, to draw. They make me think that although life may be tough, and that it breaks our illusions far too early, it never lacks magic.

For that, I am grateful.

THE WORKOUT

1. The Paranoid Universe

The universe has a message for you, which it is trying to communicate to you through small signs: articles in the newspaper, birds visiting your garden, coincidences. For ten days, pretend that you believe that the universe has such a message, and be ready to receive signs. Note down in your Book of Wonder all the possible signs you discern: for example, if you hear on the radio a snatch of a song that reminds you of a friend from school, the message might have to do with that friend, or with something connecting you both. Try to understand what the message is.

2. The Fairy Gambit

For a month, act as if you believe in fairies. You might find it difficult at first, but it will get easier after the first week. Consciously look for signs of fairy presence around you. Things you glimpse out of the corner of your eye; an otherworldly tune coming from afar; a voice in the wind; a shiver when it is not cold. Let go of all scepticism, and act as if you believe in fairies, completely and utterly. Note down in your Book of Wonder all the fairy signs you spot. After a month, look at your notes.

Is there a discernible pattern?

Is it possible that you will keep on believing? Or was it just a game?

If you already believe in fairies, reverse the exercise. For a month, act as if no fairies exist, and go out of your way to demonstrate it.

3. The Encounter with a Spirit

For a week or more, go back to the tree that you got to know for the workout for the Fourth Key. If that tree had a spirit, what spirit would it be? Would it be female, male, or somewhere else on the spectrum – or would it be something else altogether? How would it look? If you can draw, draw it. What would its voice sound like? And what would it say? Don't be too shy to address the tree as you would a person, and listen to its answers.

4. The Journey to Faerie

Take a walk in the woods, or in a stretch of countryside close to where you live. Before starting the walk, pour a libation of milk – a traditional offering for the Good Neighbours – and ask the Good Neighbours to meet you during the walk, in friendship and with no harm done. When you take the walk, look for signs and patterns. Are you still walking in our world? Are you in Faerie? Or a place in between?

The Sixth Key

The Story

* * *

We need to escape

The Sultan Shahryar had a younger brother with a smaller kingdom. They got along well: a smaller kingdom is still a kingdom, and the younger brother was content with it. The two of them had beautiful wives and loyal subjects. Life was sweet, for a while.

One day the sultan sent his vizier to his brother, with an invitation to come and spend some time with him, if the brother so wished: it was two years since they had last met. The brother thought it an excellent idea, and asked the vizier to camp out of town while he got ready for the journey.

The brother had his servants pack food, and presents for Shahryar, and he put his loyal minister in charge of the kingdom. The queen, he decided, would stay behind: it was better for her to remain at court in case there was trouble while he was away. Not that he expected any.

On the night before leaving, Shahryar's brother kissed his wife goodbye and joined the vizier's camp, next to which he had set up his own, ready to leave at first light. It was a warm, scented night, and happy as the brother was to be visiting Shahryar, he was already missing his wife's soft skin, and the husky note in her voice. He tossed and turned in his bed, under the myriad stars that shone in the night sky, until he could take it no more. He decided to sneak back to his palace and surprise her with a last goodbye.

You should never sneak in on your lovers, for you might be the one who is surprised; had the sultan's brother been older and wiser, he would have known that.

He found his wife in her rooms, asleep. She was naked; her skin, as smooth as water on a perfectly calm day, reflected the starlight coming in through the window. She was not sleeping alone. A young man, one of those bucks whose muscles have been drawn with care and pleasure, was asleep with her, naked too. They were both smiling, their limbs entangled, satiated after what had clearly been a long night.

The cuckolded brother took the only option open to him: he drew his sabre and killed his wife and her lover. He threw their bodies in a hole, and then sulked his way back to the camp. He gave the order to leave at once.

The cortège soon reached the sultan's palace. If anyone noticed that his brother was in a foul mood, they chose not to point it out. But when the two men met, all worries were forgotten. The brothers hugged, and went in to dinner, and then they smoked and drank and chatted late into the night. There is a special warmth, an iron bond, that only people who have known each other for a lifetime can share. The sultan's brother went to bed a different man.

Or so he thought.

Once in his bed, he could not fall asleep. He could not believe how stupid he had been, and how ill-fated. He got up. Yes, *ill-fated* was the word. Of all the pretty women there were in the kingdom (and there were many), he had to fall in love with the one who would not be faithful. Had he been cleverer, clever like his brother for example, he would have seen through her, and would never have married her.

Lost in thought, he paced his room, and when his room was not big enough, he paced the palace, and then he went outside and paced the gardens.

Shahryar was awake too – after having entertained the sultana in ways fitting a sultana – and saw his little brother sulking by starlight. He thought that the brother must be missing his wife: a night like this was made for love. He made a resolution to lift his brother's mood.

Starting the next day, the sultan sent his brother gifts, organized parties for him, fed him the sweetest dates and wine. But his brother continued to sulk. When Shahryar suggested they go hunting, his brother refused, saying he was feeling ill. Shahryar did not insist. He went hunting without him. And of course, his entire court went with him.

The only people of note who remained at the palace were his brother and the sultana.

The brother locked himself in his room to sulk some more. He was sulking by the window, when he saw movement in the lush gardens. A secret door opened, and twenty-one veiled women emerged from it. One of them was the sultana. They walked until they came very close to his window, and there they stopped, and undressed. Now he could see that ten of the women were not women after all, but men (of the better-looking variety) in disguise. The sultana undressed too. She called out a name.

Another man appeared, stronger than the others, taller than the others, and naked too, and quite ready for what was to come. He approached the sultana and kissed her full on her lips. Her hands gripped his waist.

That was the signal the others were expecting. The women and the men started kissing, and touching, and playing with each other in the bright sunshine, drunk on the scent of the garden. It was a beautiful orgy, and it lifted the sultan's brother's mood a little. But for the wrong reasons. He was still a cuckold, but at least he wasn't the only cuckold in the family: Sultan Shahryar's wife was unfaithful too.

When Shahryar came back, he found his brother in a better mood. He asked what had changed, and his brother told him the whole story, describing in particular detail how the sultana's careful ministrations had exhausted the vigorous young buck. Shahryar did not believe him; surely the sultana would not demean herself in such a way.

His brother suggested they set a trap, so that Shahryar could see with his own eyes what the sultana was getting up to. They would pretend they were going on another hunt, and secretly come back together. The sultan was sceptical, but he agreed to the plan to humour his brother.

The next day the two brothers departed for the hunt accompanied by the entire court, but then soon slipped away and returned in secret to the palace. Sure enough, another orgy was in full bloom in the garden, a rose of splendid bodies with the sultana at its centre. For reasons that I will never fathom, rather than join in (and I am sure the orgiasts would have welcomed them warmly), the brothers fled the scene and went off together in a sulk.

They decided to abandon their kingdoms and their palaces and seek out a land where they could sulk as much as they wanted. They vowed not to return until they had met someone more ill-fated than they were. They left behind the happy sounds and entwined bodies, and rode all day long, until they reached the sea. They set up camp under some trees.

They had just fallen asleep when a noise from the sea woke them up; a mighty bellow, like a beast on the hunt. A black column rose from the water, reaching out to the sky, and when the brothers saw it, they knew who was coming: a *jinn*, a creature of magic. They scrambled up a tree to hide.

The column of blackness eventually assumed the form of a man, more or less, who moved from the sea to the land, bringing with him a box of fine glass. The jinn opened the box and from it there emerged a woman, her hair as black as jet, her eyes dark and shining. It was clear that the jinn was deeply in love with her. He whispered sweet words in her ear and asked if she would allow him to rest his head on her legs, the softest pillow of all. She graciously permitted him to do so. The moment the jinn fell asleep, the woman shifted her gaze to the top of the tree and smiled at the sultan and his brother. She beckoned to them to come down.

While they were climbing down the tree, the woman gently moved the jinn's head so it was resting against a rock. She whispered to them to follow her, and so they did.

When they got to a secluded place, she ordered them to undress, and before they could answer, she started undressing herself.

The brothers would have rather carried on sulking (that's the sort of people they were). But they were worried that the woman might wake the jinn, so they did their best to make her happy.

I imagine that the brothers' best was not up to much, but the woman appreciated their efforts nonetheless. When their last ounce of strength was spent, and she had allowed them to get dressed again, she remarked on their wedding rings, and asked if she might have them for herself. The two men were happy to oblige: after all, they had no further use for the rings, since the wife of one of them was dead, and the wife of the other was probably still going at it hammer and tongs in the scented garden.

The woman thanked them warmly. She explained that she had a collection of ninety-eight such rings, and it was nice to get to a hundred. The jinn kept her in a glass box beneath the sea, but even so, she managed to take her pleasure whenever she wanted. Now, if the brothers didn't mind, she was pleasantly tired and needed some sleep, so she would be grateful if they could take their leave.

The brothers said a quick farewell and moved on before the jinn woke up. He was, they reasoned, more ill-fated than they were. He was more powerful than they could ever dream of being, yet he was as much a cuckold as they were.

They went back to the sultan's palace. Shahryar was so disgusted with womankind that he couldn't face killing his wife himself, which would have been the done thing. Instead, he ordered his vizier to dispatch her for him.

After that, he took his sabre and killed her courtesans. That, he could do. You might wonder why he didn't ask the sultana and her courtesans to give him a few tips – he clearly had much to learn in that department. The answer is that the sultan, like his brother, was not very imaginative. He would sooner sulk than party: you know the type.

And when a sultan sulks, he sulks mightily. No woman could be faithful, he had learned, so he would be faithful to none. He gave his vizier a terrible task: every night the vizier had to send him a new woman to marry, and the morning after, the sultan would kill her, so she would not have time to cuckold him. His brother returned to his smaller kingdom, with no such project in view, but awed by his brother's intelligent scheme.

The vizier found it, frankly, an over-reaction, and tried to talk the sultan out of it. But Shahryar didn't listen, and the vizier, who wanted to keep his head attached to his body, sent him the first woman, praying that one would be enough.

It wasn't.

Every night the sultan married a different woman, and the morning after he chopped off her head with his jewelled sabre. His subjects, who had loved him so much, now weren't quite so sure. Where there had been trust, a dangerous blend of fear and contempt was creeping in. Besides, the vizier would run out of eligible women sooner or later, and then what?

The vizier had a daughter, and her name was Scheherazade. She would have none of it: if her father could not stop the sultan from sulking murderously, then she would. She asked her father to send her to him.

The vizier was petrified. He asked her not to go, then pleaded, then ordered her not to. But Scheherazade would not hear reason: there was nothing her father could do to stop her. So, already crying for a daughter who was as good as lost, the vizier sent his Scheherazade to the sultan.

Scheherazade had a little sister, whom she asked to prepare herself.

That night the sultan admitted Scheherazade to his rooms. He was awestruck by her beauty, but puzzled when she started crying. What was all that about? Surely, a night with him would more than make up for being beheaded the following morning?

Scheherazade reassured him that it did, of course it did. She was only crying because she wished she could spend her last night on Earth with her sister in the room. Would the sultan allow her sister to sleep at the foot of their bed?

The sultan would.

The three of them awoke just before dawn. The sultan yawned and stirred and (as had become second nature to him) reached out for his sabre. As his fingers closed around the jewelled handle, Scheherazade's sister asked Scheherazade for a story. One last story, one of the many Scheherazade knew and told so well. Surely the sultan would allow one last story between sisters?

Shahryar was happy to agree. His habit was to behead his wives at the first light of dawn, and it was not dawn yet. Besides, as long as he controlled Scheherazade, as he surely did with his sabre in his hand, she could not trick him.

Scheherazade started to tell her story. It took so long to tell that when the sun rose, the story was not yet over. But Scheherazade accepted with good grace that it was time to go. She had been granted all her wishes and had had the immeasurable pleasure of spending the night with Shahryar. Now she was ready – no, happy – to die.

Shahryar, however, was no longer quite so happy about

killing her, at least not right away. He was curious to know how the story ended. He would give her one more night, one night and one only; she would finish her story, and then her neck would taste the kiss of his sabre.

One night became two, and two became twenty. Scheherazade's lips were magic even when they were weaving a story. She told of merchants and jinns, of warriors and wonders, and she talked of love, and hatred, of the pleasures of the night and the struggles of the day. She told stories within stories, and each of them was a treasure trove of unexpected new things.

A thousand and one nights went by this way, until Scheherazade announced she had finally run out of stories. I think she was lying. I think she could have continued for a thousand and one nights more, but she did not need to. By then Shahryar had forgotten all about his sulking and was madly in love with her.

As for Scheherazade, all things considered, she did not dislike him. He was handsome, and a better man now than he had been a thousand and one nights before.

Scheherazade was Shahryar's last wife. She took her pleasures abundantly until the end of her days; and he learned from her that you should never sulk when you can join in. Scheherazade's little sister married Shahryar's little brother, and both kingdoms were more prosperous than ever before, saved not by a magician, not by a great warrior, but by the most cunning enchanter of all, a teller of tales.

We are all that enchanter, though not necessarily as cunning as Scheherazade.

I took some liberties in my retelling of her story, in line with the tradition the story comes from. Folk tales were written down only when the first folklorists started collecting them; before that, they had been transmitted orally for centuries. The tales would change each time they were told, shifting with the teller, the listener and the context. They were not fixed texts in the way that the book you are holding in your hand is a fixed text; they were more like sets of footprints, clear in some cases and faint in others, which each teller would track in her own time, in her own style. What mattered was that the footprints led somewhere; that they had an end. But what was that?

To keep death at bay, Scheherazade tells us. Not her own, but the sultan's.

Scheherazade herself was never in danger. Her father was the man who found fresh victims for Shahryar, so she was as safe as anyone could be from the sultan's... sabre. If all she wanted was not to die, there was no need for her to tell stories for a thousand and one nights. She could have stayed at home. She offered herself as the sultan's latest wife to save her country.

Behind Shahryar's actions lay a hopelessness that had to be addressed. He had cut himself off from the possibility of love: he was alive, but dying inside. And his victims were dying *tout court*, so something had to be done. You cannot overpower a murderous sultan; but you can heal him.

Scheherazade entered Shahryar's bedroom as a psychotherapist, in the literal meaning of the word, that is, as someone who heals the soul (in ancient Greece, *Psyche* was the soul, and also the lover of *Eros*, love itself, while *therapeaia* means 'healing'). She went in there *expressly* to tell stories, to use them to make the sultan better, night after night. And they were not just any old stories: for a thousand and one nights, Scheherazade told wonder tales (another name for fairy tales, less common, but better fitting). The root of the sultan's problem was that he had lost his sense of wonder, he was jaded – he thought he had learned all of life's lessons. Scheherazade took him on a journey not dissimilar to ours, to show him that was not the case.

For a thousand and one nights, the sultan ambled in the maze of words that Scheherazade conjured up around him, and he found there enchantment and adventure, sorcery and magic, jinns, ghouls and other marvels. For a thousand and one nights the sultan gorged on wonder, until, finally replete, he was once again ready to live his life.

Scheherazade holds our sixth key. We are all like her, in that we tell stories to keep death at bay; but we are not as skilful at it as she is, and our stories sometimes end up working against us. Then we become like Shahryar, jaded and lost (though hopefully not murderous).

Like Shahryar, we need to escape.

I have had my own Scheherazade moments, in which stories saw me through a dark time. I have had many of them, in fact: stories in any shape or form have been both my daily bread and my refuge when the skies darken. One of the worst storms I endured was my father's illness, which began during my teenage years. I came out at the other end, I don't think unscathed, but alive, only because I was lucky enough to be surrounded by good friends. Among the many people who helped me, and to whom I will be forever grateful, is Superman, greatest superhero of them all.

In the early Nineties, DC Comics, Superman's publisher, orchestrated a multi-book saga that ended with Superman's death. It is not unusual for superheroes to die only to reappear later, stronger than before, but this time, we were told, Superman's death would be for real and for ever (in fact it wasn't).

The saga was launched with great fanfare. While that fanfare reached as far as Italy, the stories themselves did not, because at that time Superman was not yet available in Italian editions. I knew the character, of course: I had seen the films with Christopher Reeve many, many times, and anyway, *everybody* knows about Superman.

Much as I would have liked to learn how and why Superman shuffled off this mortal coil, I had to accept the fact that I never would. There was nowhere in Puglia for me to buy American books, and even if there was, I could not afford them. A more fundamental problem was that I couldn't read English.

One year later (I was twelve), on a Sunday morning, I went with my father into a newsagent's, and there, against all expectations, was one lonely copy of a fine Italian translation of *The Death of Superman*, a one-volume collection of the entire saga, just published. That it had found its way to Manduria was nothing short of a miracle.

It was far too expensive for a twelve-year-old, but my father bought it for me. You see, he liked comics too.

It was raining that afternoon, which is not very common in the heel of Italy, so I had another small miracle to savour – dark and sombre weather, perfect conditions to mourn the demise of Superman. I sat in my room, closed the door, and read the story in one go.

When I got to the end, I was in tears.

Superman had died in the arms of Lois Lane. He had died defending Metropolis, but that would not make Lois Lane miss him any less. He had died fighting against a big ugly monster with bones protruding out of its skin: the story never explained who this monster was, where it came from, or why it was set on destroying everything in its path. People called it Doomsday, but the monster itself didn't even talk. Doomsday was meaningless tragedy made flesh, the superhero version of a random car crash. Superman managed to stop it, but died in the process.

I was sorry for Lois Lane, who would never get to marry the man she loved, and I was sorry for Jimmy Olsen, who had lost his best friend in the world, and I was sorry for Superman, who, with all his powers, would not live to see another day. But I was especially heartbroken at the pointlessness of it all. Yes, Superman's death had been suitably heroic, but also meaningless, because Doomsday didn't want to conquer or destroy the world or anything like that, it wanted to kill people for the hell of it. Its violence did not seem to have any goal other than violence itself. In some respects Doomsday got what it wanted: his aim was to kill people, and he ended up killing *Superman*, the most prestigious trophy of all. As for Superman – the embodiment of the all-American ideal that there is always a reason to be cheerful, always another day to be lived and enjoyed – he was more than just killed, he was defeated.

Even so, my tears seemed disproportionate. All that I knew about Superman came from four films, and two of them were, by my own admission, pretty bad. I had only just *met* Superman, so why did his death move me so much? With the benefit of hindsight, I understand that I was not crying for Lois Lane, or Jimmy Olsen, or Superman, but for myself.

My father was not well.

The older members of my family had not noticed it yet, but I had, quite consciously. I was a child, and although children can sometimes be unobservant, they have uncannily sensitive antennae, and pick up waves that grown-ups don't. My father began to forget things, he had significant mood swings that were not in character with the man I knew. Something was not right. Doomsday was coming.

The publisher who translated *The Death of Superman* started publishing Superman stories in Italian in a regular series, twice a month. I badly, badly, wanted to know what happened next, now that Superman was gone. I wanted to know how he would return, because even at twelve I wasn't so naive as to think that he wouldn't. I *needed* to see him return.

My pocket money was not enough to buy a *Superman* comic twice a month. And so my father and I began the strangest of dances. Sometimes we would pop into the newsagent together (it had to be that specific shop, or another in the next town, because they were the only two that could be relied on to stock *Superman* comics), and he would buy it for me. Or, before sitting down on the sofa, he would put coins in his pockets, and when he got up again, the coins would fall out. They were my loot, as if I were a pint-sized Viking and the sofa an unfortunate coastal village. By hook or by crook, my father managed to buy me *Superman* twice a month, always giving me the impression that *I* was getting it by my own cunning.

Meanwhile, his health went steadily downhill. It came to a point when even my mother and my older brothers had to acknowledge there was something wrong, and they took him for tests, and he found out that he was going to die. Early-onset dementia: Doomsday was here.

When my father was too ill to continue his dance with me, my mother discreetly allowed me a little more pocket money, enough for me to keep buying *Superman*. There were superheroes whose stories I probably liked more – among them the Silver Surfer and Doctor Strange – but Superman had *something* the others did not have, a quality I could not put my finger on, and which made me feel closer to him.

Now I know what that something was. Superman is the parent that lucky children have, before that parent, inevitably, lets them down. Superman is the kind, unbeatable, invulnerable, *good* parent we have before we discover our parents are mortal, and make mistakes – and yes, that they can be beaten and beaten badly. In some way, my father had seen his defeat coming, and one of the last things he did for me was to hand the baton to Superman: *here*, he said, *take care of my son*.

And Superman took good care of me. Unlike my father, he survived Doomsday and came back, as strong and as confident as ever. As my father lost the ability to recognize me and cried all night in the other room (and once almost set our house on fire), and as my family suffered financial hardship and my padded middle-class world turned to kryptonite all around me, Superman would sweep me to Metropolis, where Doomsday can be defeated, where you can die for a while, and return, if not unscathed, at least alive.

A little after I turned eighteen, I had Superman's shield tattooed on my arm. Two years later, my father died.

Scheherazade healed Shahryar by helping him to escape. The sultan had built for himself a cage of grim certainties. He was surrounded by new, unexpected things, as we are, but he had closed his eyes to them, as we do. Adding *more* new things to his life was not the solution. He had decided there was nothing to see, so he saw nothing, and he would keep seeing nothing. When he stumbled upon a beautiful orgy in a scented garden, he could not find a way of embracing this event – unexpected, admittedly, but also potentially revealing of pleasures yet to come – in his own life. Instead he sulked, because it was not what he expected. The sultan had to be lured out of his world, into other possible lives.

The idea of escaping in a story, glorified in *The Arabian Nights*, makes modern Western culture deeply suspicious. Certain commentators routinely hurl accusations of 'escapism' at blockbuster movies, TV dramas and fantasy novels. The intellectual and writer Germaine Greer once declared: 'Ever since I arrived at Cambridge as a student in 1964 and encountered a tribe of fully grown women wearing puffed sleeves, clutching teddies and babbling excitedly about the doings of hobbits, it has been my nightmare that Tolkien would turn out to be the most influential writer of the 20th century.' Such pedestrian gatekeepers consider escapism bad, the idea being that a yearning for other worlds is a sign of intellectual weakness. Perhaps.

The fact remains that Superman saved me.

In one of the most passionate essays on fairy stories ever written, J. R. R. Tolkien (who might well be the most influential writer of the twentieth century) defined escapism as 'very practical' and went on to say that it 'might even be heroic'. He made the good point that, when a person is stuck in jail, you cannot blame them for trying to go home. Those who rant against escapism 'are confusing, not always by sincere error, the Escape of the Prisoner with the Flight of the Deserter'.

When Superman came for me, I was stuck in a small town without bookshops, with a dying father and a family in a profound crisis. Reality was overwhelming: of course I wanted out. The idea that in life you should just grit your teeth and soldier on, no matter what, is macho lunacy. None of us is strong enough to withstand reality when it has it in for you, and in those years, it was coming at me full on.

Superman believed I could make it, but he knew I could not make it on my own. He would help in any way he could. He would take me to Kandor, a city in a bottle; to his Fortress of Solitude, the ultimate kid's bedroom, self-contained in some far-flung icy place; he would take me to impossibly remote planets and beyond. I came back from these places stronger and better, for the simple reason that I had seen that other lives were possible. Even though I could not completely escape reality at that moment, reality could change.

In Tolkien's words, 'the world outside has not become less

real because the prisoner cannot see it'. Superman kept open for me a window on the world outside, and he gave me hope that I could reach it one day, in the same way Scheherazade kept open for the sultan a window on life's gourmandizing variety. As another great writer, Ursula K. Le Guin, put it, 'the direction of escape is toward freedom'.

Our wonder fades after we have been stuck in jail for too long. Fairies have shown us that we are trapped in a web made of all the things we are absolutely certain of. To obey the orders we receive, we must be absolutely certain that it makes sense to work nine to five in somebody else's office, that cash measures accomplishment, that there is a hierarchy of taste, and ultimately, that the universe is a watch. Disenchantment is the name of the cage we live in. To escape its confines, we need to learn to think like storytellers.

When Tolkien says that the confusion between the flight of the deserter and the escape of the prisoner is not always a sincere error, he means, I think, that there is a precise plan, a conspiracy if you like, to keep us all in jail. *They* actively want us *not* to escape to other worlds, so that we won't get ideas in our heads about changing this one. *They* want us to be sitting ducks, because we are difficult to control when we fly. And the worst thing is, *they* are *us*.

The conspiracy is not another sneaky scheme of Lex Luthor's. We are all in it: we are conspiring against ourselves, like Shahryar. Someone who realizes that we can stop at any time and change course, someone who knows enough stories not to be certain of anything any more – someone like Scheherazade – would never forget that we have made our social realities, and that we can unmake them. Someone like that would not fear the power of any sultan; she would be dangerous enough herself.

Superman taught me, a scrawny boy who had been served a crappy hand, that I didn't have to be a victim; that I could pull through, and be dangerous.

✳

After each flight with Superman, I landed back in my room. I closed the comic and put it away, lovingly, on the shelf next to the others, in a place where dust would not settle on them, and then continued with my day: I checked on my father, I finished my homework. I counted the weeks, months and years that separated me from university, my final escape.

I knew that I could not move to Metropolis, nor did I want to. I had friends and family I loved on this side of the page; I had projects for the future (I was thinking maybe I could become a writer); I helped as much as I could with the situation at home. I could not deny the hard facts of life, but my journeys with Superman reminded me not to take them for granted. Those flights were supply runs: I was foraging for resources to bring back to my mundane life.

I would never physically walk the streets of Kandor, and I

did not consciously model myself on Clark Kent, Lois Lane or Jimmy Olsen. But all of those things – the splendour of Kandor and the honesty of Clark, the courage of Lois and the sympathy of Jimmy – made my world vaster, and filled my head with new, unexpected things, keeping the flame of wonder alive. They made the hard facts of life a little softer.

Stories do that, regardless of whether they contain superheroes. Elizabeth Bennet is every bit as made up as Superman – and every bit as real. There are, admittedly, some differences between the two characters, but literal truth is not one of them. What they have in common is far more important to us: all good tales are paths to wonder. They give us new ways of looking of things, such as memory and perception in Marcel Proust's *À la recherche du temps perdu*; or the Italian-American experience in John Fante's *Bandini Quartet*; or the pains and joys of growing up in the Harry Potter novels. They make us think thoughts we never dared think before. They confront us with vastness. They are wonder tales, all of them; it just happens that some of them contain house-elves and dementors.

Our lives can be wonder tales also, provided we learn how to narrate them as such. Scheherazade shows us the way. There are five things she knew, five things she would be happy for us to know. By learning them, we shall break out of our cage.

✳

The first thing Scheherazade knew is that *stories make us*.

If I asked you to describe the first time that you screwed up with a lover, you would tell me a story. It would be a heavily edited version of what really happened: you would remember some of the things you said and some of the things she said, but not all of them, and not necessarily the most important ones. When you meet her twenty years later, and you are both very civilized about it, you go back to what happened, and you have very different recollections of it – so much so that it seems the pair of you were in two different stories. She is sure that her version is right, but you are just as certain that yours is. You do not want to change your story, because in the last twenty years you have made a lot of choices based on what you thought had happened, and it would be painful, impossibly so, to reconsider them. And she is in exactly the same position.

The thing we call 'identity' is a storybook, a selection of tales we tell ourselves, which have very practical consequences. The sultan's storybook was hopeless (and rather small), and he ended up chopping off heads. The larger our storybook, and the more varied its content, the more open to wonder we become.

The space between reality and fiction is a shoreline, which changes with every breaking wave. Reality and fiction are not the same (I would kill Superman a thousand and one times over if it would give me back my father), but we spend our lives on that shoreline. My memories of my father's sunset years are made bearable by the red, yellow and blue of Superman, and when I think of Superman, there is, I am sure, a touch of my father in the way I imagine him. The world and the story overlap.

The contemporary sociologist Arthur W. Frank says that 'life and story imitate each other, ceaselessly and seamlessly, but neither enjoys either temporal or causal precedence'. So-called 'real' life and stories are echoes of one another: we tell stories about the things that happen to us, and the things that happen to us are in turn shaped by the stories we tell. Real life does not happen *before* stories, it happens *together with* them. I was flying with Superman while tending to my father.

I say that I love mushrooms, but I remember (or do I?) that I only started eating them after reading *The Lord of the Rings*: hobbits adore mushrooms, and hobbits know one or two things about the finest pleasures of life. Beans are another of my favourite foods, and my liking for them also derives from stories: Bud Spencer and Terence Hill, who appeared in a series of Italian comedy-adventure films, wolfed down platefuls of beans on screen (indeed, one of Bud Spencer's films had the title *Anche gli angeli mangiano fagioli*, 'Even Angels Eat Beans'). And these are only two instances of which I am aware – there must be many, many more cases of events that happened only in stories and yet exerted an influence on my life. I would not be at all surprised to discover that the almost-monk I saw was born of some story I once read – which wouldn't mean, of course, that I didn't really see it.

In Philipp Meyer's masterful novel *The Son* there is a character, an old frontiersman, who 'always complained about the moment his cowboys began to read novels about other cowboys; they had lost track of what was more true, the books or their own lives'.

As we navigate our lives, we are continuously telling stories about ourselves and about others, which means, as Scheherazade knew, that by changing the stories we tell, we can change the way we live. Stories shape reality. Give them enough Western books, and real cowboys will start playing book-cowboys.

So what books do you give to cowboys when you want to turn them into bank clerks? What books did they give you at school, to turn you into a respectable adult? If you have never deviated from the path that was laid out for you, now is the time to do so, by searching for different stories.

There is a form of modern psychotherapy, called Narrative Therapy, which, like Scheherazade, helps people to cope with the troubles of life by giving them new stories to tell. The therapist, having established with the patient the values and characteristics that they believe make up their identity, works with that person to create new narratives about themselves that explore how they came to develop those qualities. It has been used successfully, for example, with older patients who are adjusting to a new stage of life.

Superman can haul himself up from the page and fly to our help because the veil between our world and his own is as thin as the cheap paper of a comic book. Stories bleed into reality, reality bleeds into stories. Sometimes, spectacularly so.

✳

The second thing Scheherazade knew is that poetic faith is a formidable tool of enchantment.

Grant Morrison, one of the best writers to have worked on *Superman*, once met the great hero in the flesh. Morrison was with his editor in San Diego, where a famous comic book convention is held every year. The two of them had spent a good part of the night in a hotel room, scratching their heads about a problematic storyline. At around 1 a.m., exhausted, they went for a walk. In a deserted street by the harbour, they saw two people. One was a comic book fan; the other was Superman.

Here is how Morrison describes him: 'He was dressed in a perfectly tailored red, blue, and yellow costume; his hair was slicked back with a kiss curl; and unlike the often weedy or paunchy Supermen who paraded through the convention halls, he was trim, buff, and handsome.'

Morrison and his editor asked him if they could interview him; Superman, ever the do-gooder, agreed. He sat in the relaxed position you would expect from an invulnerable being, and for the next hour-and-a-half he talked about himself, his relationship with Lois Lane, his friendship with Batman. He laid bare his life for Morrison and his editor. After getting back to the hotel, they spent the rest of the night writing.

Morrison admits that meeting a guy dressed up as Superman while there is a comic book convention in town is anything but unusual. But he also makes the point that it is less common to meet one so uncannily similar to the original, and by night. Morrison says that he had two options: he could decide that the guy was either just another costumed fan, or that he was indeed Superman, and ask him for help. He went for Superman.

This is the only part of the story that I don't buy. I don't think Morrison ever had a choice. Someone else, maybe; but not him, not a gifted writer who had long been acquainted with Superman. To him, the encounter had to be a hard-ish fact of life.

Morrison's experience had little to do with what we sometimes refer to as 'willing suspension of disbelief', defined as the idea that, in order to enjoy stories, we must make an effort to believe things that we know are not true. By this definition of suspension of disbelief, Superman won't be able to help us if we do not make an effort to believe that people can fly, broad chests can stop bullets, and dead people can be resurrected. This is a disenchanted definition, one that cultivates the illusion that we are in control. We are not.

The poet Samuel Taylor Coleridge, who coined the expression 'suspension of disbelief' in 1817, intended a rather different meaning. While writing about fantasy elements in poetry (he used the words 'supernatural' and 'romantic' to describe them), he said he wished to 'transfer from our inward nature a human interest and a semblance of truth sufficient to procure for these shadows of imagination that willing suspension of disbelief for the moment, which constitutes poetic faith'. In other words, Coleridge did not think it was the reader's job to suspend their disbelief – he was not begging people to listen to him. He was saying it was the *poet's* job to put readers in a state of mind where they are happy to surrender control. When poetry works, it sweeps readers away with no effort on their part.

The tag line for the first Superman film was 'You'll believe a man can fly'; it wasn't 'Please, believe a man can fly'. As long as you do not pull against the story, the story will work on you and for you (and even when you *do* pull against it, the right story at the right time might still work: you start watching a rom-com sneering at the clichéd nature of the plot, then you surprise yourself by laughing at a joke halfway through, and by the time the unlikely lovers are kissing at the end of the movie, you are, to your embarrassment, in tears).

Coleridge was convinced that a successful poem will instil a 'poetic faith' in the reader. You *know* that the poem is true, even when it is not literally so.

Poetic faith, as Scheherazade knew, makes all the difference. Poetic faith is what Superman instils in the likes of Grant Morrison and me, and poetic faith is what Scheherazade was cultivating in the Sultan Shahryar. The sultan was not at all willing to live and let live – quite the contrary. He was not particularly interested in stories either: after-sex murder was more his thing. And yet, he listened.

Poetic faith melts away in the heat of a direct gaze, but it can change your life when you let it work in its own time and in its own way. I am confident Grant Morrison did not try to shoot Superman when they met, to check whether the guy was indeed bulletproof. Then again, it was not a bulletproof body-guard Morrison needed, it was a helping hand with inspiration, and that was exactly what he got. A real hero helps in which-ever way help is needed.

Poetic faith allows us to travel between fiction and reality, bringing back here what we found there. It is a magic of extraordinary potency, which Scheherazade trusted with her life. We must be careful, though, because the stories we trust will become the reality we live.

※

The third thing Scheherazade knew is that reality is only won-drous when it is declined in the plural.

There was a time when we believed in Father Christmas, which means that we believed in the stories we were told about him. Then there was a time when we stopped believing, and our sense of wonder started to fade. There was a third time, though, which does not get enough attention, when we didn't quite know what to make of the whole business. This was when we slowly came to understand that the cheery man with the sack and white beard was not real in the way we had thought, and yet we could not quite bring ourselves to believe that we had been lied to so blatantly. It was a time in-between, a time of doubt and questioning, occupying a liminal position between two different types of certainty. Tales of wonder reconnect us to the vital energy of that time.

Belief in Father Christmas is not an either/or switch. Even after I had admitted the sad truth to myself, I pretended to go on believing in him for a year or two, before telling my family I had worked out what was going on. I had felt conflicted. Given the effort they went to in order to create the illusion of Father Christmas's visit, I didn't know how to tell them they might as well stop; and also, I wanted to keep the magic alive for myself. As long as I didn't say out loud that I knew that the magic gift-giver was in fact a credit card, the presents I received would still be sprinkled with fairy dust.

There was another reason, as well, not to come out as a Santa denier: although I knew that Father Christmas was not real in the same way I was real, declaring that he did not exist at all seemed disingenuous. The joy he had brought me had been real enough. To disown him would be a betrayal.

The time we stop believing in Father Christmas as a jovial fat man living at the North Pole is when we start to grow up; the time we proudly announce it to the world is when we start to get old. The preciously brief time in-between, when we dwell in ambiguity and we can't make up our minds as to what to think, is the one we need to reconnect to.

As grown-ups, we know that the moon is a grey rock in space. It lacks plants, animals, books and basic comforts such as oxygen. It is not that interesting unless you are a geologist. Once upon a time we could imagine that it might be made of cheese, or that it was a treasure trove of all the things that had been lost on Earth; but now we have sent spaceships to explore it, we know that the moon is just a large lump of rock.

But the moon is also a goddess. She is Hecate, with a torch in each hand and three heads, mysterious and fearsome; she is Diana, the virgin who hunts in the woods with her pack of dogs, and who has a temple, still standing, on the shore of Lake Nemi, not far from Rome. In ancient times, the lake was known as *speculum Dianae*, Diana's Mirror, because she is reflected in its waters in the form of the moon. Those waters are still there and the moon still reflects in them, and on special nights, someone still knows the lake as *speculum Dianae*.

The moon is a rock and the moon is a goddess: these are truths of different kinds, but equal value. The mainstream position of our culture is, more or less, that seeing the moon as a rock is a truthful perception because it is useful, while seeing the moon as Diana is not a truthful perception because you cannot do anything with it.

But Diana is useless only in the sense that we can't land on her or mine her for minerals, only in the sense that a goddess is not a resource. She is a friend, and as a friend she can shine on us after a difficult day at work, she can make us fall in love, she can inspire bad and sometimes even good art. She can soothe our darkest moods.

The healthy thing to do is hold to both truths at once. If we see only the rock, we might quickly grow disenchanted; if we see only the goddess, we might come to deny the weight of the rock. Every story we tell grows stale after a while, if it is the *only* story we tell, and hardens into another certainty. We need many different stories, every one of them true, but none of them offering a sole truth.

Here lies the genius of Scheherazade: she saved the sultan by telling him not one story, but hundreds. Each new tale was a new possibility, the seed of a new doubt; each offered a new point of view.

When we are completely sure that something is true, it is because of the pull of that particular story. You might have a poetic faith in the idea that you have a talent for tennis, or that the moon is just a rock. The story of your talent and the story of the rock appeal to you, and they might have some basis in reality, but make no mistake, they are still just stories. Believe in them too much, without awareness of their poetic layers, and you might end up shooting at a guy dressed up as Superman just to demonstrate that he is not bulletproof.

We are not poetic monotheists, but poetic heathens; not monogamists, but polyamorous. Which leads us back to Scheherazade, her many stories, and her many joys.

The fourth thing Scheherazade knew is that the root of story is pleasure.

Ray Bradbury, in a splendidly titled essay 'Run Fast, Stand Still, Or, The Thing at the Top of the Stairs, Or, New Ghosts from Old Minds', says that the question writers are asked most often – 'where do you get your ideas? – makes him laugh. 'We're so busy looking out,' he says, 'to find ways and means, we forget to look *in*': in other words, we are full of stories that we *don't* see, seeds of wonders we misplace and lose for ever.

In his early twenties, Bradbury started keeping a list of nouns. Just that, nouns: stuff like, 'the lake. the night. crickets'. These were simply words that came into his mind and which he wrote down, without thinking twice. In time, a pattern emerged: these words made him remember childhood enthusiasms, forgotten feelings. In these humble nouns he found some of his best ideas, which he would make into short stories and novels. Those nouns are floating in your mind too, unrecognized.

Bradbury could do something with them for the simple fact that he enjoyed doing it. In another essay, he says that 'zest' and 'gusto' are a writer's best friends. Stephen King is on similar terrain when he says that writing is 'about enriching the lives of those who will read your work, and enriching your own life as well. It's about getting up, getting well, and getting over. Getting happy, okay? Getting happy.'

In my own way, I have been writing professionally both fiction and non-fiction for fourteen years now, and I agree with Stephen King with all my heart. Writers try to write their way to better mental and spiritual health – even when we impressively fail. Even those of us who are keen on making money rarely have money as our prime motivator. We want to heal our hurts, feel things more intensely, and we want to do that together with readers – which means, other human beings. We write characters with zest and gusto because we want to have more of both, a lot more, we want all the zest and gusto we can find. The quest for pleasure is the ultimate form of wisdom.

✳

The fifth thing Scheherazade knew is that wonder comes at the price of certainty. In a thousand and one nights, she convinced the sultan that this was a price well worth paying.

The great Ursula K. Le Guin said that fantasy literature is all about 'the freedom of uncertainty'. I would broaden the category to include all acts of storytelling.

While learning to be adults, we are told that we should reduce uncertainty as much as possible, that we should decide once and for all what we believe, what we like, what we want to do with our lives. We are told that it is wrong not to have clear-cut opinions: what will we tweet about if we don't?

So to make the process of opinion-making smoother, we are

offered wholesale identities. We are taught to think of ourselves as 'man' or 'woman', as 'British' or 'Italian', as 'sultan' – or as 'serf'. Assuming a couple of those identities will indeed reduce our uncertainty, because each identity comes with a set of ready-made opinions. The price we pay for the privilege is our sense of wonder.

Only what is uncertain, unclear, misty, can be awesome. Scheherazade's stories taught Shahryar how to rejoice in ambiguity. The price of certainty is a loss of wonder and the price of wonder is a loss of certainty: stage magicians, witches, scientists, explorers and fairy-seers all agree that there is no way out of that.

A storyteller's world is ever ambiguous, echoing with stories that connect to other stories, a maze of crossed destinies that change with every step, every choice. By the end of any given day a storyteller has died five times, tamed a lion, welcomed aliens, slept with three good-looking strangers. Or not. While every sensible adult tries to reduce uncertainty, telling themselves that fairies do not (or do) exist loud enough to start believing it, storytellers work hard to maximize uncertainty, to embrace as many possibilities as they can. Everything is strange to a storyteller, and their job is to make your life stranger.

I read *Madame Bovary* when I was sixteen. When I got to the point at which Emma gives birth to a daughter and is not happy with her, I was flabbergasted. It dawned on me for the first time that mothers *have thoughts about their children* that are both positive and negative – that mothers are not born mothers. They are people who have children, but they are *people* first. There is more to them than their role.

It meant that my own mother was like that too. This realization was frightening: I felt as though I didn't know her any more. And of course that was correct, my knowledge of her was incomplete. Madame Bovary had revealed to me a general face of motherhood of which I had hitherto been unaware, and with that came the particular, shocking truth that my mum was a human being.

This is what we have been doing on our journey so far: we have been coming at our lives from different perspectives, thus making them stranger. We have been looking not for reassurance, but for its opposite. And we have been doing that in a storyteller's way. As Scheherazade did with Shahryar, I have told you stories and made you a part of mine, thus becoming, inevitably, a part of yours.

Before we embark on the last stage of our journey, let's recap how this has happened.

By talking to magicians, we found out about mystery, things that cannot be explained because they do not exist to be explained. If there were no mysteries in life, if everything was merely a problem to be solved, there would be no stories: we could explain everything rationally, by number and square and compass. Stories probe the borders of mystery. They hint, but they never explain. When the existence of mystery upsets us, and we deny it exists at all, we sever our primal connection to wonder.

After that, we danced with witches. They reminded us of the numinous, the feeling of something that attracts us and makes us afraid in equal measure. They also reminded us of the importance of ritual, and every well-formed story is a ritual, an attempt to hint at a deeper reality which can never be communicated directly.

Then, when we looked at science, we saw how far the asking of good questions can take us. They push us to a point at which we unlearn everything we thought we knew. In their simplest form, stories are answers to questions. What will Hamlet decide to do? What would happen if you transplanted a dog's heart into a human being? When a story does not make us wonder, it hasn't taken its questioning far enough; and when life does not make us wonder, we have stopped questioning far too soon.

Our fourth key took us into the natural world of forest and stream, to look at how our stories interact with the physical landscape we are part of.

To get our fifth key we leaped into Faerie, to begin to see the strange way in which stories influence our perceptions. Every new story is the promise of a new world.

And finally, we have seen that stories and reality collide, that we can never completely disentangle one from the other. Stories can heal us because stories can break us. We have learned Scheherazade's secret, to become better tellers of the tale of our life.

We are almost ready to wrap up our journey, but not quite.

Ray Bradbury said that 'the logic of events always gives way to the logic of the senses'. We are creatures of flesh and bone. It is all too easy to forget that wonder, like all emotions (and all life) happens in the body. We are not a ghost in the machine: we are spirits of matter. Without the other five senses, our sense of wonder would not exist.

Before returning home, we will give those senses their due.

THE WORKOUT

1. Scheherazade's First Lesson: Stories Make Us

Write down in your Book of Wonder three stories that are important to you. They might be books, films, or anecdotes passed down in your family (the time grandma disgraced herself after three glasses of sparkling wine at your cousin's wedding; how your parents met), or memorable things that happened to you. You might be inclined to write down only a short sentence or title, such as 'Charlotte's Web' or 'that epic night in Barcelona'; or you might want to narrate the stories in a longer format.

Then look at the three stories and ask yourself: how have those stories impacted on my life – in good ways and bad? Examine both sides: even your favourite story will have its negative effects.

For each story, write down at least four ways in which it has influenced your life – two positive ways, and two negative.

2. Scheherazade's Second Lesson: Poetic Faith Is a Formidable Tool of Enchantment

Find a character you love and trust – it could be Mary Poppins, Jack Skellington, Aragorn or Elizabeth Bennet. For the next month, imagine that this character is entirely real, and let him or her help you. When you are feeling unsure about something, ask yourself what the character might suggest you do. Try to catch a glimpse of the character in the street, in bars, at work, out of the corner of your eye.

Make a note in your Book of Wonder of all the ways that character has helped you out in the past, and of the ways the character is helping you out in the present.

If you happen to meet the character, and maybe even have a conversation, describe the encounter in your Book of Wonder.

3. Scheherazade's Third Lesson: Reality Is Only Wondrous When It Is Declined in the Plural

For a week, or longer, meditate on the moon. Go into your garden, or to a place where you can look at her, and gaze at her for at least five minutes every time, setting a timer in advance. If the moon is not visible every night for a week, keep trying until you have done the meditation at least seven times.

During the meditation, think of the moon as a goddess (you might want to call her Diana). Look at the face of the moon as you would the face of a friend. Acknowledge her presence with a nod. If you hear her voice in your head, in the form of thoughts and ideas, be sure to answer. Make a note in your Book of Wonder.

4. Scheherazade's Fourth Lesson: The Root of Story Is Pleasure

Forget all of your existing ideas about what books, films and stories are 'good' and which are not so. Forget all your preconceived notions of what constitutes good taste. If pleasure was your only guide, what would you read, what would you watch? Note down your choices in your Book of Wonder. Be entirely honest!

Then examine your choices. How different are those books and films from the ones you usually read and watch? And what do these stories all have in common? Do they suggest that something is lacking in your life?

5. Scheherazade's Fifth Lesson: Wonder Comes at the Price of Certainty

Write down three statements about aspects of your personality that matter a great deal to you. For example: 'I am loyal'.

Then find episodes from your life that run counter to that.

Senses of Wonder

We catch glimpses of our soul in
the thick foliage of our senses.

P hilip 'the Good', Duke of Burgundy, was not one for half measures. He had eighteen illegitimate children that we know of, established one of the most splendid courts of the late Middle Ages, and, when he married Isabella of Portugal, he marked the occasion by creating nothing less than a whole new chivalric order (the Order of the Golden Fleece, named after the ram's pelt sought by the Greek hero Jason and his Argonauts). He saw it as his sacred duty to launch a crusade to take back Constantinople from the Ottomans, who had conquered the city in 1453. To rally the support he needed, he held a magnificent feast. On 17 February 1454, he threw the party to end all parties.

Each course consisted of no fewer than forty-eight dishes, lowered from the ceiling on three tables of increasing size. The tables were laden with more than the choicest of foodstuffs. On the shortest one was a forest through which animals and human characters seemed to move of their own accord. On the next table, where the duke himself sat, was a church with four singers and an organ and a fountain in the shape of a child peeing rose-water. On the last table, the longest one, were crammed twenty-eight musicians, a castle encircled by a moat of orange water and containing the figure of Melusine (a water spirit who could take the shape of a serpent) in a tower, a wind-mill, and a desert in which, among other things, a remarkably realistic tiger did battle with a snake.

Once the guests had sat down (after entering through five different doors, each guarded by an archer), the church bell rang, and the singers started singing. Then a horse made an entrance, walking backwards. He was caparisoned in red, and on his back were two trumpet players. After the horse came a wild boar, clad in green. Riding the boar was a man, dressed half as a human and half as a griffin. A second man was doing a handstand on the shoulders of the first.

This was just the warm-up act. Now that the audience's attention had been captured, a play was performed based on Jason's quest for the Golden Fleece. It featured yet more music from the trumpeters, a young child riding on a beautiful hind, a fire-breathing dragon that could actually fly, the slaying of a monstrous serpent, and a battle between soldiers who sprang from the serpent's teeth.

After these diversions, the main business of the evening could finally begin. A huge, armed brute entered the room, dragging behind him a captive elephant on whose back stood a castle. Inside the castle stood a lady dressed in white and wrapped in a black cloak. She represented the Church; the brute was a stand-in for the Saracens. When the lady asked for protection from the brute, a small army of heralds burst in, bearing a gold-collared pheasant, which they presented to the duke. They asked him to swear on it to save and protect the Church.

Philip the Good, being good, didn't have a heartbeat's hesitation. He wrote down his solemn oath on parchment. He swore that he would fight the sultan mano-a-mano, if push came to shove. Who was with him?

It was an unqualified triumph. So many people started writing down their oaths that Philip had to ask his guests to postpone the deluge of piousness until the next day, so that the party could go on. As a thank-you token, God sent the twelve Virtues, in the form of twelve young women, to join in the revelry. And people danced, and drank, and ate, and made merry until late into the night.

The crusade never happened; the feast, however, went down in history.

※

This is the story that has been passed down by the chroniclers. But there is another story here, one that we can work out for ourselves – a story of sensuousness. This story starts with candles: the late medieval aristocracy would have used candles made of beeswax, which gives off a scent that is subtle but distinctive. Thus, even the light in that dining hall was scented, a gentle base note for the much stronger aromas vying for attention. In those days people did not wash as often as we do today, and they made liberal use of perfumes and powders. The intensity of all those scents combined would have been more than enough to put us off our food – even before the horse and the boar and the elephant brought their feral bouquet into the closed and crowded room.

None of this, however, spoiled the appetite of Philip's guests, who were happy to gorge on the sequence of heavily spiced courses. Heavily coloured too: medieval cooks used every trick imaginable to make their dishes bright and appealing to the eye. The richness of the colours on display – from fabrics, food and the pageant of entertainments – must have been astounding.

And the tactile appeal, too. Think of the warmth the guests must have felt on their skin, the warmth of candles, fire and people, so different from the clinical dry warmth given off by modern-day radiators. Think of the clothes they wore, heavier than ours, and made of natural fibres. Think of the wood on which they sat, sculpted by hand, irregular. Everything was handmade, no two things (no two chairs, no two benches, no two tables) were the same; everything they touched was new, with its own shape and quirks. The tactile experience enjoyed day in day out by these fifteenth-century nobles offered a level of variety that we would struggle to imagine.

I wonder how it felt to sit down, in rich clothes, on a chair whose shape you could not anticipate exactly, surrounded by other people wearing similarly rich apparel, eating foodstuffs of vivid hue, and watching, by the flicker of candlelight, a tiger that seemed to be real but was not so, and a boar that was definitely real and came wrapped in green silk. This visual splendour was augmented by music and song, by the speaking of lines of the play, and the voices of Burgundian noblemen steadily working their way towards intoxication.

The world has changed: as we have found at different stages of our journey, while some things have been gained, others have been lost. Our senses have been diminished to a saddening extent.

A soirée like the Feast of the Pheasant would be impossible to put together today. Insanely wealthy people are still throwing insanely hedonistic parties, but there is no escaping the fact that we have dulled our senses with neglect. At all levels of wealth, in all social classes, a certain *intensity* of experience has just disappeared. It would take a long and expensive sommelier training to gain just a fraction of the sensual awareness my peasant grandfather had for wine and the food that accompanied it.

We are afraid of touching and being touched, we are suspicious of unfamiliar smells, easily repelled by flavours that are too heady, too robust, too bitter, too spicy: in order to sanitize our world, we have reined in our senses. They have become dull and predictable – and so have our lives. To seize our seventh and last key, we are going to rewild them.

When you say that you had a great time yesterday night at your friend's dinner party, what you mean (alongside the fact that the company was congenial) is that the wine had an inviting bouquet, the beef fillet was so tender you barely had to chew it and the crispness of the accompanying garlicky green beans provided a delightful counterpoint. The music was the smoky jazz that never fails to lull you into a deep feeling of wholeness, especially when you have imbibed the better part of a bottle of Primitivo di Manduria. By definition, there is nothing you feel that you don't feel through your senses. And the same goes for wonder.

The limits of our senses are the limits of what we will ever be able to feel, learn, know and do. A person without a nose cannot smell violets, a person with no sense of touch can neither give nor receive massage. Without a tongue, the enjoyment of that Primitivo di Manduria would be beyond us, while without eyes, we could not appreciate the beauty of the Cumbrian fells. For this reason, scientists have been keen to develop tools (the microscope and the telescope, for example) that enhance our senses – to allow us to feel, learn, know and do *more*. Unfortunately, society as a whole has taken the opposite path, and has done its best to smother our senses and put them to sleep.

For most of our history as *Homo sapiens*, being attuned to our senses has been a matter of life and death: if you could not smell or otherwise *feel* the presence of the predator hiding in the bush, it would almost certainly kill you.

Little by little, we have run out of things that could kill us. We have either wiped them out or caged them in but, either way, they are no trouble to us any more. We still need sensory awareness, but not a lot of it. And we have tamed not only other beasts, but also ourselves. We are much cleaner than we have ever been, with hot and cold running water available at the turn of a tap, and cheap, safe, tried and tested products to enhance our personal hygiene, and make us smell less like the apes we are. We know the exact date by which our (pre-packaged, pre-cleaned) food has to be eaten, and we know exactly how to preserve it. When it goes off, we just chuck it in the bin. The wildest culinary risk most of us have probably taken recently is to take an inadvertent sip of some sour milk that we poured on our breakfast muesli. Our senses have become sluggish. By limiting their reach, we have made our lives much smaller: we have made a whole range of sensuous experiences impossible.

Even worse, we appear not to have realized we have done this. When Max Weber, whom we met when looking for our First Key, noted the 'disenchantment of the world', he considered it a purely intellectual phenomenon. He did not consider at all the importance of sensual, bodily experience, the possibility that we might have lost wonder because we have dulled our *physical capacity* to feel it.

He was in good company in this respect. We have spent the

last few centuries doing our best to deny that we are first and foremost corporeal beings. Descartes famously wrote that soul and body are two separate entities – and it goes without saying that he considered the soul more important than the body. The body's only function was to be a receptacle for the soul, a temple and protection for the precious thing contained inside.

This is the prejudice we still live by in practice, even when we don't subscribe to it in theory. We believe that our body is a machine we control: it is not *us*. Those who believe in an afterlife commonly say that after death souls 'leave' the body – they were in and then they're out. Those who don't believe have translated the word 'soul' into 'mind' – or even 'brain' – but the idea remains the same. The construct of flesh and bone we drag around the world is but a puppet; the important stuff is going on inside its head. This idea is hurting us profoundly.

We used to live in a sprawling mansion of the senses, with scented gardens, dazzling rainbows and divine music, but then we began to confine ourselves to the inside of the house, and allowed the gardens to decay and the musicians to leave; and we kept on retreating as the walls crumbled and the roof caved in, until, finally, we holed ourselves up in one tiny room, all alone, and let the rest go to hell. Sure, we can travel more easily than we did in the past; and National Trust membership will open the gate to many an immaculate garden. But our scared, numbed senses will be as powerless there as they are in our open-plan office; as unable to participate in the variety and splendour of the world. We cannot buy our way back to our senses.

What we need to do is rebuild the house, restore the garden, hire new musicians and get the fountains back in working order so we can see rainbows again. It takes work. Everything that we have learned so far has been leading to this.

※

Paola and I had just moved to London when we heard a baby scream. It was night and we were walking back home from the station. We stopped in our tracks; the baby kept screaming. We thought of calling the police, though the idea of speaking over the phone was daunting, considering how poor our English was at the time. The scream continued, both heart-rending and frightening; the baby's distress suggested something more sinister than a bout of colic. Paola took her phone from her pocket (Paola often wears cargo pants, for she has strong views on the lack of pockets in women's clothes). There were no other sounds, no other voices. Just a baby screaming, and screaming in unearthly fashion.

'If it's a baby,' Paola said, 'it's a weird one.'

We began to think that this banshee wailing might not be a baby. We took our phones and googled for things that scream in the London night. We immediately found the answer. The source of the screaming was indeed not human – it was an urban fox. We don't have foxes in Rome, where Paola and I had lived until a few weeks previously, and there were no foxes in

my home town either. We had never heard their shrill noctur-
nal call before, so we could only interpret the sound as that of
a distraught baby.

I thought of sly red foxes adapting to the nooks and crannies
of a city, and I felt a rush of wonder; my reality shuddered and
grew.

You could say that we misunderstood the sound, only to
correct ourselves before we wasted police time, but it would be
more correct to say that *we actually heard a baby scream*. Our
bodily experience was the experience you have when you hear a
baby scream: we were nervous, on edge and ready to act. When
we learned it was a fox, then we heard it as a fox. We adjusted
our perception, not just in our ears or our brain, but in our
whole body. We were not ready to leap into action any more; we
were amused rather than terrified. We – our bodies – reacted
in an entirely different way.

Senses are not a transparent window on the world. They
are more like impressionable siblings who tell third-hand tales
about friends of friends, and tell them so convincingly that we
buy them, no questions asked.

The neuroscientist Beau Lotto uses the expression 'space of
possibility' to indicate the space created in our brain by all the
possible ways in which we can understand the world. I didn't
know that it was possible to hear foxes in a city – a fox was not
in my space of possibility – so, when I heard a strange call, I
could not think it was emitted by *Vulpes vulpes*. Our reality is

contained within our space of possibility: we cannot conceive anything outside of that space, so what lies outside is, to us, unreal. The space of possibility is the box within which we think. Being in a new city, Paola and I were ready to at least try to think outside the box: we were both willing to let our space of possibility grow. But usually we are only too keen to remain inside it.

Stepping outside of our space of possibility is stressful: when you accept that a fox might lurk in an alley, you start wondering what else might be hiding there, unseen. Our space of possibility is like a muscle: the more we work it, the bigger it becomes. Beau Lotto says that 'if you give your plastic human brain a dull, unchallenging context, it will adapt to the lack of challenge and let its dull side come out'. Inside our box, it is warm and comfortable, but too much warmth and too much comfort will make you ill.

We have given up challenging our senses. We have banished strong smells – the era of Napoleon Bonaparte, who once asked Josephine not to wash for two weeks before meeting him, so he could intoxicate himself on the fullness of her natural bodily scent, is long past. The world we sense, the world of planted trees and straight roads and soothing jingles, is mass-produced, carefully engineered to satisfy the average person. It is a world that trains us to *become* that average person, to have average senses and an average sensibility. This destroys the best bits of us, the bits of us that make us create, explore and live rather than survive. There is nothing average about wonder; the moment we content ourselves with what we know and stop looking for more mystery, wonder is lost. To find it again, we have to make ourselves uncomfortable.

Wonder happens when our space of possibility shudders and grows. Inside that space there is nothing new or surprising; outside it, there is nothing at all. On the border, magic lies. It is fundamentally important, then, that we know that the border *exists*, that our space of possibility, the box within which we think, is only a tiny, haphazardly cut slice of a bigger reality, which is more magnificent than our grandest dreams. And it is important that we know that not only in theory. We must see and hear and lick and touch and smell that border, so as to know it physically, and sense the new, unexpected things that lie just beyond it.

It is not a matter of making our senses 'better', but of paying attention to them; of shutting up for once to let them talk. Our journey so far has had the not-so-hidden goal of making us less self-assured, but in a good way. When we are uncertain what to think, it becomes easier to stop the thinking for a while and let the body do its work. Every step of the journey has led us further down that path. Before going back home we are going to visit our senses, one by one, pay our respects to each in turn, and bond a little with them.

✳

Sight is the sense we rely on the most: we 'look' where we are going, rather than 'smelling' or 'feeling' our way. We need to be reminded that 'there is more than meets the eye' (and to challenge the impulse that makes us instinctively trust good-looking people).

Our society is over-reliant on sight at the expense of the other senses. It is tempting to say that we should care less about sight rather than more: that our sense of sight is, if anything, over-stimulated. But quantity is not quality.

Our daily activities require only a very basic level of visual awareness: we spend most of our time processing information that other humans have tailored for us by plucking out of it any last traces of ambiguity. Let's say you are working with a spreadsheet, and you need to see whether there is a number '3' in the third or fourth column. This is all you need to see, and there is no room for visual interpretation. You do not linger to evaluate the shape of the '3', its hue, the way it looks today compared to yesterday; or how it is set against a nice white background, in the context of all the shapes surrounding it, those lovely 5s and bullying 7s. Nothing like that; once you see that your 3 is a 3, you are good to go. We have been trained to a pragmatic gaze. To learn a gaze of a different sort, we could do worse than look at some art.

Alain de Botton and John Armstrong argue, in a book called *Art as Therapy*, that art can give us a deeper appreciation of our apparently humdrum reality. They cite the example of a famous work by the American artist Jasper Johns, who cast in bronze two Ballantine Ale cans, and set them on a pedestal. They are just normal cans of the sort you would have found in many an American fridge of the 1960s, but once they are cast in bronze, and put in a gallery, they become 'art'. And because they are art, the cans make you stop, and look, and what you find in them is a previously unsuspected beauty in the colour of the label, in 'the attractive proportions of each cylinder'. You look at the beer cans 'as a child or a Martian, both free of habit in this area'. You really look at them for the first time, rather than just glancing over them. They are made new, and unexpected; and your world gets a little larger.

You can take from this experience much more than the joy of looking at art in a gallery: you can take, if you are lucky, the joy of seeing art in your fridge. Remember what we learned from Christina, the High Priestess? Your kitchen can be more amazing than a levitating monk. We are circling back there.

What if you are someone who finds art boring? You drag yourself to a gallery, you go through the motions of looking at the works on display, but your heart is not in it. One or two paintings are nice, sort of. But frankly, you would rather be at home watching TV after a long day at work. In theory, you appreciate that art is important, but in practice, you don't know what to do with it. I had the same problem for a long time, until something very simple dawned on me.

Sight-based forms of art first developed in societies in which people, at all levels of wealth, had more free time available than almost anyone does today. They also had a much slower rhythm of life. We prize velocity; sight-based art comes from a world where slowness was the norm, and it is on slowness that it thrives. To appreciate art and let it work on us, we need to approach it at its own pace, which is a slow one.

Our instinctual response to a painting in a museum is to briefly look at it and move on. We want to bag as many paintings as we can in our visit, to get good value for our money and time. But when it comes to art, value is a matter of *seeing more of one thing*: five paintings, carefully selected, would be plenty for an exhibition. John Armstrong points out that 'it can seem strange to treat lingering as a virtue', because when you linger, you are not accomplishing anything. But art invites you to linger, and sensuously dawdle.

A dawdling experience I remember fondly was with a painting by Jackson Pollock. Until that moment, I had refused to like Pollock's work: I saw in it a jumble of colours and chaos and nothing more, a cheap trick for people with too much money for their own good. That particular time, for no particular reason, I happened to linger on *Reflection of the Big Dipper*, and something odd happened: I could feel the inner rhythm of the work. I didn't actually hear any music, but it was as if I was remembering a long-lost tune. I gazed at the work and started noticing – or projecting – patterns: the tune in my mind made the colours beat and shift almost visibly, but not quite so. I was in a light trance. By slowing down, I had found a new artist I liked, and a new opportunity, if nothing else, for pleasure.

Through art we learn to let our sight linger, and notice the miracles that are already happening – quite literally – in front of our eyes.

✳

Other miracles manifest as vibrations in our eardrums. We live immersed in an aural reality we scarcely consider unless we are forced to by the wail of an ambulance or someone shouting our name. At any moment, there are sounds around us that our ears are perfectly equipped to pick up, but never make their way into our consciousness. There is an immense potential for wonder here.

When I was thirteen, the headmaster of my school organized a classical music concert, which all students were required to attend. Having to endure a bunch of old buffers playing Beethoven was excruciating, a shocking act of institutional violence. I sat down, brooding, in an uncomfortable lumpy chair and braced myself for excruciation.

The orchestra took just a handful of minutes to exorcise my angst, and then they went on relentlessly enchanting me. Soon the music captured me, and after a while I started to see the music as colour in movement, brushstrokes of red and yellow and electric blue appearing in the air above the orchestra: every movement of bow on strings created a visual echo. The room was bathed in psychedelic light. I didn't see any of this with my physical eyes, but the colours appeared in my mind's eye, like vivid memories, in an experience that anticipated and mirrored the one I would have years later in the presence of *Reflection*. Classical music makes you sit and listen; it is a sensuous experience before it is an intellectual one.

I am not a music expert. I can read music and for a while I used to torture a saxophone pretending I was playing, but I don't have a musical ear, I don't have any musical culture to speak of, and I definitely do not have discerning tastes. I don't *know* the first thing about music, intellectually speaking. I enjoy it for the sheer sensual pleasure that it gives me.

The fiddle was once known as 'the Devil's instrument', because, when played with suitably diabolical fervour, it would arouse yearnings of a sinful nature (a desire to dance, or – God forbid! – to roll in the grass). The violin virtuoso Niccolò Paganini was refused a Catholic burial when he died in 1840 because he was rumoured to have made a pact with the devil. A similar story was told about the bluesman Robert Johnson, who was rumoured to have acquired his musical gift after selling his soul to the devil at a dusty crossroads. Music – visceral and sensuous – belongs to the devil, and so do the pleasures of the body.

Marsilio Ficino, a marvellous Renaissance priest, mage and philosopher, believed that we have a body, a soul, and also a 'spirit', an intermediary between them. Music, for Ficino, is made of the same substance as the spirit, it is spiritual itself. As a consequence, music, through the spirit, moves our whole person, body and soul – and it could *change* our whole person.

Ficino held the belief, common in his time, that the universe is held together by a beautiful network of connections. The stars have special virtues, and in a form of cosmic echo, these virtues are also present, in diluted form, in plants, trees, rocks and other components of the natural world. Ginger and chamomile, for example, were considered to share the virtues of the Sun, which had the power to heal.

So it is with music. For Ficino, each of the stars in the heavens is playing its own tune. The cosmos as a whole is endlessly singing and playing a stunning harmony, a 'music of the spheres', which we never notice because it is always – and has always been – present. The mage, the artist, could mirror the harmonies of the Sun itself, and its virtues. A mage could summon up the music of a star to heal a friend.

This magical world view might (or might not) be too much for our modern sensibilities. But it certainly tells us at least two important things. The first is that by paying attention to our senses, we can enter into a deeper communion with the world we are part of. The second is that we are surrounded by an aural reality we have stopped listening to. In a world of building sites, roaring cars, and adverts screaming at us from television and computer, we have grown as deaf as we have ever been to the harmonies of the spheres.

The spheres still play. The composer John Cage shut himself in 'an echoic chamber', a chamber that blocked all sounds, and in that perfect silence, he heard a silence that was all but perfect: he heard 'two sounds, one high and one low'. He explained it as the twinned sounds of his nervous system and his blood circulation, but as Sara Maitland has noted, this is far from being a scientific fact. The same sound has been heard by all sorts of people who have gone searching for silence (Maitland herself among them), and no one knows for sure what it is. It may be not a problem, but a mystery.

As above, so below. As the universe, so everything it contains. I have already mentioned that one of my favourite pastimes when I was growing up was to sit on the beach and look at the sea. Sometimes I would close my eyes, and rather than look, I would listen. I would do this especially as summer was drawing to a close, when a deep sadness at the dying of the season took hold of me. The waves came ashore with a broken rhythm, never exactly the same. It was a very different sound from the one the beach had made just two weeks before, when electric tunes and human voices had obliterated the sea and the wind. The tunes and voices only lasted a couple of months each year; the waves were there before the beach-goers came, and they were still there after the beach-goers left.

The waves will still be there after I leave.

By tuning in to them, I was tuning in to a cosmic time span that was too big for me to understand. I did not need to; I could just sit down, and listen.

※

'The lower classes smell,' wrote George Orwell. These 'four frightful words', he explained, sum up the essence of the class system. The lower you are on the social scale, the worse your smell.

Orwell's words reflect a continuing reality. Seeing a homeless person prompts a variety of reactions in us, ranging from charitable concern to discomfort. *Smelling* a homeless person, however, can tilt us in the direction of suspicion. Old clothes and a dishevelled appearance are one thing (there are Oxbridge dons who are happy to sport such a look, after all), but the sour tang of an unwashed body suggests 'outcast' status. The person emitting this animal scent is not 'one of us'; surely they lie beyond the pale of society.

Remember what we said about social realities? They are the stories that our society tells about the world, and that come to define our reality. Smell can reinforce them strongly. Luckily, it can challenge them as strongly: we can use smell to go against the grain of disenchantment.

We think of smell almost exclusively in negative fashion. When you say of something, 'that smells', you mean *it smells bad*; if you want to indicate the opposite, you qualify your statement by saying 'it smells nice'. The smells we appreciate the most are the ones that we don't notice. The chief requirement for our friends is that they do not smell – we appreciate them wearing some nice cologne, but that is not necessary in the way, say, that it is necessary for them to wear trousers. Town planning aims to create visually interesting environments, and in the best cases even quiet ones, but it does not concern itself at all with the smell of those localities, other than to ensure that no smell is present. We take it for granted that odours are unpleasant, and our main concern about them is how to get rid of them. This is what we must change.

Smell takes us into uncharted waters. It feels alien to us, a leftover of a bygone era.

Charles Foster, author of *Being a Beast*, described the frustration he felt when he tried to create a map of an area of woodland the way badgers do, by using smell rather than sight. Badgers take paths marked by odours: there are no visible signs to indicate that a specific line across a field is a path, but the badgers passing through that field will know a path is there, and will walk it. To them the line is... we could say 'visible', but that only goes to show how bad we are at talking about smell. An olfactory line is not a line you can see. The best verb we have is 'to perceive', which is annoyingly generic. We lack the most basic words to even conceive the world of aromatics.

Our sense of smell is weaker than other animals', and yet, after some training, Foster was able to distinguish trees by

smell, and in more general terms he gained an olfactory understanding of his patch of woodland. He found, though, that he
always translated that understanding into visual terms, using
metaphors like 'walls' and 'paths': he was unable to stay at the
level of the scent, to appreciate odours for what they are. Our
difficulties with smell are not only a matter of physical perception (or the lack thereof); in modern Western culture at least,
smell has been largely erased from consciousness.

This has happened because we have stopped using our
sense of smell. We use sight for spreadsheets, and hearing to
have meetings, but in our safe and healthy world smell is not
crucial. Besides, those of us who live in a city are surrounded
by mostly unpleasant odours: of course we would rather avoid
them altogether.

The authors of a study on smell, *Aroma*, argue that smell
destroys the illusion that each of us is a separate entity, with
clearly cut boundaries separating us from each other. To smell
a person, or an animal, is to know them intimately, to a degree
that we are uncomfortable with. To smell skin is almost to
touch it, to feel close to the animal reality of our fellow human
beings; smell is scandalous. Our society, terrified of intimacy
as it is, would rather do without it. And yet smell stubbornly
exists, and it connects us to invisible realms.

We have seen how difficult it is to speak of the numinous, or
to describe it, but smells are not words, and the numinous can
manifest itself through them. In ancient Egypt, a type of incense

called kyphi was sacred to the Sun, and was burned as an offering. There were different recipes for making kyphi, some of which were considered important enough to be inscribed in stone in temples. The use of incense and the pungent smoke it produces for spiritual ends is still widespread: I spent my childhood in a Catholic country, and although I was bored by the mass on Sundays, I was thrilled by the smell of frankincense that accompanied its celebration. It gave me a sign, at least, that a numinous experience might be possible.

In the tradition of *grimoires* – textbooks of magic containing, among other spells, instructions for the summoning of spirits – incense played a key role. Practitioners of this kind of magic still burn specific mixtures of gums, resins, oils, herbs and wood, in a triangle drawn on the floor, where the spirit they are conjuring is supposed to appear. The spirit uses the pungent-smelling smoke to fashion a shape for itself.

But why would a spirit need a *visible* shape? A spirit *scented* can be as real as a spirit *seen*. The numinous experience is impossible to put into words, so the magician resorts to a visual metaphor to describe it, as Charles Foster had to do when he tried to live like a badger.

The Chewong, a tribe of the Malay peninsula, have no such qualms. They burn perfumed wood for the spirits every night; this ritual feeds the spirits, and must never be neglected. When a shaman calls up a class of spirits called 'leaf-people', they come carrying a sweet fragrance with them, and although only the shaman can see the leaf-people, everybody can smell them. Their smell is so sweet that it might cause you to weep tears of joy.

Smells can provoke tears in other contexts, also. It is devastating to inhale the scent left on a pillow by a departed lover. Suddenly that person is there with you again; if you close your eyes, you can feel his presence, absolutely real. You can sense the bulge on the bed where he used to lie, the gentle warmth of his body. And when you open your eyes, and he is not there, you feel betrayed by the diminished reality in which you live.

By defining scent only as an absence, we are renouncing endless possibilities of wonder. Sight and hearing are certainly more useful in terms of our physical survival, but to reject your sense of smell because of that is like cutting off your left arm because the right one is all you need to change the channel on the TV.

✳

The trajectory of taste is a cautionary tale. As the animals we are, we need food to survive. Gradually we discovered that some foods taste better cooked; then, that particular combinations of flavours are especially pleasing; then we learned that we could record those combinations in the form of recipes. In terms of strict necessity, we only needed food, and maybe some rudimentary cooking to make food safer. The next steps were exquisitely useless: they were driven by our desire to broaden our spectrum of experience and make our world vaster. Our sense of taste followed and nourished our sense of wonder, and what started as fuel became a source of pleasure. Then, unfortunately, there came a time when, under the weight of disenchantment, we reverted to using food almost exclusively as fuel again, and today we have better things to do than cook, or take time to eat. My own life has followed a similar trajectory.

Some of my fondest childhood memories are infused with flavours. Italy is perhaps unique in its variety of regional produce and recipes: a tourist from Rome could visit Puglia for a week and every day sample a dish she had never even heard of before. Some local flavours – the bitterness of certain mushrooms, for example, or the deliciously rotten tang of *ricotta shcante* – are too much for those who have not grown up with them.

A regular summer breakfast in my family entails *pane e pomodoro* (crusty bread with the juice of tomatoes squeezed directly on it, a drizzle of olive oil, and a pinch of salt), fruit just picked from the trees in the garden (apricots, peaches or figs, depending on how late in the season it is), milk, coffee, warm focaccia and croissants, and biscuits. Cured meat is often on the table as well – especially prosciutto crudo and mortadella. A lot of flavours come together at our small table, from the sweetness of tomatoes to the chocolate in the biscuits, from the sharpness of coffee to the wholesome freshness of milk. I like to alternate between savoury and sweet flavours, from a bite of *pane e pomodoro* to a juicy peach, while others are more conservative, and move methodically from a savoury start to a sweet ending. The one thing everybody agrees on is that figs wrapped in prosciutto are divine; some make sandwiches with them, to take to the beach.

I wouldn't say there is a food culture in southern Italy as much as that southern Italy *is* a food culture, where flavour matters almost as much as family, and, in practice, more than religion. It is entirely normal for friends to debate the quality of the varieties of olive oil produced that year, and how they compare with those of the previous crop. Do you prefer a stronger, more piquant note, that tickles your throat in a pleasant way, or are you one for mellow sweetness?

Italians regularly converse about *other* food while they are eating, exchanging ideas on all the dishes they are going to try in the next few days, or memories of those they tried recently, or that they used to eat in the past. It is the sensuous equivalent of the free association technique championed by Sigmund Freud, in which patients give their memory and imagination free rein. Certain flavours remind you of other flavours, and you let your senses lead you down memory lane, or into the future.

For good eating, mindset is as important as produce. London, in theory, is food heaven. I can jump from my favourite Chinese restaurant, which does *real* Chinese food and sits discreetly in a garish tourist area, to a place where I can get good chips and fresh fish deep-fried in a light batter, to the Turkish restaurant in Brockley that initiated me into the forbidden delights of lamb and yogurt conjoined. This abundance of food, however, does not translate into an abundance of pleasure.

In London, lunch is all too often a sandwich or other fast food bought in a supermarket or chain restaurant, utterly bland garbage. In the evening, we eat watching television, and we barely notice what we are putting into our mouths. Even when we visit a good restaurant, we eat quickly, because the next customers need the table, or because we have more activities to squeeze into our scarce free time.

Eating this way is surely effective, if you measure effectiveness by how much you get done in one day: this is yet another face of the 'cold philosophy' of disenchantment that John Keats deplored, the approach to life that made 'all charms fly'. The disenchanted mindset has as little patience for the pleasures of the body as it has for the wildest flights of imagination.

Food, like art, requires us to slow down, and food, like art, helps us to do that. The slowness demanded by food is the wild tranquillity of nature: eating means bringing inside things that were outside, making them part of us by breaking them with our teeth and mixing them with our bodily fluids. As Anthony Bourdain put it, 'good food, good eating, is all about blood and organs, cruelty and decay'. The paradox is that on the one hand, food dispels the illusion that we are not like other animals, while on the other, cooking is the sort of quirky idea that only a nerd like *Homo sapiens* could come up with. Eating is a matter of survival; preparing linguine all vongole is a sign of civilization; buying pre-cooked soggy pasta is a herald of decline.

A simple strategy to eat counterculturally is to eat seasonal food. In southern Italy there are of course supermarkets that make certain types of fruit and vegetables available all the year round, as in England and the rest of Europe, but it is still common to buy vegetables from smallholders, and cook seasonal recipes. On one level, this means that you are eating produce whose flavours are more intense. On another, eating seasonal food puts your body in step with the rhythms of the land. The bitterness of aubergines heralds summer: when you bite into the flesh of the year's first aubergine, your mouth tastes sunshine, and your body prepares itself for the sensuous explosion the season will bring. Globe artichokes, with their metallic sobriety, tell you that the cold is coming and you better cosy up. Through flavour, you can pierce the human-shaped bubble we have created around us.

Taste allows us a pagan communion with the world, and not only with the world. The essayist Diane Ackerman has written that 'taste is largely social': when you eat for pleasure, you eat in company. Families are kept together by bonds of loyalty and love, and also by bonds of flavour: they sit down together to break bread, and the pleasure of food nurtures the pleasure of conversation, of being present together in the same space, breathing the same air, drinking the same wine. Taste is an under-appreciated cure for loneliness. Then again, loneliness is exactly what a disenchanted society wants us to feel: we are better workers, better drones, when we eat quickly, when we eat garbage, when we don't mind our senses, when we are alone.

Taste is, it turns out, a matter of resistance.

※

Look at me: I am hugging a tree. It is a dismal sight. I am a shaven-headed guy pushing forty, with a face that recalls an expendable extra in a Mafia film more than a hippie sage. I wear a battered jacket, old jeans and wellies, and I have spread my arms as far as possible around the trunk, and rested my cheek against it. A dismal sight indeed. I don't care. I am touching and being touched, and if you don't like what you see, you can look away; being here, being the one doing the hugging, feels amazing. Let me explain how I got here.

The story I have charted thus far is a parable of defeat. Sight and hearing are reduced to an impoverished state, smell has been exiled, and taste survives only in remote corners of Europe. Touch fares even worse: it is the object of fear and ridicule, and it has been bound and gagged by the tightest social norms. Being 'touchy-feely' is an insult: feeling is wrong, touching is not the done thing.

Touch is frightening to the atomized society that capitalism thrives on, because touch, more than any other sense, more even than smell, cannot help being intimate. In a world in which too many people (and too many morons with too much power) still believe in zero-sum games, with winners and losers, touch reveals the lie. You cannot touch without being touched. The universe is touching you at all times, you are touching the universe.

The other senses might still allow us to labour under the delusion that they are detached reporters of the world out there, but touch shatters that delusion once and for all. Touch is an act of communication. Every time we touch we are making ourselves vulnerable. Every time we touch we are having a conversation with whoever we are touching, allowing them to touch us in turn. Touch makes the magical universe of Marsilio Ficino, in which everything is connected to everything else, palpable.

The art of touch was valued in classical times: the goddess of sexual pleasure (Aphrodite for the Greeks, Venus for the Romans) was not intellectually inclined, which does not mean she was dense. She possessed a wisdom of the body, and it was a powerful wisdom at that. It was not by chance that she had great sex with Ares/Mars, god of war, who was not exactly a thinker either, and was the bringer of a different sort of wisdom of the body, geared towards violence rather than pleasure. Eros and Thanatos always went together.

The art of touch has been lost. We say that good sex is in the mind; that imagination and mental connection are far more important than skin and sweat. But *are* they? When you are naked in bed with your lovers, you need more than telepathy.

I have often heard it said, and I have said it myself, that good conversation leads to good sex. That is true, and yet the contrary is true as well. Sex might be as good a way to make new friends as conversation, if only we were more touch literate.

The main way in which we represent sex, that is, pornography, has contributed to this lack of literacy. What looks good on screen doesn't always feel good on the skin: one of the most often seen positions for performing oral sex – the so-called '69' (or soixante-neuf) – became ubiquitous for the way it looks, even though, from a physical perspective, it is far from ideal for actual mutual stimulation. A lot of unsatisfactory sex happens when we do with our partners things that *look* good, rather than things that *feel* good. In our minds, we are continuously watching the film of our life, to the point that we forget to enjoy starring in it.

Lydia Daniller and Rob Perkins came to realize, after many long conversations about female sexuality, that no one knows the first thing about the female orgasm. Reaching orgasm during sex is notoriously difficult for women, but why? Daniller and Perkins found a possible answer in the fact that most people, men and women alike, are not too sure how to get *physically* there. So they interviewed a sample of women and, starting from their experience, they created OMGYes, a website aimed at educating people about pleasure. It is fascinating to navigate, for its clear, laser-like focus on physicality. Learn to touch, it says, and a brave new world will open up for you. Yes, it is important to set the mood, and yes, state of mind matters; but we still need to learn how to touch, skin against skin, and how to be touched.

It was this line of reasoning that led me to hug a tree. The art of touch goes beyond sex: I wondered how it would feel to try to understand a tree through touch. The very thought of this can make sceptics laugh and scoff. You must be touchy-feely to be a tree-hugger, right?

I selected a day midweek, when I had a good chance not to be interrupted (or seen), and I went to Oxleas Wood, in Greenwich. My plan was to hug a random tree, but then I surprised myself by trying to select the *right* tree to hug. I wanted it to be an oak, because I have a fondness for oaks; I wanted it to be far from the entrance to the woods; I wanted it to be old enough to have some history to it. In the end, I settled on an oak not too far from a dried-up stream bed. I took off my glasses, put them in my jacket pocket, and before I could change my mind, I hugged the tree. I rested my cheek against the rough surface of the bark, and waited.

I spent the first few minutes silently cursing myself. Common sense urged me to let go, to stop being stupid and act like an adult. I waited, until the awkwardness passed and was replaced by boredom. Still I waited and still I carried on hugging *Quercus robur*. Then something snapped.

I became aware of the feeling only when it was over: while it was happening, I did not have a clear sense of time, or of myself. It was a sensuous feeling that words are not made to describe: the best way I can translate it is by saying that my body understood that I was part of the woods. My feet rested on the same earth the oak tree had planted its roots in, and my lungs breathed in the oxygen it produced.

There was nothing revelatory about this realization, nothing mind-blowing. It is common knowledge that trees and people are joined in one ecosystem. What was new was the intensity with which I *felt* the connectedness, in my arms, my cheek, my guts – not as an idea, but as a physical sensation as palpable as thirst. I was, I realized, embodying every last hippie cliché, but I didn't care, because while I was holding on to that tree, every last hippie cliché was true. If I had to use a word to describe what had happened, I would say I had *opened* myself in a way that was out of character for my bookish, doubting self. The tree was doing that to me.

Our fear of touch is fear of being touched; of opening ourselves to the new and unexpected. When we move beyond that, when we train our skin to feel again, we can sense wonder with our whole body; we can embrace wonder, and we can, at last, let wonder embrace us.

✳

I am convinced that human beings have a soul. I couldn't possibly say whether it survives the death of the body or not, and I don't think anybody can answer this question. But we do have a soul: there is a part of us that is not body and it is not mind, and it is not Marsilio Ficino's 'spirit'. It is far, far stranger than that. While scientists and philosophers have explained many things about our body and mind, and will explain many more in the future, there is little to say about our soul. It is just there.

In his poem 'The Tyger', William Blake considers the remarkable physical reality of a tiger, and wonders who could have created such a beast. The poem takes the form of a series of questions that come together to describe the creature at its core. The questions are asked and never answered; we never get to know 'what immortal hand or eye' framed the beast's 'fearful symmetry'. Some questions are just too good to be belittled by answers.

'The Tyger' is one of the most perfect celebrations of wonder I have ever encountered. It revels in sensuousness: every time I read it aloud, I feel the tiger prowling savagely from line to line. There is beauty in the sounds of this poem, and fear also: in the last line, the 'could' of the opening stanza's question 'what immortal hand or eye could frame thy fearful symmetry' is replaced by the more disquieting 'dare'. The unashamed sensuousness of the tiger leads us to the heart of mystery, and mystery is dangerous, for it destroys our certainties without ever giving us the consolation of new ones.

The tiger is a wonderful image for our soul.

Our soul, too, is a mystery. We cannot define it precisely and we cannot decide what it is exactly, but we feel it when we are kissing a person we love, biting into an apple in a Somerset orchard, smelling the fragrance of jasmine, looking down on our city from high above, or listening to Bach's Mass in B Minor. We catch glimpses of our soul in the thick foliage of our senses.

In a book celebrating uncertainty, American Zen philosopher Alan Watts said that we can understand an experience in two different ways. One way is just having it: you are happy when you are happy. The moment at which you think 'I am happy', you are already filtering the experience, you are already interpreting it through the lenses of words and culture. Which brings us to the second mode, the most common, in which we have the experience and 'compare it with the memories of other experiences, and so to name and define it'. In so doing, we doom ourselves never to enjoy an experience that is entirely new, because the moment something new happens, we define it in terms of experiences we have had previously. How does the juice of this particular apple taste? It's nothing special; you have had apples before. You translate *this* apple here, special and unique, into the abstract category of 'apple'. You ignore your senses to listen to your own ideas, and you seal yourself off from the world.

As we grow older, we do this more and more. We stop sensing the new and unexpected, and thus we stop sensing wonder. We have tasted so many different apples that we become utterly incapable of appreciating that we have never tasted that particular apple before, and we shall never taste it again.

This journey we are taking, which we have started but can never really finish, is *a journey of unlearning*. At every step of the way, we have rid ourselves of more certainties, we have shed another layer of our armour, to make us ready to step into the world naked and vulnerable, to feel the wind caress our skin, and open the door to wonder.

Alan Watts remarks that our culture is not at all materialistic, 'if a materialist is a person who loves matter'. We have the opposite problem: 'the brainy modern loves not matter but measures'. We have created a maze of abstractions to surround and protect us, so that we can ignore the material reality of the world. Children are awake to that reality: they don't yet know enough of the world to have learned to rein in their senses. We can be awake to that reality too, with a little effort and a lot of courage. Through a fuller engagement with our senses, with the material reality of scents and flavours, we can rediscover our soul, the mystery we carry within.

We can be the tiger, and burn bright.

THE WORKOUT

1. Slow Down

For a week, make a conscious effort to feast your eyes on things you enjoy looking at. When you are out walking and you notice a car you like, deliberately stop to look at its shape, its colours, its movement. When you see a pleasant image, linger on it. When you see your lover's face, look at it for more than a few moments, and appreciate what you see.

Do the same with especially displeasing images and shapes.

Note down in your Book of Wonder how this affects your feelings.

2. Tune In

For a week, three times a day, stop whatever you are doing and *listen*. Make a note of all the sounds and voices you hear. How many would normally go unnoticed? Keep doing the exercise for the entire week, even though you may think you have 'got it' after the first day; it is a way to attune your body to your environment. Select different times of the day to do the exercise. How does the soundtrack of your life change at different times of day?

3. Smell That

For a week, smell as many things as possible. Smell food, phones, chairs, trays and (politely, with their consent) other people. Smell the air in your house, the air on your commute, the air in your workplace. Make a note of all these smells – try to describe them, in writing, in your Book of Wonder. This way, you will build up a mental encyclopedia of aromas that will help you perceive more smells, and in turn, broaden the encyclopedia itself.

4. Don't Bolt Your Food

This exercise will require two weeks.

During the course of the first week, eat as you would normally do, and focus on each flavour. Does the flavour of crisps give you deep pleasure – or not? Is the sugary sweetness of doughnuts pleasant on your tongue? Is the texture of this refrigerated ham sandwich satisfying to you? As usual, make a note of your findings in your Book of Wonder.

In the second week, eat only food that you really enjoy, even if this means having to spend time cooking it. While you eat, do not do anything else, except for talking with friends. Do not send emails, do not check your phone at all, do not watch TV, do not work. That goes for all meals throughout the day, even snacking (if you eat snacks). How does this change your attitude to flavour? And how difficult would it be to accommodate this way of eating into your daily routine?

5. Touching Skin

Find a comfortable, warm space and get naked. Close your eyes, and for five minutes, touch yourself gently, without any specific intent. You are not aiming to arouse yourself, though arousal might happen. All that you are doing is touching your own skin, meditating on the feeling. If five minutes is too short a time, try seven, or even ten.

When the exercise is over, immediately record your feelings in your Book of Wonder.

Repeat the exercise for a week.

Then, if you have a willing partner, do it with them. If possible, both of you should be blindfolded. On at least seven occasions, with no more than three days between them, spend ten minutes together, naked, touching and being touched. Negotiate boundaries, if any, beforehand: once the exercise begins, it is better not to talk at all.

Do not try to be sexy. Just touch, be touched, and focus on the feeling.

6. Burning Bright

When is your soul at its brightest?

Spend a week with this question. Write down in your Book of Wonder any answers you might find, even when (especially when) they are contradictory. Write down any random thoughts, any ideas that the question might inspire.

The Portals

A new breed of rebels was quietly rising

Y ou look better,' said Paola. The cab had left. I was on the threshold of home.

I was back from the remote place where I shut myself away to write. I had almost finished this book. When I am in my hermitage I stick to a brutal schedule, which sees me working from the moment I get out of bed to the moment I have to crawl back into it. That does not make me *look better*. I knew for a fact that I was tired and sleep-deprived, I had a beard too long to be handsomely rugged and too short to be wizardly wise; my eyes were half-closed, and the half that was visible was reddish. 'Sure,' I said.

'I mean it,' Paola insisted. 'You seem… happier.'

I stepped inside and glanced at myself in the mirror hanging next to our front door. She had a point. I wasn't going to be targeted by any Hollywood director for the starring role in a romantic comedy, but then again, that wouldn't happen even on my best day. Nonetheless, I seemed at ease with myself in a way I hadn't been for a long while. The book was almost done. The process had caused a fundamental shift to take place inside me.

It would be a plump lie to say that writing had been easy. Writing is the best job in the world, and the best things in life are never easy. The plans you have never survive the impact with reality. I did not write this book in an unbroken state of wonder and I am not promising you that by reading it, and working your way through the Wonder Workouts, you will effortlessly achieve such a state. And thank goodness for that. Sadness, boredom and worry are also part of a well-lived life.

But something had changed. I had re-immersed myself in one of my oldest passions, the study of wonder. I had written and tested a series of exercises, I had talked to people and read books and tried new things. I had opened myself to surprises and I had been, indeed, surprised. For example, the last key did not figure in my original plan: I realized the importance of embodied wonder while I was searching for the Fifth Key. What seems obvious now was not obvious at the time. The journey was completely real to me, and it had changed me in positive, rather than predictable, ways. Where before I had been on the defensive, and had felt anxious about the difficulties in my life and the world in general, now I was ready – even eager – to fight back. I felt larger, open to whatever new and unexpected things might come my way. And also capable of making new and unexpected things happen.

Meanwhile, the world had got worse.

*

In Britain, politicians of both the right and left seemed to be intent on stoking tensions between native Britons and immigrants – and on sowing discord between people of different faiths and cultural traditions. They said that the free movement of nomads like me was the root of all evil, and that curbing freedom was a good thing; they said that the country should take in only those who brought 'useful' skills – and of course, they were the ones who would decide what was useful, and to whom. They also decided that the likes of me – the foreigners – would have to apply to receive a number, which would identify us from then on. They decided that we will have to show that number when we need a GP, or to have any of our rights secured; and that we would have to pay for the privilege out of our own pockets. Some of us foreigners were asked to trial this new scheme, and in exchange they would receive their little number first; and some of us were terrified enough, or well-trained enough, to oblige. The situation carried uncomfortable echoes of tragedies past, and very few voices, from either left or right, were raised against it.

Italy, my other country, was faring no better. Its new rulers, a gang of illiterate bullies, allowed migrants to die at sea, and campaigned for parents to stop vaccinating their children in the name of long-debunked pseudoscience, spreading ignorance so that they could prey on it. While the United States, a country regarded for decades as the rock and pillar of the West, continued to be ruled by that most dangerous creature known to humankind, an idiot trying to look smart.

The values that had defined my life – inclusivity, the importance of higher education and universal access to it, a globalism based on a joyful celebration of diversity rather than a fearful push for assimilation – were under attack from all sides. What had changed was that, as I watched myself in the mirror, unshaven and pale, for the first time in a long time I thought, *let them come.*

Fear and hatred were not *all* that was rising in the world. Falcons were soaring over the rooftops of major cities, secret societies were fighting back against disenchantment, fairies were creeping back to sabotage our clockwork universe, science was discovering frontiers stranger than our strangest dreams. Of course there were people desperately trying to stop this surging wave. They were afraid; as they should be. A new breed of rebels was quietly rising against them. Our culture, our way of life, our financial situation too, would change massively in the years to come, but they might still change for the best. *We* could make them change for the best.

In conversation with Neil Gaiman, the novelist Kazuo Ishiguro made the observation that since the Industrial Revolution children have been allowed fantasy, have even been encouraged to pursue it, only as long as they are children: 'but then, when they get to a certain age, they have to start getting prepared to be units of the labour force'. When we come of age, we are told to let go of our imagination and stick to the harsh facts of life, which were decided for us before we were born, and will accompany us to the grave. We must develop 'useful' skills, and we are made to believe that we can never decide for ourselves what is useful and what is not. When people start imagining a different world, they might end up building it, and getting rid of the old one.

The psychologist Paul Piff rigged a game of Monopoly in order to carry out an experiment relating to entitlement. At the beginning of the game, he gave some players much more money than others. The 'wealthy' players knew that they had more cash than the 'poor' ones, and vice versa: all the players were perfectly aware that the game was rigged. The wealthy ones won, as was inevitable. When they were asked to explain their victory, however, they did not factor in their initial advantage. Rather, they spoke about how cleverly they had played, and how much they deserved their win. It is desperate to see how easily we convince ourselves that we deserve the privileges we have; how self-centred we are.

And yet.

A team of psychologists, of which Piff himself was part, wanted to study the effect of awe on 'prosocial behaviour', the behaviour we display when we put other people's interests before our own. They took a group of students into a wood, and invited them to look at some majestic trees for a minute. When asked what they felt, the students reported high levels of awe.

The psychologists then ran some tests. For example, one of

them dropped a bunch of pens apparently out of clumsiness. He then counted how many pens the students helped him to pick up. Also, the students were asked how much money they thought they deserved for participating in the experiment.

The experimenters ran the same tests on a second group, the only difference being that they placed this second group in front of an unremarkable tall building, where they did not report high levels of awe.

The first group, who had felt awe, helped the experimenters to pick up more pens than the second group, and asked for less money. They had become appreciably keener to help, and less entitled, after one meagre wonder-filled minute. Just think what effect a lifetime of wonder could have.

And this is why wonder is shunned.

It challenges the dispiriting notion that selfishness and greed is humanity's default setting. A minute of wonder is enough to show that this is *not* a dog-eat-dog world if we don't make it so: being small-minded is a choice, not a necessity. A re-enchanted world would have less space for the hatred on which so many politicians and media moguls are feeding.

Before I let you go, let me tempt you with three quick ideas on how to use your new sense of wonder to make the world a slightly better place. These are three portals to open with your keys. I am sure you will discover more of your own.

✳

The first portal is Creativity. We can define it as the capacity to find new ideas that work. It takes creativity to write a good novel, it takes creativity to fix a flawed relationship, or to find a fairer way of running a country. To be truly creative, new ideas have to get the job done better than the old ones.

Being creative is hard because of something we discovered in our journey: we have locked ourselves in a very narrow reality. We look at the world through the distorting prism of the stories we have been told, and we believe that prism shows us the world as it is. We even train our senses to be less sharp than they would be naturally, so as not to dispel that illusion. We live in a cramped box, which cuts us off from a large part of our astounding universe.

In order to be creative, we need, first, to fully accept that we live in that box; second, to map its boundaries; and third, to look for effective ways of extending them. When, in 2004, the novelist Susanna Clarke published *Jonathan Strange & Mr Norrell*, she believed it was possible to write a fairy tale in the way Jane Austen would have written one, had she written such stories. Clarke's publisher believed that a literary fantasy novel could find a large audience (a point of view that many 'sensible' people might have said lacked supporting evidence) and printed a huge number of hardbacks. The book was a critical and financial success, and quickly came to be considered a classic. Believing that such a book was *possible* in the first place took a breathtaking amount of good ideas at all levels of the production process. It took chutzpah too.

Wonder makes us find the ideas, and gives us the chutzpah.

With a heightened sense of wonder, you are always aware that you live in a box, no matter how big it is. You keep pushing against its walls; you never stop questioning what you think you know, you never stop sailing against the current of common sense, you cultivate doubt about what others consider the most obvious certainties. An enchanted life is organically creative.

The psychologist Mihaly Csikszentmihalyi famously identified a state of mind he called 'flow', in which we are completely focused on the task at hand. In a state of flow, we create our best work. We can write ten thousand good words in a day, or break a world record at the Olympics, or solve an elusive equation; or have the kind of mind-blowing sex that makes you wobble for a week afterwards. In a state of flow, it is easier to be focused than distracted. The secret to flow is engagement: to be in flow is to be fully engaged with what we are doing.

We cannot generate a state of flow at will, but a heightened sense of wonder gives us a profound level of engagement with life that makes flow more likely to happen. When you understand that everything around you carries the seeds of the new and the unique, and that every situation you encounter is different, that level of engagement becomes second nature to you.

It will still take an effort to come up with good ideas, and test them, and discard those that are not effective. But that effort forms part of the adventure of discovery, and as such it will be bearable. Susanna Clarke took ten years to write *Jonathan Strange & Mr Norrell*, and her publishers took a huge financial gamble with it, a gamble they could have lost regardless of the novel's quality. I am sure that Clarke endured many sleepless nights, and her editor at least as many; I am sure that her agent anticipated publication day with a mixture of elation and terror – that day was for everyone involved truly a *mysterium tremendum et fascinans*.

Susanna Clarke and the people around her opened themselves to the mystery, and thus made something extraordinary happen. As witches do; as we have learned to do.

✳

The second portal is Stress. In a study of high achievers in different fields, from the military to the arts, the psychologist Angela Duckworth observed that they all have one quality in common, which she called 'grit'. High achievers were not necessarily cleverer or more talented than other people, but they were persistent. They were the ones who, after suffering a setback, would bounce back and try again; and then, when they suffered another setback, they would bounce back from that as well; and so on. High achievers can cope with stress.

This attitude is necessary if we are to see through to completion every long-term task we set ourselves. A marriage requires grit, writing a novel requires grit, making our organization more environmentally sustainable requires grit. There are other factors that might help one to succeed (a privileged background and luck, to name two), but whereas other factors we cannot control, we can strengthen our levels of grit.

In 1990, England were playing Cameroon in the quarter-final of the World Cup, a match that would become legendary. England were losing 2–1 when they were awarded a penalty. The responsibility of taking it fell to the striker Gary Lineker. He was under an immense amount of stress. He dealt with it by embracing it in full. Before he took the penalty kick, Lineker thought about how wonderful it was to be there, to be playing for his country, and becoming part of the history of his chosen sport; the pressure he was feeling was part of the game, it was part of the beauty of the situation. Lineker went on to score with his penalty, and then, for good measure, to score a second goal, and England won.

A sense of wonder does not make stress go away, but rather it helps us to engage with stress productively, and so turn it into an ally.

Sometimes that won't be enough. The story of Lineker in the Cameroon game has the kind of happy ending we like. We love the story of J. K. Rowling and of how, after her first Harry Potter had been rejected for not being 'commercial' enough, she eventually found a publisher for it and went on to achieve wealth and success beyond dreams, to turn millions of children the world over into book readers, and to found a charitable trust to fight poverty and disease. It's a true story, and an uplifting one.

Another true story is that of Edgar Allan Poe, author of some of the most extraordinary tales in the literary canon – still cherished nearly two hundred years after they were written. Poe did not become successful and wealthy. Quite the contrary: he died a wretched death in the street at the age of just forty, impoverished and broken by alcohol. This is the kind of story we do not tell often enough.

We have an unfortunate relationship with defeat. We try to erase it as a fact of life; inspirational quotes tell us there is always something to learn from a failed venture, that every curse is a blessing in disguise, that obstacles show the way. This is disingenuous. While refusing defeat seems to add to our grit, it actually detracts from it. To bounce back from a setback, it is fundamentally important that we admit that it was, indeed, a setback.

It sometimes happens that an obstacle is a giant bloody obstacle and nothing less than that. A healthy person who has never smoked a cigarette in their life gets lung cancer at twenty-seven; you are by far the best candidate for your dream job and you still don't get it, and it is not a blessing in disguise, because the next job you find is pretty bad, and it takes you three years to get out of it. Such things happen. There is nothing to learn there, except that luck matters.

The ancient Romans held the goddess Fortuna, *Luck*, in high regard; she could make or break the plans of mortals and gods alike. When Fortuna is raging against you, as is bound to happen at some point, then you need your sense of wonder more than ever. A sense of wonder comes from a full engagement with life in all its aspects, darkness as much as light, fear as much as joy. Knowing that the mystery of reality is indeed *tremendum et fascinans* will help us not to despair when we are seeing its more frightening face. It will help us to look at defeat square on, and hang on, until the wheel of luck turns, and the storm dies down; or until we reach our life's end at last, and we have nothing to worry about any more.

✳

The third portal opens a thousand more. It is Communication.

We give this word an almost predatory connotation. Effective communicators should be able to convince the other side to do their bidding; they outsmart their opponent in a competition in which one person's victory is the other's defeat. But the word 'communication' comes from the Latin *communicare*, 'to share': communication is an exchange of gifts. Both sides are trying to create a new reality together, and effective communication is about finding a solution that will leave both of them happy.

Wonder is connected to a capacity to live in ambiguity: a life of wonder will leave you with very few certainties. It will make you able to understand that other people's reality is not yours, and even when you think they are wrong, or ill-intentioned, you will still be able to see why they have acted as they have. You will see them as *Thou* rather than *It*. A wonder-based approach to communication sees it as an encounter rather than a contest.

I have been working with communication for my entire professional life and the misconception I have encountered most frequently is the belief that good communication is a matter of self-expression. If you focus on what you need to say and you articulate it clearly, so the misconception goes, you will be an effective communicator. That is not the case.

Real communication requires you to focus on the other side; not on what *you* need, but on what *they* need. Your words are a rope you give them so that you both can climb together, rather than one they should use to hang themselves.

Deepak Malhotra, Professor of Business Administration at Harvard Business School, says that empathy leads to successful negotiation, and all the more so when the negotiations are tough. When the other side's interests go against ours and there seems to be no chance of compromise, Malhotra argues, what we must do is put ourselves in their shoes, and ask ourselves: 'How does the other side see their own behaviour?'

That might be easier said than done in the heat of a negotiation, be it with armed criminals holding hostages or with your partner who wants to go to Mallorca while you favour Venice. We are like the Sultan Shahryar: we think we have it all figured out, and if the other side does not agree, we must, alas, chop off their head. Like Shahryar, we might even have the power to do that. The sultan, though, was not happy.

Those who cultivate an enchanted world view are open to other realities. By habitually seeking wonder, they have enlarged their space of possibility so often that it won't hurt them to do so one more time. By having learned that our reality is small, we will forgive others the smallness of theirs, and we might just have a chance to change both. Wonder fosters empathy – and we are going to need a lot of it in the coming years.

＊

We are the species that invented jewels and fireworks. With jewels, we make wonder eternal: we lovingly sculpt rocks and bend metals to create objects that exist only to be forever wonderful. With fireworks, we make wonder transient: we lovingly sculpt fire, one of the elemental forces of nature, to create art that is beautiful for a fleeting moment only. We long for transience and eternity; we are made of both.

Human life is filled with paradoxes. We can only see (and smell, and lick, and touch, and hear) a small part of the universe but we want to know it all, we say that we will love someone for ever even though we know we are going to die, we cleave to certainties that hold only as long as we refuse to see the exceptions. A life of wonder is one in which we embrace these paradoxes. It is a messy life, a life that accepts ambiguity and celebrates mystery; a life that runs counter to the narrative that would leave us disenchanted, satisfied with our lot – and obedient.

There is no denying that the world is darkening. We seem to

be forgetting what it was like to live in a society in which dictators were condemned without ifs and buts. The day I wrote these words, a major national paper carried an opinion piece arguing that democratic leaders had one or two things to learn from autocrats; or, to quote the article, from 'strongmen'.

I believe we have one or two things to learn from those who *resist* strongmen.

This is what we have been doing: we have armed ourselves to fight against the definition of reality that others want to impose upon us – a bland, grey caricature of our dazzling universe.

Wonder is the fuel we need in order to be Blake's tiger burning bright. Every disenchanted day we live is a day we surrender to those who want us divided and lonely. A life of wonder is a radical life, for wonder is not childish, little, or cute.

Wonder bites, and so do we.

Acknowledgements

A mentor named Piers Blofeld set me on the journey: on a windy winter afternoon we sought refuge in a tiny tavern, and there he listened to my vision. He wisely counselled me on how to prepare, and found me a place where to start.

A champion named Richard Milbank was with me at every twist and turn, accepting patiently all the detours and the assorted strangeness that comes your way when you travel with someone who aims at making the world weirder.

A companion named Paola Filotico shaped the vision with me, and when I got lost she got lost with me, and when I found my way back it was because of her.

My mother gave me food, my brothers gave me Father Christmas; Ferdinando Buscema taught me the secret of magic; Christina Oakley-Harrington keeps open the door on the sacred; Simon Young knows the way to Faerie; John Milbank reminds me that 'meaning' is a meaningful word. Kate Baylay weaved magic, both inside and outside, with her pictures. They were all with me, and to all of them I say a heartfelt *thank you*.

And I say *thank you* to my father, too, who left me with Superman so long ago.

It was a good call.

Notes

The First Key: The Mystery

p.29   'Drawing the line is not easy.' This reconstruction is based on the one found in Jim Steinmeyer (2005), *Hiding the Elephant: How Magicians Invented the Impossible*, pp.47–69.

p.33   'society has been through a process of disenchantment'. Max Weber, 'Science as a Vocation', *Daedalus*, Vol. 87, No. 1, Science and the Modern World View (Winter, 1958), pp.111–134.

p.36   'The performance is on YouTube'. www.youtube.com/watch?v=405xMmDpCZs.

p.38   'a redemptive feeling, a reminder of many potential wonders'. Jim Steinmeyer, cit., p.21.

p.38   'custodians of a sacred knowledge of fire'. Georg Luck (1994), *Il Magico nella Cultura Antica*, p.49.

p.48   'gasps for air rather than grasps for a method.' Ken Weber, 'The Hierarchy of Mystery Entertainment: Essential Essays for Magicians', in Joshua Jay, *Magic in Mind: Essential Essays for Magicians*, p.512.

p.49   'it is taken away from most of us at a very early age.' Charles Reynolds, 'On a Definition of Magic', in Joshua Jay, cit., p.32.

p.51   'an interview with Erik Davis and Maja D'Aoust'
        expandingmind.podbean.com/e/062410-magic-and-meaning.

The Second Key: The Shadow

p.64   'weird and terrible figures were often seen.' Quoted in
        Richard Kaczynski (2010), *Perdurabo: The Life of Aleister
        Crowley*, p.67.

p.66   'magic had all but disappeared from British life'. Ronald
        Hutton (1999), *The Triumph of the Moon: A History of Modern
        Pagan Witchcraft*, p.69.

p.68   'something that you did'. Karen Armstrong (2010), *The Case
        for God*, p.60.

p.70   'the first new religion home-brewed in England'. Ronald
        Hutton, cit., p.vii.

p.79   'the numinous in him perforce begins to stir'. Rudolf Otto
        (1958), *The Idea of the Holy*, p.7.

p.83   'We don't have our Tertullian, our Augustine'. Tertullian
        (*c.*160–*c.*240) was an early Christian theologian who lived
        in Carthage. St Augustine (354–430) was bishop of Hippo,
        also in North Africa. His writings, including *Confessions* and
        The City of God, have exerted a huge influence on Christian
        thought.

p.86   'without any irritable reaching after fact and reason'.
        www.bl.uk/romantics-and-victorians/articles/
        john-keats-and-negative-capability.

p.92   'Religious fundamentalists appeal to a *logos*-based view of
        their faith'. Karen Armstrong, cit., p.7.

p.108   'midwives of other people's discoveries'. F. W. Gibbs,
         'Itinerant Lecturers in Natural Philosophy', *Ambix*, Vol. 8,
         No. 2 (1960), p.111.

p.110   'help her to remedy the weakness of her own mind'. Lisa
         Shapiro, 'Princess Elizabeth and Descartes: The Union of
         Soul and Body and the Practice of Philosophy', *British Journal
         for the History of Philosophy*, Vol. 7, No. 3 (1999), p.504.

p.112   'Empty the haunted air, and gnomèd mine'. 'Lamia', in John
         Keats (2007), *Selected Poems.*

p.113   'it's only dull and stupid folk who are not naturally disposed
         for wonder.' René Descartes (2017), *The Passions of the Soul*,
         www.earlymoderntexts.com/assets/pdfs/descartes1649part2.
         pdf.

p.120   'Respectable physicists argue that parallel universes might
         exist'. Michio Kaku (2005), *Parallel Worlds: The Science of
         Alternative Universes and Our Future in the Cosmos.*

p.120   'a prediction based on past experiences and cultural
         expectations'. Lisa Feldman Barrett (2017), *How Emotions are
         Made: The Secret Life of the Brain.*

p.121   'The article is from an urban birdwatcher'. David
         Lindo (2015), 'Pecks and the City: How to Be an Urban
         Birdwatcher', www.theguardian.com/lifeandstyle/2015/
         jul/10/urban-birder-birdspotting-cities-david-lindo.

p.121   'In a novel I wrote more than ten years ago, *Pan*'. Francesco
         Dimitri (2008), *Pan.*

p.126   'questions about things that had until then seemed entirely obvious'. Philip Ball (2012), *Curiosity: How Science Became Interested in Everything*.

p.130   'similar to those found in monasteries.' Philip Ball, cit., p.316.

p.131   'rather than simply seeing better what they already knew.' Philip Ball, cit., p.290.

p.131–2   'by giving us a glimpse of what we don't know'. Stuart Firestein (2012), *Ignorance: How It Drives Science*.

p.132   'science produces ignorance, possibly at a faster rate than it produces knowledge'. Stuart Firestein, cit. p.28.

The Fourth Key: The Wild

p.154   'achieve fulfilment'. Victor E. Frankl (2004), *Man's Search for Meaning*, p.49.

p.164   'a gift relationship with nature'. Lewis Hyde (1999), *The Gift: Imagination and the Erotic Life of Property*, p.27.

p.165   'nature is not a place to visit, it is *home*'. Gary Snyder (1999), *The Practice of the Wild*, p.18.

p.167   'cultivate a healthy poverty and simplicity'. Annie Dillard (2011), *Pilgrim at Tinker Creek*, p.17.

p.169   'the prejudice induced by a powerful map'. Robert Macfarlane (2007), *The Wild Places*, p.10.

p.171   'a place as it is perceived by an individual or by a culture moving through it'. Robert Macfarlane, cit., p.141.

p.176   'All real living is meeting'. Martin Buber (2013), *I and Thou*, p.9.

p.176   'central to the experience of religion, politics, nature, and art'.
          Jonathan Haidt, Dacher Keltner (2003), 'Approaching Awe,
          a Moral, Spiritual, and Aesthetic Emotion', *Cognition and
          Emotion*, Vol. 17, No. 2, p.297.

The Fifth Key: The Lore

p.186   'and nothing else is known of her'. This telling of the story
          comes from the reconstruction, from different sources, to be
          found in John Clark, 'Small, Vulnerable ETs: The Green
          Children of Woolpit', *Science Fiction Studies*, Vol. 33, No. 2,
          (2006).

p.190   'He is a good man, Thomas the Rhymer'. From the
          reconstruction in Carolyne Larrington (2015), *The Land
          of the Green Man: A Journey Through the Supernatural
          Landscapes of the British Isles*, pp.50–53.

p.191   'a brush with mortality'. Simon Young (2018), 'Confessions of
          a Fairy Hunter', world.edu/confessions-of-a-fairy-hunter.

p.191   'It contains five hundred entries'. Dr Young and I had been
          briefly in touch before I started writing this chapter. He
          wrote to me more than three weeks later, just as I was writing
          this paragraph. It feels like too much of a resonance not to
          mention it.

p.194   'priests routinely identified fairies with demons, devils and
          witches'. Richard Firth Green (2016), *Elf Queens and Holy
          Friars: Fairy Belief and the Medieval Church*.

p.198   'bacteria and radiation readings were normal for this
          material'. Jacques Vallée (2014), *Passport to Magonia: From
          Folklore to Flying Saucers*, p.35.

p.201   'in the hope of making some sense of them'. Patrick Harpur
        (2003), *Daimonic Reality: A Field Guide to the Otherworld*,
        p.268.

p.202   'just a vaguely humanoid flowing mass of soil, rock, and
        mud'. Simon Young (2018), 'Fairy Census 2014–2017'.

p.205   'as professionals who need to probe into strangers' memories
        (police officers, for example) know all too well.' See, for
        example, Giuliana Mazzoni (2003), *Si Può Credere a un
        Testimone? La Testimonianza e le Trappole della Memoria*.

p.208   'we have not even a rush candle to guide our steps'. W. B.
        Yeats (1902), 'Belief and Unbelief', in *The Celtic Twilight*.

p.212   'To this day, she swears that she saw a gnome'. Simon Young,
        cit., § 18.

The Sixth Key: The Story

p.242   'the most influential writer of the 20th century'. Johann Hari
        (2003), 'The Wrong Lord of the Reads', www.independent.
        co.uk/voices/commentators/johann-hari/the-wrong-lord-of-
        the-reads-82201.html.

p.243   'are confusing, not always by sincere error, the Escape of the
        Prisoner with the Flight of the Deserter'. J. R. R. Tolkien
        (2001), *Tree and Leaf*, pp.60–61.

p.243–4 'the world outside has not become less real because the
        prisoner cannot see it'. J. R. R. Tolkien, cit.

p.244   'the direction of escape is toward freedom'. Ursula K. Le
        Guin (2017), *No Time to Spare: Thinking about What Matters*.

p.248   'but neither enjoys either temporal or causal precedence'.
         Arthur W. Frank (2010), *Letting Stories Breathe: A Socio-*
         Narratology, loc. 494.

p.250   'he was trim, buff, and handsome'. Grant Morrison (2011),
         Supergods: Our World in the Age of the Superhero, p.403.

The Seventh Key: Senses of Wonder

p.271   'that went down in history'. Jean Verdon (1999), *Il Piacere nel*
         Medioevo, pp.126–131.

p.278   'space of possibility'. Beau Lotto (2017), *Deviate: The Science*
         of Seeing Differently, p.163.

p.279   'it will adapt to the lack of challenge and let its dull side come
         out'. Beau Lotto, cit., p.86.

p.282   'as a child or a Martian, both free of habit in this area'. John
         Armstrong, Alain de Botton (2014), *Art as Therapy*, pp.59–60.

p.283   'it can seem strange to treat lingering as a virtue'. John
         Armstrong (2000), *The Intimate Philosophy of Art*, p.98.

p.287   'two sounds, one high and one low'. Sara Maitland (2009),
         A Book of Silence: A Journey in Search of the Pleasures and
         Powers of Silence, p.197.

p.288   'wrote George Orwell'. Cit. in Constance Classen, David
         Howes, Anthony Synnott (1994), *Aroma: The Cultural History*
         of Smell, p.8.

p.289   'by using smell rather than sight'. Charles Foster (2016), *Being*
         a Beast: An Intimate and Radical Look at Nature, pp.55–59.

p.290   'a study on smell, *Aroma*'. Constance Classen et al., cit.

p.292   'Their smell is so sweet that it might cause you to to weep
         tears of joy.' Constance Classen et al., cit., p.131.

p.295   'about blood and organs, cruelty and decay'. Anthony
         Bourdain (1999), 'Don't Eat Before Reading This', *The New
         Yorker*.

p.296   'taste is largely social'. Diane Ackerman (1995), *A Natural
         History of the Senses*, p.127.

p.303   'and so to name and define it'. Alan Watts (1951), *The Wisdom
         of Insecurity: A Message for an Age of Anxiety*, p.92.

p.304   'the brainy modern loves not matter but measures'. A. Watts,
         cit., p.93.

The Portals

p.314   'they have to start getting prepared to be units of the
         labour force'. Neil Gaiman, Kazuo Ishiguro (2015), 'Let's
         Talk About Genre: Neil Gaiman and Kazuo Ishiguro in
         Conversation', *New Statesman*.

p.315   'how cleverly they had played'. www.youtube.com/
         watch?v=bJ8Kq1wucsk.

p.316   'after one meagre wonder-filled minute'. P. Dietze et al.,
         'Awe, the Small Self, and Prosocial Behaviour', *Journal of
         Personality and Social Psychology*, Vol. 8, No. 6 (2015).

p.318   'In a state of flow we create our best work.' Mihalyi
         Csikszentmihalyi (2002), *Flow: The Classic Work on How to
         Achieve Happiness*.

p.319   'which she called "grit"'. Angela Duckworth (2016), *Grit: The
         Power of Passion and Perseverance*.

p.320   'score a second goal, and England won'. As reported by Alastair Campbell (2015), *Winners: And How They Succeed*, p.170.

p.323   'how does the other side see their own behaviour?'. Deepak Malhotra (2016), *Negotiating the Impossible: How to Break Deadlocks and Resolve Ugly Conflicts Without Money or Muscle*, p.126.

Bibliography

Diane Ackerman, *A Natural History of the Senses* (Vintage Books, New York, 1995).

John Armstrong, *The Intimate Philosophy of Art* (Penguin, London, 2000).

John Armstrong, Alain de Botton, *Art as Therapy* (Phaidon Press, London, 2014).

Karen Armstrong, *The Case for God* (Vintage Books, London, 2010).

Philip Ball, *Curiosity: How Science Became Interested in Everything* (Bodley Head, London, 2012).

Lisa Feldman Barrett, *How Emotions Are Made: The Secret Life of the Brain* (Macmillan, London, 2017).

Walter Benjamin, *L'Opera d'arte nell'epoca della sua riproducibilità tecnica* (Einaudi, Turin, 2000).

Peter L. Berger, *A Rumour of Angels: Modern Society and the Rediscovery of the Supernatural* (Allen Lane, Penguin Press, London, 1970).

Anthony Bourdain, 'Don't Eat Before Reading This' (*The New Yorker*, 19 April 1999).

Ray Bradbury, *Zen in the Art of Writing* (Harper Voyager, London, 2015).

Derren Brown, *Absolute Magic: A Model for Powerful Close-up Performance* (H&R Magic Books, Humble, Texas, 2002).

Derren Brown, *Pure Effect: Direct Mindreading and Magical Artistry* (H&R Magic Books, Humble, Texas, 2002).

Jerome Bruner, *La fabbrica delle storie: Diritto, letteratura, vita* (Laterza, Rome and Bari, 2002).

Martin Buber, *I and Thou* (Bloomsbury Academic, London and New York, 2013).

Alastair Campbell, *Winners: And How They Succeed* (Arrow Books, London, 2015).

John Clark, 'Small, Vulnerable ETs: The Green Children of Woolpit' (*Science Fiction Studies*, Vol. 33, No. 2, July 2006, pp.209–229).

Constance Classen, David Howes, Anthony Synnott, *Aroma: The Cultural History of Smell* (Routledge, London and New York, 1994).

Mihaly Csikszentmihalyi, *Flow: The Classic Work on How to Achieve Happiness* (Rider, London, 2002).

Lorraine Daston, Katharine Park, *Wonders and the Order of Nature 1150–1750* (Zone Books, New York, 1998).

René Descartes, *The Passions of the Soul*, translation © Jonathan Bennett (2017), www.earlymoderntexts.com/assets/pdfs/descartes1649part2.pdf.

Pia Dietze, Matthew Feinberg, Daniel M. Stancato, Dacher Keltner, Paul K. Piff, 'Awe, the Small Self, and Prosocial Behaviour' (*Journal of Personality and Social Psychology*, Vol. 108, No. 6, 2015, pp.883–899).

Annie Dillard, *Pilgrim at Tinker Creek* (Canterbury Press, Norwich, 2011).

Francesco Dimitri, *Pan* (Marsilio, Venice, 2008).

Angela Duckworth, *Grit: The Power of Passion and Perseverance* (Scribner, New York, 2016).

Mircea Eliade, *The Two and the One* (Harvill Press, London, 1965).

Mircea Eliade, *The Sacred and the Profane: The Nature of Religion* (Harcourt, Orlando, 1987).

Stuart Firestein, *Ignorance: How It Drives Science* (Oxford University Press, New York, 2012).

Philip Fisher, *Wonder, the Rainbow, and the Aesthetics of Rare Experiences* (Harvard University Press, Cambridge, Massachusetts, and London, 1998).

Charles Foster, *Being a Beast: An Intimate and Radical Look at Nature* (Profile Books, London, 2016).

Arthur W. Frank, *Letting Stories Breathe: A Socio-Narratology* (University of Chicago Press, Chicago and London, 2010).

Viktor E. Frankl, *Man's Search for Meaning* (Rider Books, London, Sidney, Auckland and Johannesburg, 2004).

Robert C. Fuller, *Wonder: From Emotion to Spirituality* (University of North Carolina Press, Chapel Hill, 2006).

Neil Gaiman, Kazuo Ishiguro, 'Let's Talk About Genre: Neil Gaiman and Kazuo Ishiguro in Conversation', (*New Statesman*, 4 June 2015).

F. W. Gibbs, 'Itinerant Lecturers in Natural Philosophy' (*Ambix*, Vol. 8, No. 2, 1960, pp. 111-117, DOI: 10.1179/amb.1960.8.2.111).

Eric T. Goodcase, Heather A. Love, 'From Despair to Integrity: Using Narrative Therapy for Older Individuals, in Erikson's Last Stage of Identity Development' (*Clinical Social Work Journal*, Vol. 45, No. 4, 2017, pp.354–363, https://www.scie-socialcareonline.org.

uk/from-despair-to-integrity-using-narrative-therapy-for-older-
individuals-in-eriksons-last-stage-of-identity-development/r/
a1Cofoooo05KG3DEAW).

Jonathan Gottschall, *The Storytelling Animal: How Stories Make Us
Human* (Mariner Books, Boston, 2013).

Richard Firth Green, *Elf Queens and Holy Friars: Fairy Beliefs and the
Medieval Church* (University of Pennsylvania Press, Philadelphia,
2016).

Pierre Hadot, *The Veil of Isis: An Essay on the History of the Idea of
Nature* (Belknap Press of Harvard University Press, Cambridge,
Massachusetts, and London, 2006).

Jonathan Haidt, Dacher Keltner, 'Approaching Awe, a Moral,
Spiritual, and Aesthetic Emotion' (*Cognition and Emotion*,
Vol. 17, No. 2, March 2003, pp.297–314).

Johann Hari, 'The Wrong Lord of the Reads', www.independent.
co.uk/voices/commentators/johann-hari/the-wrong-lord-of-the-
reads-82201.html (2003).

Patrick Harpur, *Daimonic Reality: A Field Guide to the Otherworld*
(Pine Winds Press, Ravensdale, 2003).

Ronald Hutton, *The Triumph of the Moon: A History of Modern Pagan
Witchcraft* (Oxford University press, Oxford, 1999).

Lewis Hyde, *The Gift: Imagination and the Erotic Life of Property*
(Vintage Books, London, 1999).

Joshua Jay, *Magic in Mind: Essential Essays for Magicians* (Vanishing
Inc., online).

Richard Kaczynski, *Perdurabo: The Life of Aleister Crowley* (North
Atlantic Books, Berkeley, 2010).

Michio Kaku, *Parallel Worlds: The Science of Alternative Universes and Our Future in the Cosmos* (Penguin, London, 2005).

John Keats, *Selected Poems* (Penguin, London, 2007).

Carolyne Larrington, *The Land of the Green Man: A Journey through the Supernatural Landscapes of the British Isles* (I. B. Tauris, London and New York, 2015).

Ursula K. Le Guin, *No Time to Spare: Thinking about What Matters* (Houghton Mifflin, Boston, 2017).

David Lindo, 'Pecks and the City: How to Be an Urban Birdwatcher', www.theguardian.com/lifeandstyle/2015/jul/10/urban-birder-birdspotting-cities-david-lindo (2015).

Maria Rosa Loretelli, Roy Porter, 'Società Scientifiche di Provincia e Opinione Pubblica nell'Inghilterra dell'Età dell'Illuminismo' (*Quaderni Storici*, Vol. 14, No. 42 (3), September/December 1979).

Beau Lotto, *Deviate: The Science of Seeing Differently* (Weidenfeld & Nicolson, London, 2017).

Georg Luck, *Il Magico nella Cultura Antica* (Mursia, Milan, 1994).

Robert Macfarlane, *The Wild Places* (Granta Books, London, 2007).

Sara Maitland, *A Book of Silence: A Journey in Search of the Pleasures and Powers of Silence* (Granta Books, London, 2009).

Deepak Malhotra, *Negotiating the Impossible: How to Break Deadlocks and Resolve Ugly Conflicts Without Money or Muscle* (Berrett-Koehler Publishers, Oakland, 2016).

Gabriel Marcel, *The Mystery of Being, Vol. I: Reflection and Mystery* (Harvill Press, London, 1950).

Gabriel Marcel, *The Mystery of Being, Vol. II: Faith and Reality* (Harvill Press, London, 1950).

Giuliana Mazzoni, *Si Può Credere a un Testimone? La Testimonianza e le Trappole della Memoria* (Il Mulino, Bologna, 2003).

Philipp Meyer, *The Son* (Simon & Schuster, London, New York, Sidney, Toronto and New Delhi, 2013).

Grant Morrison, *Supergods: Our World in the Age of the Superhero* (Jonathan Cape, London, 2011).

Rudolf Otto, *The Idea of the Holy* (Oxford University Press, London, 1958).

Mary-Jane Rubenstein, *Strange Wonder: The Closure of Metaphysics and the Opening of Awe* (Columbia University Press, New York, 2008).

Kirk J. Schneider, *Rediscovery of Awe: Splendor, Mystery, and the Fluid Center of Life* (Paragon House, St. Paul, 2004).

Lisa Shapiro, 'Princess Elizabeth and Descartes: The Union of Soul and Body and the Practice of Philosophy' (*British Journal for the History of Philosophy*, Vol. 7, No. 3, 1999, pp.503–520).

Gary Snyder, *The Practice of the Wild* (Counterpoint, Berkeley, 1999).

Jim Steinmeyer, *Hiding the Elephant: How Magicians Invented the Impossible* (Arrow Books, London, 2005).

Alex Stone, *Fooling Houdini: Adventures in the World of Magic* (William Heinemann, London, 2012).

J. R. R. Tolkien, *Tree and Leaf* (HarperCollins, London, 2001).

Jacques Vallée, *Passport to Magonia: From Folklore to Flying Saucers* (Daily Grail Publishing, Brisbane, 2014).

Jean Verdon, *Il Piacere nel Medioevo* (Baldini & Castoldi, Milan, 1999).

Daniel Pickering Walker, *Magia spirituale e magia demoniaca da Ficino a Campanella* (Nino Aragno Editore, Turin, 2002).

Marina Warner, *Once upon a Time: A Short History of Fairy Tale* (Oxford University Press, Oxford, 2014).

Alan Watts, *The Wisdom of Insecurity: A Message for an Age of Anxiety* (Vintage Books, New York, 1951).

Max Weber, 'Science as a Vocation' (*Daedalus*, Vol. 87, No. 1, Winter 1958, Science and the Modern World View, pp.111–134).

David Wootton, *The Invention of Science: A New History of the Scientific Revolution* (Allen Lane, London, 2015).

Miles D. Wyndham, 'Public Lectures on Chemistry in the United States' (*Ambix*, Vol. 15, No. 3, 1968, pp. 131-153).

W. B. Yeats, *The Celtic Twilight: Faerie and Folklore* (A. H. Bullen, London, 1902).

Simon Young, 'Confessions of a Fairy Hunter', world.edu/confessions-of-a-fairy-hunter/ (2018).

Simon Young, 'Fairy Census 2014–2017', www.fairyist.com/wp-content/uploads/2014/10/The-Fairy-Census-2014-2017-1.pdf (2018).